Brass Instruments

Brass Instruments
Their History and Development

ANTHONY BAINES

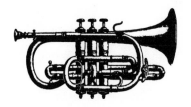

DOVER PUBLICATIONS, INC.
New York

Published in Canada by General Publishing Company, Ltd., 30 Lesmill Road,
Don Mills, Toronto, Ontario.
Published in the United Kingdom by Constable and Company, Ltd., 3 The
Lanchesters, 162–164 Fulham Palace Road, London W6 9ER.

This Dover edition, first published in 1993, is a republication of the edition
originally published by Faber and Faber Limited, London, 1976, as reprinted
with corrections in 1978 and 1980. An appendix which appeared in the 1980
reprint has been incorporated into the main body of the present edition as
footnotes. A preface to the Dover edition and a supplement to the Bibliography
have been added to the present edition by the author. Several minor corrections to
the text have been made tacitly by the author.

Manufactured in the United States of America
Dover Publications, Inc., 31 East 2nd Street, Mineola, N.Y. 11501

Library of Congress Cataloging-in-Publication Data

Baines, Anthony.
    Brass instruments : their history and development / Anthony Baines.
        p.   cm.
    Reprint. Originally published: London : Faber and Faber, 1976, as reprinted
with corrections in 1978 and 1980.
    Includes bibliographical references (p.   ) and index.
    ISBN 0-486-27574-4 (pbk.)
    1. Brass instruments.   I. Title.
ML933.B33   1993
788.9'19—dc20   93-19988
                                                                              CIP
                                                                              MN

TO MY WIFE

Contents

—

Illustrations

===

c. 1770; horn by Rodenbostel, end of eighteenth century; horn by Hofmeister, pre-1754; set of slide crooks, for horn by Goodison, *c*. 1830; horn by Haltenhof, 1776, crooked in E flat.

X. Hand-horn, Courtois, *c*. 1820; 'Caporal Cornet des Chasseurs', Dutch print, 1815; *Jakthorn*, modern Swedish; post-horn with transposing hole, German, nineteenth century.

XI. Trade-card of Piattet & Benoit, Lyons *c*. 1836, showing dragon-bell *basson russe, trompette demilune*, trombone with bell to rear, etc.; demilune trumpet, Guichard; circular trumpet, Jahn; the Distin family quintet, *c*. 1834 (trombone, cornopean, slide trumpet, two hand-horns).

XII. Slide trumpet, Clementi & Co., *c*. 1820; mouthpieces of serpent, the above trumpet, ophicleide (Turton, 1829), keyed bugle (English), cornet (early type); short-model 'Inventions' trumpet, Missenharter; keyed trumpet, Riedl, *c*. 1820; keyed bugle, D'Almaine; bass keyed trumpet; an ophicleide player.

XIII. Valves, Périnet (early type), Berlin, double-piston, Stoelzel, square, rotary; horn by Schott; Schuster-type square valves; bass trumpet by Schuster; bass trumpet ('Tenor H.'), *c*. 1825; trumpets in B flat (1837) and E flat by M. Saurle.

XIV. The Besses-o' th'-Barn band, 1860; alto ophicleide, Printemps; clavicor, Guichard; saxhorn baryton; saxhorn basse with independent pistons.

XV. Tenor-base trombone, J. Saurle; Ton-wechsel on tenor horn; Vienna horn; Wagner tuba (tenor), Alexander; two celebrated London players of the past, John Solomon; Aubrey Brain.

XVI. Valved Ophicleides and Bombardons by Beyde, Bachmann, Finke; helicon, Stowasser; Bass tuba, Zetsche; saxhorn contrebasse; BB flat tuba, Saurle.

FIGURES IN TEXT

Preface to the First Edition

To all who love the sounds of instruments, the history of brass instruments must have a curious fascination as it passes through long phases when the instruments have meant a great deal to life and death, but less to music, up to the times when they have musically come to mean very much indeed. Small wonder that they and their music have latterly been attracting much historical research, mainly of specialized nature, probing confined areas in depth. From this we all profit, and we must hope that it will always continue. A short introductory survey of the evolutionary field as a whole, however, does not seem to have been attempted for some considerable time, and this is what I am now offering to musicians and music lovers in general.

Here I have tried not only to set down the broad historical facts as they are known but also to give due consideration to things which are not known. On the other hand I have given hardly any space to certain matters. Acoustics, for instance, has grown into a huge experimental and mathematical subject to which scant justice would be done by picking out the morsels here and there which I myself can follow. Secondly, with regard to music for brass my chief concern is with formative stages, whether of a repertory or of a technique of playing, which leaves me with no room to discuss repertories as a whole. Thirdly, for the modern period, say the last hundred and fifty years, I have confined myself to first-hand knowledge (museum collections, brass-instrument sounds etc.), and since this has been almost wholly within Europe, less than due attention is paid to developments in America, even though in some instances these have produced the weightiest results in world practice today.

Hoping that the reader will find something interesting in what is left, I must acknowledge the great amount I owe to musicians and scholars, many more than I can name, from days when professional brass players were my constant companions in London and men like Blandford, Carse, and Morley-Pegge (our latest loss) my mentors in history. Over the last few years my debt has been particularly to Dr. Laurence Picken, Mrs. Joan Harrison, Dr. F. J. de Hen, Anthony Spurgin, Reine Dahlqvist, Marcello Castellani and Robert Minter, and also indeed to the directors and staffs of museums who have generously allowed me to work on their instruments, while my greatest debt is declared in the dedication.

ANTHONY BAINES, *Oxford, 1974*

Preface to the Dover Edition

Apart from light revision in many places, the main change in this edition is the dispersal of the Appendix which was added to the first paperback edition (Faber, 1980) to appropriate points in the main text, mostly as new footnotes. Further to this, footnotes marked 'Note to the Dover Edition' briefly notice a few of the more important instances where the recent years have seen revision or reassessment of the historical status of some particular instrument or type. A supplementary bibliography has been added.

ANTHONY BAINES, *London, 1993*

Naming of musical notes: c' represents Middle C on the piano and b is the note below it. The octave above is c'' and the note below it b'. The octave below is c and the note below it B; two octaves below is C and the note below it is B'.

ONE

Introduction

The fundamental distinction of brass from other wind instruments, namely that they are sounded by vibration of the player's lips, stresses the central factor in a chain of several. Behind the lips a pressure of air is supplied by the body. Against the lips is placed the mouthpiece of the tubular resonator, the air in which will, through reflection and superposition of waves of local oscillatory motion, vibrate as a standing (or 'stationary') wave with nodal and antinodal conditions at certain points along the length, and a set of frequencies dependent upon the distances between such points, which are in turn dependent on the tube-length. Between air-pressure supply and tube-air, the lips are held partially closed so that their central surfaces will vibrate by yielding to pressure and rebound as they impede the dissipation of the air pressure into the tube. On their first tremor the corresponding tremor in the force of emergent wind is instantly sensed by the tube-air, which will then resonate at whichever of its potential frequencies most closely matches that of the lips at that moment. On the lowest level this calls for no skill: if one merely puffs hard and crudely into an instrument the tube-air will usually guide the lips into vibration sufficiently close to one of its own frequencies for a sound to be emitted. But a trained brass-player's mouth and lips know in advance the correct muscular control for selecting whichever is required of the possible frequencies, whether the instrument is a 'natural' one (with no mechanism) offering only one set of frequencies, or one provided with valves or slide through which momentary additions to tube-length are made whilst playing, making six or more further sets available.

An essential requirement for Western music is that the main frequencies of a set be such that they provide as truly as possible the primary intervals of the octave and the fifth, on which our music is based. For this, these frequencies must lie as close as possible to those of a harmonic series, with values standing in the ratio 1:2, musically the octave, and 2:3, the perfect fifth, and so on, even though the continuation of the series upwards leads to various problems of intonation that may have to be overcome, as will be noticed later. A harmonic series is rooted, both in traditional theory and in players' experience, on a fundamental pitch which may be counted as No. 1 of the series (h1). The next pitch, h2, is the octave above, the next, h3, a fifth above that, then h4 a fourth above h3, and so on, the successive musical intervals progressively diminishing as the numerical ratios become smaller. But a simple plain tube provided by nature will seldom give the essential intervals. If blown as a flute, open to atmospheric pressure at both ends, it might. But blown as a brass instrument the expected octave from the fundamental will be nearer to a tenth (as with the Australian didjeridu) and the interval h2–h3 an uncertain sixth instead of a fifth. Certain expansions of the tube are necessary. There may be an expansion throughout, as in various instruments ultimately derived from animal horns, for instance bugles; or at one end, or better still both ends, with cylindrical tubing between, as with most of our brass instruments, even where the initial expansion is confined to the cavities inside the mouthpiece as with baroque trumpet and trombone.[1]

The expansions must be properly matched to the plain tubing, and here the bell profile is particularly important. The bell was introduced early in the history of brass instruments to strengthen and radiate the sound, but often in plain conical shapes which do not by any means bring harmonics in tune. There are still oriental trumpets which possess a handsome and purposeful-looking bell—and also a conical mouthpipe (i.e. the section of tube which follows the mouthpiece)—but nevertheless fail to give sounds in harmonic relationship. In the circumstances this is not a blemish, since most oriental trumpeters are not concerned with producing accurately tuned intervals. But in the West, from at least the High Middle Ages, trumpets have been required to sound true octaves and fifths, and generations of makers have passed down profiles by which a series is accurately focused to these intervals.

Early patterns for bell profiles must have been found by eye.

[1] For more advanced explanations reached by modern acoustics, see A. H. Benade, 1976.

Soon geometry must have helped. How far back one cannot tell, though some traditional measuring procedures for laying out a bell profile have continued in use into modern times—as where the width is reduced by increments proportionally to increasing distance from the bell mouth, whence to draw a curve resembling a hyperbola (see Bahnert et al., 1958, p. 110). In a tenor trombone by Drewelwecz of Nuremberg, dated 1595 (Pl. VI), the effect has been to achieve a bell in which successive diameters at distance x from the rim, multiplied by $x^{.6}$ give a constant quantity. In a bell of a century later by Paul Hainlein, also of Nuremberg, the factor works out by inspection as $x^{.7}$, i.e. a rather narrower bell with more pronounced flare, likewise bringing harmonics in tune over the musical compass required but with slightly brighter tone-quality. Not, however, that a straightforward formula guarantees a perfect result in every case; troublesome intonation faults are still liable to beset certain types of instrument, while as all players know, even the most expensive hand-made model will sometimes disappoint over the intonation of one note or more. But modern acoustics has refused to accept such things as inexplicable, and experimental and mathematical research by manufacturers has begun to identify the causes of, for instance, irregularities in the location of nodes and antinodes in this or that harmonic.

In times before seamless drawn tube became available, the tubing was made from sheet metal obtained from the rolling mills, or earlier, before the eighteenth century, from battery mills where ingots made from copper mixed with some zinc ore (calamine) were hammered into brass sheets. In Germany, J. Samuel Halle (1764) specified sheets of No. 8 or 9 Latun-brass, 6 feet by 1½ in size and of the thickness of writing paper (the brass thickness is in fact usually about 0·5 mm.). This is formed into tubing over mandrels and brazed with spelter, filed and polished—arduous work over which an old Nuremberg maker might have to work into the night, helped by his wife, to complete a large order of trumpets from a crowned head: work requiring enormous experience and skill with the different hammers, anvils, etc. to make the metal do exactly what is wanted.[1] Narrow

[1] Scenes of old maker's workshops are shown in Weigel, 1698, p. 230, and in Diderot & D'Alembert's *Encyclopédie*, 1763, the latter reproduced in Morley-Pegge, 1960. A practical German account of processes is in Bahnert et al., p. 109ff.

tapers, as in mouthpipes, are made by shrinking the tube over a tapered mandrel, pushing it through graded holes in a fixed block and smoothing off in a lead die. Tubing is bent into bows (U-bends) after filling with molten lead, oiling or dousing with whitening to prevent the lead sticking, or filling with a mixture of pitch and resin. Creases may be taken out by working the bend in countersunk holes in a steel plate before melting out the filling. Where sections of tube are joined, by lap joint or by butt joint under a collar or ferrule, soft solder is used in order to facilitate dismantling for repairs (on which subject generally Erick Brand's *Manual* is helpful). Sockets for receiving detachable parts (mouthpiece, crooks etc.) are provided with a tapered shank secured under a ferrule ('chemise'); or the tube itself may be expanded and covered by a ferrule. Standard tapers like 1 in 20, or No. 1 or 2 Morse, are now generally used in the hopes that players' mouthpieces will fit well.

The mouthpiece is by origin an adaptor, needed where the starting diameter of a bore is too small to allow efficient vibration of the lips. It would have first been required with animal horns, where having sawn off the end a blowing cavity is made, for instance burning it out with a hot implement. Then followed the separately-made metal mouthpiece built to suit whatever the instrument had to do and leading in course of time to an array of specialized patterns as illustrated in Fig. 1 (Nos. 1–6) from the Late Romantic Period. Among these No. 1 stands alone, a deep funnel with neither distinct throat nor backbore. The rest vary from true cups (5, 6, though subsequently both these have lost the sharp-angled throat) to cups with much rounded-off throats (2–4). Each might be said to look very much as the instrument sounds. But mouthpieces are among the most difficult of brass-instrument components over which to generalize. Their acoustic function is still under scientific investigation (see for example in *MGG*, 'Horninstrumente'), though their different profiles certainly encourage to varying degrees the formation of overtones in the instrument's standing wave. One knows that tone-quality is objectively explained as a function of the number and strength of such overtones, which can be quantified by scientific apparatus in the form of a 'tonal spectrum'. A mouthpiece cup in which the walls meet the throat at a steep angle encourages strong overtones (bright quality) more than the flowing contours associated with mellow sounds. In some cases an instrument has been played with either type, each the 'correct' mouthpiece for its time or place, and neither, if properly-designed, impairing response and intonation. The tone-quality may then vary noticeably, as with the two types of cornet mouthpiece shown in the figure (Nos. 2, 7); or yet barely perceptibly, as when an English trombonist used a cup mouthpiece where a Frenchman, following his national tra-

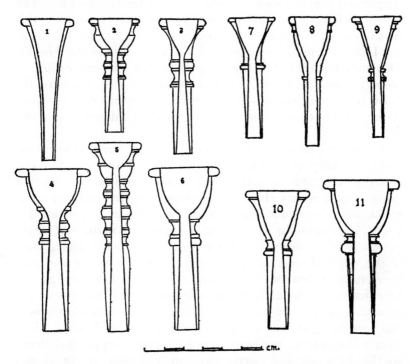

Fig. 1 Mouthpieces in section. Nos. 1–6 by V. Mahillon, *ZfI*, 1883: 1. horn; 2. cornet; 3. flugel-horn; 4. euphonium; 5. trumpet; 6. trombone. Others for comparison: 7. cornet, earlier French model; 8. horn, modern German; 9. *trompe (cor) de chasse*; 10. trombone, French traditional; 11. serpent.

dition, would play the identical instrument and likewise produce characteristic trombone sound with a mouthpiece more conical (10) than that with which a German horn-player now produces horn sound (8).

Some specimen tonal spectra can be seen in the works of Bahnert *et al.* (pp. 74–6) and of Bate (p. 17). They concern modern designs only: historical spectra do not seem to have been published as yet. Tonal spectra have been found useful by manufacturers over questions of design and over adjustment of an instrument's performance. To a layman they demonstrate in an interesting way, and partly explain, why our brass instruments, each possessing this or that form of tubing and bell, should sound so splendidly different from each other. Indeed, by juggling with shapes and proportions one could of course create new ones. The inventive freedom of the last century made men very alert to this possibility. At the time when Wagner was envisaging his tubas, the London firm of Key, Rudall & Co. advertised in the *Musical Directory* for 1857: 'By the application of a scientific calibre of bores in the Solo Cornu, an instrument has been produced [in E flat] of a rich, sonorous, and brilliant quality of tone, combined with great sweetness, freedom and power.' What more could one want?

But a more important concern over the last hundred years has been over the dynamic range of the standard instruments. The sound of any musical instrument becomes brighter or rougher when played loudly through increasing predominance of overtones, and as more and more volume has come to be demanded of brass instruments in large orchestras and vast halls, bores have generally been widened so that an instrument, while losing some of the 'edge' of traditional small-bore tone, can be sounded very powerfully without undue loss of musical quality through the tone scattering in a flurry of over-strong high overtones. For overtones do not necessarily all belong to the harmonic series of the note being sounded. Especially when playing loudly, inharmonic (discordant) overtones appear, partly through turbulence in the tube-air, and partly through vibration of the metal, through which sound travels about eight times faster than through air to produce high-pitched overtones which bear no musical relation to those of the tube-air. They can be so predominant that in the words of one acoustician a trombone on *ffz* becomes almost a percussion instrument. The reference is here to a modern trombone with wide bore and bell-section; on older models with narrower dimensions the shattering sound appears at a much lower dynamic level, and one remembers how careful players once had to be not to overblow above a moderate *forte* if the harmonies of the music were to be distinct and pleasing. On the other hand, with too vacant a tonal spectrum an instrument can lack life and colour, especially when sounded loudly, and one reason for retaining the F side of the double horn is to preserve the means to give the old brassy sound in a strong *tutti*, dependent upon the proportionately narrower dimensions of the instrument while played in F. It was very exciting in Brahms's Haydn Variations at the second half of Variation VI when the old French horns used to be suddenly blown hard, sounding brassy so easily and naturally.

Tube-length and pitch. The pitch or tonality of an instrument, as spoken of, is the sounding pitch of its harmonic series; if provided with valves, etc., it is the 'open' series given without operating the mechanism. Often it is useful to correlate pitch with tube-length, both for description and also in historical work where one may have to estimate the pitch by measurement, as in pictures or with old instruments which are not in a condition to be sounded.

Wave-length can be defined as the distance between two nearest points in the air-column which are vibrating in the same phase. On the fundamental the two ends of the column vibrate in opposite phase, so that the wave-length of the fundamental corresponds to a journey down the tube and back again, i.e. twice the tube-length. By an elementary equation of physics this distance divided into the speed of sound should give the frequency of the fundamental: thus for a trumpet with 4-foot tube-length, 8 divided into 1,120 gives 140 vibrations per second. In practice, however, its pitch comes some 20 vibrations lower or nearly a semitone (due to mouthpiece volume, 'end correction' at the bell, but partly to acoustic behaviour more like that of an oboe, which is also short for its pitch). The discrepancy varies with tube-proportions and bell shapes, and in fact an F tuba may be at least six inches shorter than an F horn. Also, where two instruments of like kind are pitched an octave apart, the tube-length of the deeper is greater than twice that of the higher, whether or not the mouthpiece is included. Hence an adjusted correlation can be more useful. The table below, based on 200 cm. for a fundamental of *E* flat and a ratio of 100:94 per semitone difference, gives an approximate guide to the pitch of most instruments except the wide-bore tubas etc. at the modern performing pitch of A = 440 v.p.s. Mouthpiece length is not included.

At the old British 'sharp pitch' (A = 452·5) and similar high pitches common on the Continent in the last century, one reckons about three per cent shorter; sharp-pitch instruments were often supplied with an alternative slide for 'flat pitch' (modern pitch). Pitches of the baroque period could be three-quarters of a tone lower or more (Chap. 5). Much of the valuable data on past tuning pitches compiled by Ellis (1880) is easily accessible in Rockstro's well-known book on *The Flute*, §298.

Table 1

Fundamental	Length cm.		Example
d'	49		
c'	55		
b♭	62		piccolo trumpet
a	66		
a♭	70		
g	75		
f	85		
e	90		
e♭	96		soprano cornet
d	102		D trumpet
c	116	('4-foot')	C trumpet
B♭	131		B♭ trumpet, cornet
A	139		
A♭	148		
G	157		
F	177	('6-foot')	classical F trumpet
E	188		
E♭	200		alto trombone
D	212	('7-foot')	baroque D trumpet
D♭	225		
C	239	('8-foot')	
B♭'	270	('9-foot')	trombone, B♭ horn
A'	288		
A♭'	306		
G'	326		G bass trombone
F'	369	('12-foot')	F horn
E'	390		
E♭'	416		E♭ horn
D'	442	('14-foot')	
C'	500	('16-foot')	
B♭"	563	('18-foot')	contrabass trombone

For rapid description a well-established method is to refer to tube-length by the nearest foot (or half foot) as indicated in the table in brackets. Thus the present C trumpet is in '4-foot C', but an old natural trumpet in C is '8-foot C'. Tubas and other wide-bore instruments may be thus spoken of similarly.

The fundamentals themselves have a relatively small yet often indispensable part in brass playing. In only a few cases is it impossible or very difficult to produce even the open fundamental, as on the F horn, where its frequency is too slow for the lips tc match with the width of mouthpiece provided. Fundamentals are particularly important on trombone, B flat horn and the tubas, while on the ophicleide they supply a full third of the compass. Ex. 1 is an example of the use of the fundamental on a smaller

Ex. 1 Bugle (*Halbmond*) call, Prussian Light Infantry (after Kastner).

instrument, in a Prussian Light Infantry call from 1846 for bugle in 4-foot C. On cornets and modern trumpets it may at first seem flat and unfocused, but many teachers of the first rank have required pupils to learn to produce it firmly at its correct pitch, as part of the principle that command of sounds both well below and well above the ordinary range helps to develop security and tone throughout that range. Some famous cornet soloists of former times used to astonish audiences by gravely ending 'The Carnival of Venice' deep in the bass, using the fundamentals.

Higher harmonics. A series as far as h27, the highest to occur in written music, is shown in Ex. 2. The choice of *C* as demonstration fundamental brings the series into line with the original notation of music for trumpet and horn, the written *c'* denoting h4 (but h2 usually appears in the bass clef as *C*, seldom as *c* before recent periods; hence in bass clef, the octave *c*, *C* for two horns signifies h4 and h2). The old, *c'* = h4, notation is usually retained today when writing for the horn (representing the 12-foot F series, in actual sound a fifth lower) and for cavalry and other natural trumpets. But for most of the post-classical instruments, such as cornets, modern valve trumpets, and the brass-band instruments, the series is placed an octave higher, middle C representing h2, in accordance with the notation which was adopted in the eighteenth century for the bugle. The sounding pitch of the notes, dependent on the tonality of the instrument, is very often to be found by the same transposition in either case. Thus 'Trumpet in

D' sounds a tone higher whether in a classical part written in the old notation or in a modern D trumpet part written in the later notation, though the harmonics employed to obtain the notes are not the same in the two instances, the actual instruments being pitched an octave apart (Table 1).

Ex. 2 Harmonic series on fundamental *C*. Approximate notation in musical symbols.

Ex. 2 cannot show the harmonic series accurately throughout, since each interval in it is smaller than the preceding interval by an ever-decreasing amount, which is not how any musical scale runs. Even, for example, the whole-tone D–C, frequency ratio 9:8, is greater than E–D, ratio 10:9, by an amount equivalent to a good inch of tubing on an F horn. The series thus calls for examination in smaller units. This is most conveniently done by division of the Equal Temperament (E.T.) semitone into 100 cents (a unit introduced by Ellis); thus there are 1,200 cents to the octave (table 2, left-hand column). Harmonic intervals are then converted into cents by dividing the larger harmonic number by the smaller (keeping within the octave) and multiplying the logarithm of the result by 3,986. The middle column in the table shows to the nearest cent the interval that each harmonic theoretically makes with the C below. Values for other intervals are found by subtraction, thus for the smaller tone, E–D, 386–204 = 182 cents. The very slight sharpness of the Gs and Ds to E.T. has no practical significance; but the prime number 5 (E and B) brings the series into conflict with E.T. which puts the major third about a sixth of a semitone (14 cents) above the value which nature gives it, and this is an appreciable difference to the ear. It is equivalent to a tuning-slide movement of about 5·5 mm. with B flat trumpet and 15 mm. on F horn.

There was no problem here for brass players of the eighteenth century. The natural major third was then, as J. J. Rousseau described it, 'the soul of harmony'. The same feeling is expressed in the contemporary Mean-tone tuning of keyboards, which in its normal form (right-hand column), in order to provide pure major thirds throughout, sacrifices the true fifth to the extent of

Table 2

Pitches above C in cents (to nearest whole number). Harmonics numbered in **bold** figures.

Equal Temperament	cents	Harmonic series (1 to 27)		Mean-tone
C	1200	**2, 4, 8, 16:** 1200		1200
B	1100	**15:** 1088		1083
B♭	1000			{ 1007 (B♭) 965 (A♯)
		7, 14: 969		
A	900		**27:** 906	890
		13, 26: 840		
A♭	800		**25:** 773	{ 814 (A♭) 773 (G♯)
G	700	**3, 6, 12, 24:** 702		697
			23: 628	
F♯	600			580
		11, 22: 551		
F	500		**21:** 471	504
E	400	**5, 10, 20:** 386		386
E♭	300		**19:** 298	{ 311 (E♭) 269 (D♯)
D	200	**9, 18:** 204		193
C♯	100		**17:** 105	{ 118 (D♭) 76 (C♯)
C	0	**(1, 2, 4, 8):** 0		0

shrinking it, in theory by 5·4 cents (a quarter of a comma) or in practice by 'as much as the ear will bear'.[1] From this insistence upon the natural third follow related things heard by Baroque ears: the low leading notes, for example, and with this the low tuning of all sharps (G sharp for instance, major third above E, coming at 773 cents). A further corollary is the high tuning of all flats (a third down from C gives A flat at 814). Each sharp comes at Mean-tone some 42 cents *lower* than its enharmonic flat, and though on an ordinary keyboard a black note could serve only in one capacity, a good performer on non-keyboard instruments was expected to observe the difference. Brass-players committed to a natural instrument, horn or trumpet, would have borne such distinctions and such leading notes in their ears even if only certain of the notes in question ever normally came their way.

But by the late eighteenth century on the Continent (later in England) E.T. was increasingly used in keyboard tuning whereupon, as Altenburg tells us (pp. 74–5), great care had to be taken when playing the trumpet with the organ. Moreover ideas on melodic intonation were undergoing changes not all of them connected with E.T. There had grown a feeling that major and minor keys might be more pleasantly contrasted through slight widening of the major third and shortening of the minor (which in fact E.T. does). In 1811, Fröhlich of Würzburg, on whom like Altenburg we shall depend a great deal further on, warns against a common beginner's fault of sounding h5 too flat on the horn ('vom Horn', p. 8). Some ears may be offended by young buglers today when they blow h5 naturally, 'flat'. In some cases among valved instruments the flatness to E.T. may be so pronounced that players normally avoid the open h5 by making the note from h6 with the valves, for example on the B flat side of a double horn, and often on the C trumpets used in France and Spain.

The next three prime numbers bring intervals which do not

[1] The derivation of mean-tone can be worked out by adding intervals, either in the old way by multiplying their ratios or more quickly by adding the cent figures given in the table for the harmonic series. A major third from c′ to e′ must be 386 cents. But a pure fifth, 702 cents, added upon itself through g′, d″, a″, reaches e‴ at 2808 cents, which, deducting 2400 for two octaves, puts e′ at 408 cents, or 22 cents (the comma, almost an eighth of a tone) above the pure third. The fifth was therefore reduced by a quarter of this to 697. The note D, two of these fifths from C, now comes at 193, making the 'mean tone' which eliminates the natural difference between the 9:8 and 10:9 whole tones.

fit any recognized musical system, for example h7, nearly a third of a semitone below B flat. In non-literate music h7 is much employed, e.g. on alphorns, usually transcribed as a submediant (Ex. 6 a, f). Orchestrally, a former player might be required to pinch it up to a passable B flat, as in many classical trumpet parts. It is also important in trombone-playing, where it is tuned with the slide, while on the hand-horn it is indispensable.

Ascending higher than this, it can be most instructive to play slowly up the open notes of, say, an F horn from h8 to 16—the great melodic octave of pre-valve days—and to listen critically to the natural pitches as they come. Among them h11 and 13 each lie about a quarter-tone away from the nearest semitones of the scale and are, strictly speaking, unacceptable in diatonic music. On the natural instruments they nevertheless had to be employed, and h11 frequently in two capacities, as F and F sharp. For French and other players of the large *trompe* (or *cor*) *de chasse* this harmonic serves unabashedly as the fourth degree of the scale, here demonstrating the often overlooked fact that wrong intonation is not so when it occurs knowingly. The same goes when a composer has specifically demanded the misfit pitches of the series, as Britten in the *Serenade for Tenor, Horn and Strings*, with h7, 11, and 13, all dwelt on, written for Dennis Brain and recorded by him when he used the French horn with the F crook.

Above h16 a run of gradually diminishing semitones leads to h19, by coincidence a good E flat. At h21 we meet the twelfth of h7, and when *f'''* occurs in eighteenth-century virtuoso works for trumpet or horn this is the harmonic which no doubt served to produce it. On the old horn when crooked in one of its lowest keys the series can be climbed yet higher and at h27 at last offers a genuine A. Murray Barbour (1964, p. 112) shows this note written for Horn in low C (so sounding *a''*) in a *Symphonie russienne* of the 1770s by A. Veichtner. There are indeed cornet players who can reach h32, almost the top note of the pianoforte, though as little more than a squeak.

Embouchure history. Descriptions of players' methods of holding the mouth and lips are not known before the seventeenth century, but it is possible to gain a small idea of early embouchures from pictures and allusions to it in literature. Up to, and partly including the sixteenth century, we find almost invariably an inflation of the cheeks, still in the manner of Roman trumpeters more than a thousand years before. Too constant a feature to be interpreted as caricature, it must perpetuate a primitive obedience to the animal instinct to feel at one's most formidable when making the loudest possible noise. With cheeks distended and lips under no further restraint than the pressure of the mouthpiece, a great blast produces a vibration of vast amplitude and the ear-splitting sound required of a military trumpeter by the ancient practices of warfare: 'to inflame the army' as Machiavelli put it, and likewise to scare the enemy out of his wits. Today there are, mainly in jazz, successful brass players who inflate the cheeks and do so without detriment to either range or control. For this some tightening of the corners of the mouth is necessary, and medieval trumpeters very likely practised control along similar lines when circumstances demanded it, though it is equally likely that the purely military trumpeter, when his duty in the field lay in delivering sounds of utmost ferocity over a limited range of pitch, simply blew as hard as he could, with minimal constraint from facial muscles.

On the trumpet there are signs among sixteenth-century pictures of some reform. The trombone was then played in softer circumstances and in a more controlled manner by which 'you make the different notes not simply by force of breath and inflating the cheeks, but by moving a slide'. This, from Nicot's *Trésor de la langue français* (1606), is in a dictionary article 'Trompette', however, and not necessarily up-to-date as a general observation, since from such times the anatomical term *buccinator* enters for the 'trumpeter's muscles' at the sides of the mouth which pull back the corners and prevent the cheeks blowing out. To Bendinelli, a leading trumpeter of the same time, distending the cheeks was the worst of faults. His objection was that it was deforming; but Speer, later in the seventeenth century, adds (p. 218) that it also denies the breath its proper projection and moreover weakens the player.

Embouchure had by then reached its classic phase, still very different from the modern: 'tightly close the teeth and lips, leaving only a small opening...' (Altenburg, p. 121); 'draw the lips tight over the teeth, extending the mouth, and leaving a space between the teeth so as to admit the tip of the tongue' (Tully's *Tutor for the French Horn, c.* 1840). Such was the pedagogic basis of 'ambousure', as Hyde's *Preceptor* calls it *c.* 1798, through one of the greatest periods in brass history, and the portrait of

Reiche, eleven years Bach's principal trumpet in Leipzig, seems to show physiognomic evidence of it (Pl. VII). Its precepts were widely observed in traditional band-instrument teaching in Germany into the present century and are found in British instructions for bugle and cavalry trumpet which are still in print.

The early nineteenth century reveals some hints of revised thinking on the subject. Fröhlich tells hornists to use light mouthpiece pressure to avoid unnecessary fatigue of the lips ('zum Horn', p. 8). Yet, to judge by other works, this was well in advance of its time. In the great series of *Méthodes* emanating from the Paris Conservatoire, Dauverné, the trumpet professor, wrote just before the mid-century as Domnich had done for the horn some forty years before (1808) namely that it is the relative pressure of mouthpiece on lips which selects the pitch of notes; or, emanating from Germany in the same period, 'the trumpet should be grasped as close as possible to the mouthpiece, that the proper pressure may be given to the lips' (Roy and Muller's Tutor). The great Arban more or less repeats this for the cornet (1864), only adding that 'by pulling back the corners of the mouth one obtains a more open sound'. Sax's tutor for the saxhorns (1851) is exceptional in advocating freedom to tighten and relax the lower lip for high and low notes as being 'much better and less tiring than the method which consists in *la simple pression*'.

For the real advances, most of the credit goes to the wide world of the cornet player and brass band around the turn of the last century. About fifty years ago *The Easy Way to play Brass Instruments*, published by Wright & Round of Liverpool, could then distinguish between the Wrong Way, which 'seeks for tension of the lips by pressing the mouthpiece harder upon them' and the Right Way, 'the means provided by Nature, viz., muscular action: at each side of the lips are muscles which contract or relax at will, drawing the lips more tense or permitting them to relax, as may be desired... there is no strain on the lips,... the blood circulates without hindrance, and the lips do not become tired quickly, or eventually paralysed'. The reaction against pressure had by then reached its extreme in the 'No Pressure System' by which one learnt to sound the cornet or euphonium over the whole compass with the instrument suspended by a string, unsupported by the hands; or a no-pressure attachment could be bought, a spring-loaded telescopic shank which similarly made mouthpiece-pressure on the lips impossible. Many today use 'no pressure' in teaching, and even though in orchestral brass-playing some small pressure is usually accepted (and when practising without instrument or mouthpiece a metal ring may be held against the lips), the embouchure precepts stated in *The Easy Way* and similar publications have led directly to the modern methods which students know from their teachers and from thoughtful works like those of the distinguished American horn-player Philip Farkas, explaining the 'puckered smile'. To attempt to say more here would be out of place, but a further word is due on the question of breathing from the historical point of view.

Today regarded as the most important single factor of all, breathing seems to have been treated very casually throughout the older period. Dauprat, author of the Parisian Horn Méthode held in highest repute (1824), could have given this matter no thought at all, merely quoting from the Conservatoire's singing tutor: 'to breathe in, the belly must be flattened, swelling the chest, and to breathe out the belly returns slowly to its natural position and the chest is lowered'. This, he states, is applicable to all wind playing, and Arban repeats it. One is reminded of Shake-speare in *Troilus and Cressida*, 'Thou, trumpet . . . Come, stretch thy chest, and let thy eyes spout blood'—were it not that the Paris professors stress that no appearance of strain should be visible. It marks the extreme opposite to that which is taught today, though to be fair, Domnich mentions the diaphragm inhalation, and achievement of a 'well-controlled and efficient expiration' as opposed to the 'old manner of blowing with the chest'.

Again, the cornet player came to the rescue. Seventy years ago, pupils of Petit in France were made to place a hand upon the stomach to check that air is drawn in by pulling down the diaphragm, not by raising the chest. The same period recognized correct breathing as a conscious act, controlling air-pressure in exhalation by contracting the abdominal muscles to push the diaphragm upwards (instead of merely letting it rise as in natural breathing). This, mastered under proper instruction and with the lower ribs helping, could be said historically to have played the largest part in the abolition of plain mouthpiece pressure as the backing for the embouchure.

To hit the right note an old instruction was to 'think' the note. This works because with experience the 'thought' lip frequency will usually be close enough to the pitch for the tube-air to do the rest. Had it not worked we would hardly possess the centuries of brass music which we treasure today. But the operative word is 'usually'. Particularly under the stress of orchestral playing it was, up to less than fifty years ago, only players of exceptional talent who invariably pitched the right note. One remembers orchestral trumpeters who never throughout their professional lives felt absolutely confident in striking the sounding f'' which begins Beethoven's *Egmont* Overture; and the anxiety of the audience, equally in London or Vienna, as a famous solo passage for horn was approached, and the relief and admiration, in that order, when all went well. A player could win high repute through no other musicianly quality than of never hitting the wrong note. But today, experience is preceded by more accurate training; pupils are taught to produce very deliberately and positively the exact lip frequency required, learning to do so by extensive practice on the mouthpiece alone (though this is in itself not new, being recommended for the horn by Fröhlich) or with the lips alone (lip buzzing). A teacher may say that if one cannot play through a study or orchestral excerpt accurately in such ways, then one cannot be sure of playing it on the instrument. And so, thanks to rationalization of teaching, musical feeling and accuracy can now walk happily hand in hand for everyone, while on the historical wing of brass playing no one is likely to blame an artist if he baulks at restoring the historical embouchures which, if one has read the old sources correctly, should go with the past types of instrument now being revived. Yet if one has done so, the tight-drawn embouchure may have raised the high-overtone content, with some effect upon the tone-quality.

TONGUING is normally employed, as in all wind-playing, to strike any note which is not slurred to from the preceding note. In former times a strong emphasis was placed upon it while learning horn and trumpet; it was regarded almost as the primary action in producing the sound—'the tongue is to the player as the bow is to the violinist'. This arose in the first place through the ancient requirements of military calls with their manifold vigorous tonguings. Essential though tonguing will always be (the brisk T, more gentle D, and the double-tonguings based on $T-K$) a present trend is to allow it to develop fairly naturally, even practising attacks without it while focusing attention on the breathing and the embouchure.

VIBRATO is always a contentious subject. Musicians have tended to prefer the pure sounds of brass instruments and to suspect vibrato as being used *au fond* to make cantabile playing easier (which it does). Wherever vibrato has been regularly employed, on the cornet in British brass bands, or on the horn in France and Russia, it has aroused some criticism from outside. Ways of producing it amount broadly to four. With the diaphragm it can sound polished and stylish, but may be considered to interfere with the function of the diaphragm in pushing air into the instrument. With the lower lip or chin, somewhat as lip trills are usually made, it may interfere with embouchure, especially on instruments with small mouthpieces like trumpets: some eminent orchestral players have advocated that if vibrato must be used at all (as sometimes it must in caricature passages) the best means is by rocking the wrist on the valves to make a light wavering pressure on the lips. Finally, on trombone, the pitch-vibrato made with the slide, not mentioned in the older tutors, can as everyone knows have a pleasing effect, especially on modern suave-toned designs of the instrument.

'FALSET'. The latitude for a player's pitch-control of a harmonic, while only just sufficient in middle and high registers to allow for care over intonation, becomes in the low register very wide in the flattening direction; indeed without this the conventional system of three valves would have had a very limited future owing to sharpness of the valve combinations required in the low register (Chapter 8). At h2 the pitch can sometimes be dropped by a fourth or more by means of what is often termed 'loose-lipping', a sort of dragging embouchure which produces 'factitious' pitches not allowed for by the simple theory of the harmonic series. A useful historical term for this is from the German of Praetorius (II, 36) in connection with the cornett: playing 'in falset'. Horn-playing has known it from the eighteenth century, for instance notes down to low G (written in bass clef as G') met in classical parts. Mathematicians from Mersenne onwards have suggested explanations for these sounds, in some cases recently requiring a considerably revised view of the structure and genesis of the harmonic series which will surely lead in time to satisfactory elucidation of corresponding anomalies that crop up in the early history of sounding small horns and other instruments with the lips.

TWO

Foundations of Tradition

===

IN WOOD, SHELL AND HORN

It seems absurd that one can still be frightened by 'unearthly' echoes within a great cavern and 'ghostly' howls in the chimney. We feel a presence which is not natural and which places us in a position of danger. We hear ghosts, and having had in the past a great fear of the dead, our first thought is that they are male-volent. But primitive peoples who know ghosts better and hear them everywhere know also that some are friendly, among them the spirits of ancestors upon whose good will the strength of the folk and growth of foodstuffs may depend. The ancestors were buried and their voices are, as we say, sepulchral, and when their participation is needed in a tribal ceremony it may be invited by appropriate sounds made through instruments. The instrument may then even become temporarily the ancestor himself. Among such sound-makers are very large and crude tubular instruments which are blown into like a sort of trumpet to produce deep grunt-ing or booming sounds. They may be termed 'trumpet tubes', partly to follow Curt Sachs, the greatest of musical ethnologists, who writing in German used the term *Längstuba* (1928, p. 31).

Instruments of such kinds are widely distributed over the tropical world though not densely, and are deeply associated with tribal ritual, especially with the two great rites which span adult male life: initiation (severance from maternal protection) and ceremonies after death (departure to join the ancestral spirits). A notable region comprises the forests of the Amazon and its tri-butaries, where the ceremonial customs of the Tukano people, recently summarized by Donald Tayler (1968, xxviiiff.) provide a good illustration. At every major Tukano ritual ancestors are present, embodied in the trumpet tubes and great flutes. Both are of well-known Amazonian types. For the trumpets, a tree bark which sticks together like glue when dry is coiled into a wide tube.

Into the narrower end is stuck a thinner tube about a foot long, cut from the paxiuba palm, and this serves as a mouthpipe. Two sticks are bound to the exterior to strengthen the construction (Fig. 2, a). The instruments are intensely sacred, hidden until required. When a new one must be made, the spirit of the tree, deep in the forest, must be asked permission for removal of the sacred bark; a myth tells that the tree springs from the ashes of a sacrificed youthful musical prodigy, a theme not unfamiliar elsewhere.

The trumpet is sounded by blowing strongly but with minimal embouchure, the tube-air and the breath taking the lips with them. The effort is such that each sound is of short duration, which may explain the invariable pairing of instruments, one man blowing after the other in close repetition. Meanwhile on the great flutes, tuned a tone apart, one player follows the other up and down his harmonic series in a regular my-blow-your-blow alternation to unfold an unhurried melody above the grunting bass of the trumpets, all proceeding at the unhurried pace of a long-established religious ritual.

At a Tukano initiation the boys are first shown the secret place where the flutes and the trumpet mouthpipes are hidden in a stream bed; the coiled bark portions, which would not stand long immersion, are hidden nearby. All bathe, after which the party returns in procession with the music playing, whereupon the womenfolk remove their maternal presence on pain of death. The procession circles at a half dance round the group's dwelling house until nightfall, the men taking turns to sound the instruments. Thus the ancestors are brought to the house. Later, in the rite itself, the boy is whipped, the vine lash having been stirred about inside one of the trumpets to draw out the power of the ancestor for virility. Then the other trumpet of the pair is rolled along his back, this ancestor bestowing promise of growth in stature. Finally all return in procession to replace the flutes and mouthpipes in the stream.

At mourning ceremonies held a year after burial of a leading and respected man both men and women are present. The largest bark trumpets, up to 15 feet long, are now produced and form the most sacred element during the three-day rite. The ancestors embodied in the trumpets will guide the spirit to its ancestral home— a recurring theme in trumpet history over most of the world in higher societies and one major strand in its continuity.

Among other Amazonian tribes, trumpets dedicated to similar purposes are made of joined pottery bulbs, sounding 'very dark and deep'; or they may be hollow canes with their ends dipped into a jar which acts as a reverberator or primitive bell. 'No words can describe the awful darkness and dismal moaning which the breath draws from these canes,' wrote the eighteenth-century Jesuit, Gumilla, exploring the forests of the Upper Orinoco and experiencing a chill of fear at the unearthly sound of these 'devil's trumpets' which however to their owners perhaps represented the friendly embodiment of benign ancestors.

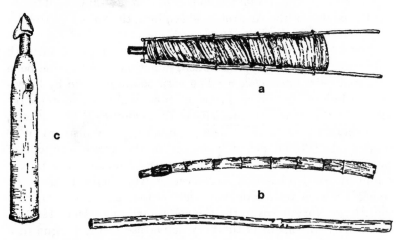

Fig. 2 a. Bark trumpet, Amazonia; b. didjeridu, North Australia (two specimens in Pitt Rivers Museum, Oxford); c. vertical wooden trumpet, Lower Congo (height 3 feet).

From a technical point of view this elementary method of sounding a tube by holding it firmly to the mouth and blowing into it, requiring no conscious element of embouchure, could have been discovered by anyone anywhere that suitable vegetable material came to hand. It is known in Africa, for example among the Nilo-Hamitic Labwor people (Wachsmann, 1953, p. 347) where metre-long wooden tubes, *aporo*, are sounded by the women to welcome the men back from a successful hunt, and also at rain-making and other dances. They blow with puffed cheeks, lips pouted into the instrument, making a wu-wu sound of deep pitch 'not unlike a foghorn'. Curt Sachs suggested, but did not insist, that such trumpet blowing has an origin in the 'megaphone' effect. At seasonal ceremonies of certain Brazilian tribes, as the Iawa (recorded by Flornoy for the Musée de l'Homme), benign spirits protecting the crops are embodied in large flutes to which are opposed malevolent spirits acted by droning vocally into coiled bark reverberators which somewhat resemble the body-section of the bark trumpets described above. The voice becomes mildly disguised, like that of a theatrical spectre spoken through a cardboard megaphone. But this voice disguiser and the primitive labrosone (to coin a handy term for 'lip-vibrated instrument') are so close to each other physically that undoubtedly they are of much the same age, and in the traditional techniques of that best-known of trumpet tubes, that of the Australian aborigines, the voice and the lips play an important part together.

This Australian instrument is made of a cane cleaned out with a firestick, or of a eucalyptus branch, sometimes one that has been hollowed by ants (Fig. 2, b). The basic sound is made by lip vibration induced by blowing into the tube, while the vocal chords vibrate at the same pitch, usually in the region F–A. Sometimes, however, this vocal ingredient is lacking. The instrument is played solo (Pl. I), not in pairs, or to the accompaniment of clashed boomerangs and song, the player achieving a continuous sound by nasal inhalation, a reserve of wind being held in the cheeks—a rare technique with labrosones, also reported with some large ivory horns in the Congo (quoted by de Hen, 1960, p. 177). Most important is the very active use of the tongue in a syllabic and compellingly rhythmic manner which has onomatopoeically given rise to the instrument's name in English, 'didjeridu'. In 1914 Baldwin Spenser described the sound as 'biddle an bum' with a strong accent on the 'bum'; Basedow later (1925) gave it as 'didnodiddo diduardu'—which comes closer to the result obtained recently when some players were persuaded, much to the amusement of their children, to record the syllables independently of the instrument (A. Moyle, *Instit. Aboriginal Studies*, M-001/5). Now and then the performer flicks the note up to the next pitch at which the plain tube will sound, about a tenth higher. But the most extraordinary feature of the music is a second tier of sounds produced high in the treble register by shaping the mouth cavity selectively to bring out different overtones, somewhat as other people play the Jew's harp or the musical bow held to the mouth. As with these, the loudest sound is the rhythmically uttered low note, and at first one may miss the corona of the mouthed harmonics which, once recognized, thenceforth draw one's attention. Whether the aborigine brought the didjeridu across from Asia during the late Ice Age or invented it in his subsequent isolation we may never know. But its complex technique was evolved because it is the only non-percussive instrument which, so far as we know, he has ever possessed. It serves for every kind of ceremony and magic from initiations and corroborees to casting love spells, while latterly it has been proudly played before the General Assembly of the United Nations to plead the aborigine cause.

A more artificial ritual trumpet is made by hollowing out a small tree trunk. People at the mouth of the Congo blow it through a hole in the side (Fig. 2, c) holding the instrument, called *ludi*, clasped vertically against the body: they sound its grunting note at funeral ceremonies. It is described by Söderberg (1956, p. 210). Another is the *mabu* of the Solomon Islands (Pl. I). Beatrice Blackwood (p. 411) tells how in former times the trunk was hollowed with a hardwood spear assisted by fire. Now it is done with an iron pig-spear. A fair-sized specimen is three feet long and about 15 cm. wide at the base, where the wood is about 6 mm. thick. To the top end a half-coconut is gummed on with putty-nut kernel and in the centre of this is a hole for blowing, 3 cm. wide. To sound it requires a knack, basically an embouchure. As in South America, a pair or more emit their powerful deep sounds in alternation, sometimes overlapping to make chords such as *G d f*, which is also the pattern of notes on some of the region's large panpipes. At funeral dances, melodies are played above the *mabu* on panpipes, joined by a chorus of mixed voices. The instrument is also sounded at initiations, and at quite minor ceremonies like hair trimming it is played with the panpipes like a village band.

The *mabu* may also be substituted for the more highly venerated wooden slit-drum, which is interesting in view of other suspected transfers in the past of different ritual instruments, for example under the influence of a stronger tribe accustomed to different sound-makers. Thus in Amazonia the boom of the bullroarer may have in some instances been replaced by that of trumpet tubes. It is chiefly through their present distribution and numinous roles that these tubes were considered by Sachs to be among man's earliest ritual noise-makers, younger than the bullroarer but older than the more powerful and sonorously efficient drum, which for all we know may have in some areas displaced the tubes.

Conch. Three principal kinds of marine mollusc are used for making shell trumpets: *Triton* ('trumpet shell') with long-pointed apex like a giant whelk; *Cassis* ('helmet shell', also used for

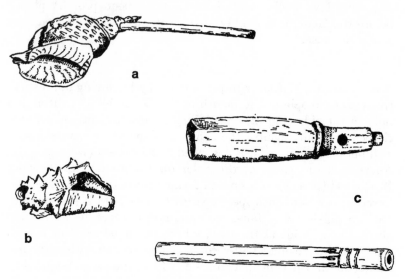

Fig. 3 a. Side-blown *Triton* with wooden mouthpipe, Polynesia; **b.** End-blown *Strombus*, Europe; **c.** two wooden conch substitutes, New Guinea.

cameo-making) with a thick brim surround; and *Strombus* ('true conch') with short sharp point encircled by spiky rings and one of the best-known to European peoples past and present (Fig. 3, b). The blowing hole is made by breaking off the point (for an end-blown conch) or, as usually across the Pacific, by making a hole in the side near the point. In some localities, such as the New Hebrides, either method may be employed. Inside the shell are 4½ turns making an expanding windway of flattened oval section and about 2 feet long. This is often increased by fixing in the hole a straight mouthpipe of wood or bamboo (Fig. 3, a), to make an average-sized shell give the note of the cherished very big ones. Acoustically the conch much resembles a horn and can be made to sound harmonics up to h3 or 4 with an effort. But the normal note is the fundamental, sounding low in the treble clef. Often this note is lowered by placing the hand across the mouth of the shell: thus the conchist of the Santander stick dance, accompanied by his dexterous side-drummer, repeats a slurred d' e'flat d' —, hand-stopping $+$ 0 $+$ on a strombus shell from the ocean nearby. Or in Fiji a large fingerhole is cut in the side of an end-blown Triton near the mouth, providing an alternative note through which the vocabulary of fishing boat signals can be enlarged.

Conch blowing has gone on at some time or another almost everywhere: in Eurasia back to neolithic times and as far inland as Tibet and Central Europe, where the shells were brought by traders, as they still are for the gift shops. In Asia this has been partly for priestly service, a reminder that the conch has had a place in tribal ritual, in defence against spirits of sickness, in rain magic (water association) and to ward off storms, as in Western Bohemia where the storm conch, *Wetterhorn*, was sounded until recently and guarded with the most stringent precautions lest it should lose its power (see, e.g., Ziskal, 1896). Such functions may or may not be the first for which the conch was blown, the issue being complicated by the fact that the instrument possesses a property which is unique on most early cultural levels, being the only small portable sound-maker which can deliver a really loud noise that can be heard two miles away. Amidst thick forests and hostile neighbours this can be immeasurably important for communication and safety. In New Guinea the conch signal can be part of daily life and every man knows the knack of sounding it. Calls are distinguished in the obvious way, by long and short notes. From a tribe on the Mamba and Gira rivers, Beaver (1916) noted the following calls:

after a killing in a fight in camp: — ∪ — ∪ — ∪ — ∪ etc.; summons to a fight, or alarm: — ∪ ∪ ∪ ∪ ∪ ∪ ∪ (re-peated); men bringing a pig: — ∪ —.

From the Kiki river, Chinnery (1917) found that a call of the second type above announced a dance; the alarm was a series of shorts, and 'death of an important person' was a series of longs. Where a shell is unprocurable or too expensive, a substitute is made of a wooden or bamboo cylinder, making a short trumpet a foot long with blowing hole in the side or the end (Fig. 3, c).

In higher cultures the conch has been sounded for everything from calling labourers from the fields in North Wales, to serving an Andalusian ducal huntsman in the boar hunt, and announcing the daily opening of the public baths in Persia. Quasi-ritual usages have grown from this, as in Jersey where, as elsewhere, the shell trumpet has served to keep fishing boats in touch in bad weather, midsummer night used to be celebrated by a festive blowing of conches all over the island (Marett, *Folklore*, 1927, p. 178).

The shell trumpet has the further importance of being man's first war trumpet, for when blown as strongly as possible its normally attractive note becomes harsh and savage. In New Guinea the conch has formed an indispensable item of equipment for every man setting out at nightfall on a war party. Captain Cook heard it as the Hawaiians strove to scare off his ships; so likewise the Spaniards in Peru, the French in Madagascar, and the early Moslem invaders of Central India, who are said to have been rather amused at the conch-blowing Hindu army mounted on elephants. In the Chinese army of the last century the conch was sounded on watches, and in the British Vice-regal guard at Calcutta it served as a bugle. But also, through the peculiarly cyclic paths of conch history, it has come to the Indian temples as an attribute of the war god Vishnu who will sound it on the Day of Judgement as the earth is devoured in flames, like the war trumpet in Western religions. The Indian temple conches are as a rule very special, made from the uncommon *Turbinella* or 'chank' shell, harvested off Ceylon and sold in the Calcutta market where great sums are paid for the rare left-handed specimens, which are then mounted in gold. War is forgotten and the conch softly punctuates the priest's recitation: 'its clear, mellow, humming notes, heard every morning and evening from the temples and the groves about them have a peculiar though melancholy effect, not without charm,' wrote Meadows Taylor in 1864. So too felt the Naga boy in Assam who used to take his conch on his walks, stopping now and again to sound it just for pleasure.

Horn. An animal horn is prepared for blowing by first removing the bony core with hot water or simply leaving the horn exposed to the air and the flies. Hence there is little hope of tracing back the blowing horn archaeologically since a fossilized core does not reveal whether the horn was further prepared for sounding by cutting a blowing hole (and not used only for drinking or putting things in). Though horned herbivores were hunted during the glacial period, horn-blowing has not been found in Palaeolithic art, so whether the mimetic association so deeply implanted in the words 'hunting horn' goes back much further than the Bronze Age is hard to tell. Africans, the only people who now extensively make blowing horns from wild game, are historically known to have done so only from the time of the first Portuguese visitors to the West Coast. Their use of the horn, however, can tell much about the place of the instrument in early society.

African horns are made principally from elephant ivory and from the horns of wild antelopes; cattle horn is a poor man's substitute. The koodoo horn is smooth with a graceful double twist. That of the sable antelope is curved and corrugated— though the horn-maker may partly erase the corrugation. The gemsbock horn is straight and slender, needle-pointed and corrugated at the base only. All are beautiful objects and the African does not regularly spoil them by cutting off nearly half the horn, which would be needed to reach a point in the bore wide enough for a terminal blowing hole. Instead he carves a large hole in the side, which serves just as well if not better. The harmonics usually sound with a flat fundamental and at stretched intervals, though often h2 and h3 can together give a good impression of a fifth, as demonstrated by A. N. Tucker's jotting (pp. 10–11) of horn motifs played during a funeral dance of the Shilluk in the Southern Sudan (Ex. 3a), the first on a koodoo horn, answered by

Ex. 3 a. Prelude to a funeral dance, Shilluk (after A. N. Tucker); b. Five ivory horns played at a feast, Middle Congo (from an old recording).

the deep note of a much longer horn with gourd bell, approached in falset. For most signals and music, however, only the clearest and best-carrying note will be used. Sometimes the point of the horn is cut off by the amount required for piercing a narrow hole through to the tip of the bore. This can be opened and closed with the thumb to raise the note by a tone or more, and is used sometimes in quick hunting calls, message sending and music.

Horns are blown in Africa for as many purposes as the conch in Melanesia. Kirby (1953) mentions witch-doctor's magic, calls to a dance, initiations, hunting, pleasure; also, and very important (p. 77): the Pedi chief (in the Transvaal) 'had his own player of the sable antelope horn who acted as his standard bearer. This official would sound the call to arms in case of war, when the men would rally to the chief, while the women would take to the hills. For in olden times all lived within hearing for safety's sake; it is only since the coming of the white men that the people have spread over the countryside.'

A striking musical use of horns in Africa is in bands, where each player is responsible for one note (Ex. 3b), save when the leader may use the tip hole for a second pitch. A bigger range is offered by substitute horns of gourd or wood or both. The gourds, specially grown in elongated shapes, have the pulp ground away by rattling pebbles inside and flushing out with water. With their hard thin walls they make good free-speaking instruments (like our metal flutes) and are cheaply expendable if falsely tuned. Sets made from hollow tree-branches have the longest horns, reaching three metres, as may be seen in a photograph from Tanzania reproduced in *MGG*, 'Ostafrika'. All band horns are side-blown, as well they might be when the band performs spectacular antics while playing, rolling on the ground and so on, very dangerous if not impossible with end-blowing.

For the end-blown horn of West Asia and Europe material was early on provided by the wild goat *Ibex*, domesticated from about the sixth millennium B.C., the wild sheep, and the wild ox *Aurochs* from the Caspian steppes, domesticated some thousand years later and subsequently the bull of Minoan fame. With domesticated herds and flocks on open pasture the custom, indeed the necessity, has ever been for the herdsman or boy to control them and to guard them against human and animal predators by the sound of his horn, suitably uttered through this token of the bull's or ram's strength and authority, and through the older periods of horn history it is probably true to say that more notes have been sounded by Little Boy Blue than by all the St. Huberts and Rolands put together. It is always a worthwhile experiment to sound a horn (even orchestral) at the gate of a meadow with cattle at the far end, and await what develops; the beasts will have never heard the sound before unless in the deep memory of instinct. From Roman times Polybius (*Hist.*, 12.iv.6) tells of the astonishing skill of Italian swineherds with the horn; how from a vast herd, the pigs of a particular breed or age-group would answer without fail to their particular call and sort themselves out for their nightly quarters. Still in remoter parts of Europe, the herdsman sets forth in the morning with his dog and his horn or substitute in wood or tinplate. Some strongly rhythmic setting-forth calls noted down in Hungary by Bartók employ three or four harmonics including the fundamental which sounds flat to the others (printed in Sárosi, 1967, p. 100).

The shepherd's horn was naturally found other uses, sounding alarms, calling to defence or war, keeping touch when hunting. Ritual use seems less pronounced. The horn was evidently sounded in some Sumerian temples along with the shepherd's flute; but more prominent in Bronze-Age Western Asia is the complete bull's horn (not cut for blowing) or its effigy in clay as it appears as a power and fertility emblem on the altars of Crete.

The horn pierced with large fingerholes is a rare European variety belonging again especially to shepherds. A four-hole cowhorn found in a Swedish bog has been dated to *c*. 900 A.D. in the Viking period (Dalarna Museum; see Crane, 1972, p. 59), while pictures suggest that the species was fairly wide-spread across Northern Europe from the tenth century to the twelfth, and then numbered among the instruments used by itinerant entertainers. In modern times it has been little known outside Scandinavia and the Baltic countries. Typical Swedish tunes like that in Ex. 4 are

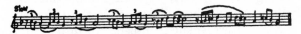

Ex. 4 Herding tune on four-hole cowhorn, Dalarna, Sweden (Swedish Radio RELP 5017, played by P. Jakobsson, 1961).

genuinely pastoral, apparently modelled on the ancient melos of herdswomen's calls with the voice. La Borde gives a similar example from Norway (1780, II, p. 418). In Finland, Estonia and some districts in Russia the horn is made of wood covered with birch-bark, about 40 cm. in length and perhaps a surviving form of the prototype of our cornett. In Vladimir, east of Moscow, a bass size, an octave lower, is made also, and with its help the villagers form three- or four-part *rozhok* choirs, in a tradition which has been said to spring from improvised part-singing and may be comparatively recent; numerous transcriptions are in Smirnov, 1959.

Bone. Bone trumpets are not very common but have been reported in Amazonia, where the thighbones of a slain enemy chief may subsequently be turned against his people as a screeching war trumpet (Rowbotham, *Musical Opinion*, 1894). In the Himalayan countries the same instrument has served in the performances of local witch-doctors (Pl. I) and in Lamaist and other sectarian rites including funerals, where the sound 'attracts the soul and guides it in the right direction'. The bone is usually of a deceased monk or executed criminal and preferably a tall one. Hooker (*Himalayan Journals*, p. 120) wrote of how in Sikkim one of the first Europeans to be buried near Darjeeling, being a tall man, was promptly dug up by members of a local sect 'for his trumpet bones'. The femur makes a serviceable trumpet up to 40 cm. long and a handsome one when overlaid with leather, ornamental brass-work and coloured stones.

Pottery. Small earthenware horns have been found in Egyptian burials. From medieval Europe more are known, and they were evidently used for sounding signals, since they have been discovered beneath castles, rather than in graves as votive objects. Pottery trumpets or horns remained up to recently familiar articles in Southern Europe, sold at fairs particularly at Carnival time. Some are curled in a small loop, perhaps to be less easily broken. The greatest variety is from Pre-Columbian America, especially Peru. Among those illustrated by the d'Harcourts (1925, Planches, X-XIII) are small trumpets, up to 52 cm. long; decorative conch-shaped models with human or animal mouths; horns coiled in a loop; and tubes coiled several times round a vase. The coiled designs, which well lend themselves to the potter's craft, could scarcely have been conceived in imitation of anything else except perhaps the interior of a conch.

Composite trumpets. In widely-separated regions of the world long trumpets are made of wood and cane, distinguished from the more primitive instruments by different handling of the raw material and by sounding with strong embouchure on high or fairly high harmonics. The instruments of wood or tall grasses are generally made by halving longitudinally in order to carve the bore or remove pith and knots. The two halves are then united under a binding of fibres, sinews or bark—a method also used in making such things as blow-pipes. A bell of gourd, pottery or cowhorn is attached, though in most wooden instruments the terminal expansion which steadies and strengthens the sound is fashioned integrally.

In Asia cane trumpets from 90 to 150 cm. long are known mainly from Assam, where Naga herdboys used to make them for scaring elephants off the crops. Sometimes they sounded imitations of British bugle calls, for which the average length of the instrument is about right. But it has also been reported to bear the name 'horn of death' and to have been blown at funerals (Regensburg, Hoerburger Coll. A.506) which links it, as a surviving prototype or perhaps a later imitation, with the metal trumpets of the Himalayan states and China. As on many composite trumpets, the blowing end of the Naga instrument is cut diagonally to make an oval opening of a good width for blowing, and in some examples the tube is given a 'conical' profile by joining together many short lengths of bamboo of increasing diameter (Fig. 4, a). Very much larger instruments are made by Andean peoples. The *trutruca* of the Araucano Indians in Chile, is two to three metres long, with cowhorn bell (Fig. 4, b). The Araucano, who were pushed south to their present homeland while valiantly resisting the Spaniard, retain many of their old musical intsruments, which are ethnologically much on a par with those of the Naga. This trumpet is intensely ceremonial and religious, blown at all feasts, funerals, rain-makings and dances, in some ways recalling the trumpet-tubes of the forests. Still larger trumpets, *clarín*, are made in Bolivia and sounded at church festivals. Some of these are made of two long tree-grass stems placed parallel and connected by a short cross-tube secured with strips of cloth and thongs (Fig. 4, c), or have a complete, much-elongated 'folded' shape with two cross-tubes. A narrower stem with lateral blowing hole is inserted in the end. Another *clarín* was reported, allegedly from Mexico, in *Caecilia*, 1828, 8 to 10 feet long with oblique embouchure.

The cowhorn bell is of course post-Columbian, but it could have come to replace the gourd-neck bell which has also been met on these trumpets. No European observer mentions any huge native trumpet in the Americas before the eighteenth century. Yet a pottery trumpet found among pre-Columbian objects (d'Harcourt, Pl. X) shows the replicated shape: it is only 46 cm. long but presumably a votive model. So one cannot be too certain that the big cane trumpets appeared in the first place as imitations of the Spanish trumpet, though the sounds of the latter may have brought new life and style to a depressed native tradition. This

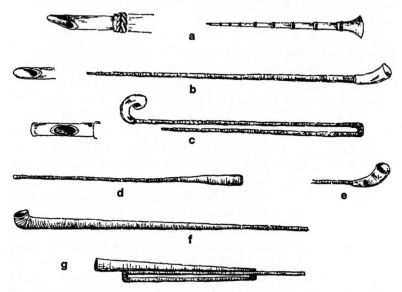

Fig. 4 a. Naga cane trumpet, Assam; b. *trutruca*, Chile; c. *clarín*, Bolivia; d. alphorn, *trembita*, Ukraine; e. with horn bell, Russia (Viatka); f. *bucium*, Rumanian Carpathians; g. *bucium*, trumpet shape, Rumania.

might account for the hint of European cavalry calls in present *trutruca* tunes, in their fast repetitions of h4 with h5 interjected (Ex. 5), recast in vigorous $\frac{6}{8}$ rhythms which, however, are certainly indigenous, being met in Araucano songs as well.

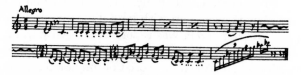

Ex. 5 Part of an Araucano dance-tune on *trutruca* (after C. Lavin, *Anuario musical*, 1961).

Certainly there can be no direct connection with the European alphorns. In a fine study of these, Szadrowsky (1867, p. 297) mentioned vague reports of such instruments in the Pyrenees, said to be fairly short—and he mentioned Scotland also—but in neither case has the species since been confirmed.

Alphorns. These long wooden instruments of the European shepherd and herdsman, here conveniently grouped together under the familiar Swiss name, have a present distribution which follows a horseshoe from Norway and Sweden, across the Baltic countries and parts of Russia, the western Slav countries and Rumania (Pl. I), round to the Alps themselves. Up to late in the last century they were still found in the Vosges and in many of the German highlands from the Black Forest to Thuringia,

The present horseshoe thus represents the surviving fringes of an alphorn area which once extended over most of North and Central Europe from Alsace eastwards, mainly in regions of fir and birch. The well-dried young trunk is halved by saw or axe, and after hollowing the two halves are spirally bound with strips of bark or sliced fir roots. Other woods are employed too, like poplar. The bore in most cases is cylindrical, expanding towards the bottom, though sometimes conical throughout. The form is straight, save where the custom is to select a mountainside tree curved at the base, so as to obtain a turned-up bell. Often a detachable mouthpiece is carved or turned, for instance from a cotton reel.

After a few unclear words alluding to a rustic *tuba* by the younger Ekkehard of St. Gall (*Casus S. Galli*, 3, eleventh century) the earliest reliable evidence of the alphorn is also from Switzerland, where tradition takes the instrument back to the fourteenth century with a length of about five feet. From 5 to 7 feet is, or was in the past, the common size in all parts and in some the only size: *cf.* Praetorius (Fig. 18), who ascribed the instrument to shepherds of Vogtland (Upper Saxony) and Switzerland. The giant alphorn, far exceeding these in length, is first mentioned in 1555 by the Swiss naturalist Gessner, who observed the 11-foot size in mountain villages round Lucerne—a size which is confirmed musically in a sung version of the 'cow-round-up' (*ranz des vaches*, etc.) from Appenzell in Rhaw's *Bicinia Gallica*, 1545; this rises to an implied h12. More such instruments, many larger, are found in the Carpathian regions. Slovakian shepherds win the record at over 17 feet. But in the east and north, seven feet has not as a rule been exceeded, and the tunes do not usually rise above h6 to 8.

In many parts, including Sweden, Russia, Rumania and Austria, the alphorn has been alternatively made in the 'folded' shape of the natural trumpet (Fig. 4, g) and patently in direct imitation of it. The historical evidence here goes back to the Schloss Ambras (Innsbruck) inventory of 1596 (Schlosser, 1920, p. 11). This lists a large *Allgewisches Waldhorn*, and there is little doubt that the trumpet-shaped alphorn from Ambras in the Vienna Collection (A. 279) is this very instrument.

One notices, with this model, how rural communities separated by great distances have independently copied the shape of the military trumpet. One possible explanation of the ordinary alphorn is that people may have done a similar thing before, reproducing the form of post-Roman straight trumpets, having been encouraged to do so by the working properties of wood and the greater sound-carrying power over that of the common run of small horns of cowhorn or wood.[1] There is some evidence, noticed in the next chapter, for early medieval wooden trumpets, but these were different, being associated with kings or with literate iconography.

A more widely-held view is that some of the Indo-European-speaking pastoralists possessed long wooden horns prior to the last great migrations. Ritual use, which could point to great antiquity, is not however very marked among alphorns; they may proclaim a death or, formerly, gather people to defence, but these are signal functions. There survived up to recently among the Mari in Russia an association with tree-worship: the victor in the Spring steeple-chase earned the right to carry the 5-foot horn of that year to the sacred grove and there hang it on the sacred tree or set fire to it in sacrifice to the harvest god (Nikiforov, p. 34). But these Volga Finns have borrowed many instruments from their neighbours (their very word for a wooden horn, *puch*, must have been brought from the south) and the alphorns in this and some other of their old rites may have come to be substituted for something more primitive and expendable like a reed-horn of coiled bark.

A few examples of alphorn melody are in Ex. 6, chosen at random along with some from the giant types. Their extraordinary

---

[1] The word *bucium* which denotes the alphorn in certain parts of Rumania no doubt derives from Latin *bucina*, but this then meant a horn of some common small size.

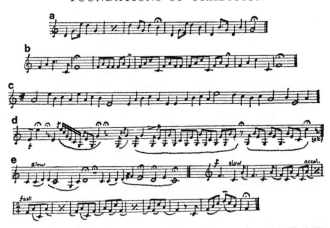

Ex. 6 Alphorn calls and tunes. **a.** Norway (*Journ, English Folk Dance & Song Society*, 1935); **b.** Estonia (*Atlas*); **c.** Ukraine (*Atlas*, transposed a third lower); **d.** Rumania, Moldavia (from a recording by Electrecord); **e.** Slovakia (after Leng); **f.** Rigi, Switzerland, 1855 (after Szadrowsky, transposed a fifth lower).

freedom and variety make the strongest contrast with the constrained formulae which marked old traditions of the military trumpet so far as an idea of these can be recovered. If in fact herdsmen copied some ancient trumpet they made free with the sounds, no doubt on the basis of the mountain cattle-call and yodel. Musical imitation has been, rather, the other way round, from country to town, as one knows well in works from Vejvanovsky to Filtz (Op. 2, VI), Beethoven (*cf.* Ex. 6f) and others later. The last section of Ex. 6c, calling the cattle to evening milking and heard in Switzerland also, may strike a concert-goer as slightly familiar.

IN METAL THROUGH ANTIQUITY

Short trumpet. The discovery of two trumpets in the tomb of Tutankhamen confirmed the metallic reality of the trumpet seen in Egyptian reliefs and paintings from the end of the fifteenth century B.C. The two instruments have short expanding tubes and funnel bell, the longer (58 cm.) of silver, the other (49·4 cm.) of sheet bronze partly clad with gold.[1] The bells are incised with the

[1] Cairo Museum. Other dimensions, putting the silver trumpet first: tube less bell, 47·4, 40·3 mm.; diameter of blowing end inside, 17, 13 mm.; outside, 25, 19 mm.; at base of bell, 26, 23 mm.; bell rim, 82, 84 mm.

king's name and with the godly emblems of leading military divisions. In all but four of the seventeen representations cited by Hickmann in his exhaustive monograph of 1946 the trumpet is seen in the hands of a trumpeter directing a squad of marching or parading soldiers; in the remainder it serves in some regal ceremony. With each Tutankhamen trumpet is a removable core of solid wood which the player kept inside the instrument to preserve it from damage until he actually had to blow it. Three scenes show this object tucked under the trumpeter's arm as he blows grasping the instrument in both hands, one by the mouthpiece, the other close by the bell (Fig. 5, a). A third specimen, of bronze, survives in the Louvre; this dates from much later, possibly from the Roman period. Its size is much the same, 54 cm., or about a cubit (elbow to fingertips, variously standardized as a measure in the ancient world); but it may be part of an incense holder.

Searching for an earlier representation, Hickmann later believed that he had found one of a thousand years before Tutankhamen in a Saqqara relief of *c.* 2500 B.C. (illustrated in his 1961 book, p. 41). The end where the bell should be is defective, leaving only what appears to be a short thin tube, held by a youth in one hand at a sacrificial procession crossing the Nile in boats. Sachs deduced from comparative chronology that musical instruments seen in Ancient Egypt were, generally speaking, known in Mesopotamia up to two millennia earlier. The nearest material remains from the latter which have any possible bearing on trumpets are some very small (10 to 20 cm. long) silver and gold 'problematic devices, perhaps signal horns' found squashed flat in excavations at Tepe Hissar (E. F. Schmidt, 1937, IIIc.). They may show that something akin to trumpet-making was in progress there, but their date is not earlier than *c.* 2000 B.C. However, Rimmer (1969, p. 30) notices a Sumerian carved stone from Khafaji, *c.* 2600 B.C. (Fig. 5, b). One cannot tell much of its shape from the eroded outline, but the size is about that of the Egyptian trumpet. It was no doubt a royal instrument of metal, or of wood encased in precious metal as the contemporary reed-pipes from Ur may have been and as some aulos pipes of later times in fact were. Cladding with metal is not rare: thighbone trumpets in Asia, cane flutes in Africa, horns in ancient Europe.

A Mesopotamian trumpet of the fourth millennium B.C., as implied by literal reading of Sachs's theory, has not yet been discovered, leaving one only to imagine a slow sequence of evolution from the early Caspian neolithic some three millennia previously, when people perhaps sounded wooden or bark trumpet-tubes at certain rites, conches and wooden substitutes for communication and alarms, and possibly thighbone trumpets (the splayed ends of which suggest a bell), all of these becoming superseded as metal crafts developed and the ruling castes of populous stratified society

Fig. 5 a. Egyptian trumpeter, relief from Abu-Simbel, c. 1200 B.C.; b. limestone fragment from Khafaji, c. 2600 B.C. (after Rimmer); c. Relief from Nineveh, c. 700 B.C. (British Museum); d. Greek bronze statuette, S. Italy, 5th century B.C. (British Museum); e. *Tuba* player, state sacrificial procession, Rome, 1st century A.D. (Vatican Museum); f. Synagogue of Dura-Europos, mural, c. 250 A.D. (Nat. Museum, Damascus).

demanded, among articles of luxury and display, a trumpet to match: the little straight trumpet with which to sound the rasping, incisive shout of command thenceforth to be associated with authority of state and the marshalling and encouragement of large military forces. To such a line of development, that which took place in Ancient America, briefly noticed earlier, offers some analogy. In Mexico the eventual trumpet is seen in the Late Maya wall paintings of Bonampak, by Chiapas (reproduced in Bushnell, *The First Americans*, 1968, p. 49): a pair of ceremonial trumpets rather larger than the Egyptian, wide-belled, and not unlike an earlier trumpet of painted clay, 52 cm. long, preserved from Nasca, Peru (illustrated in d'Harcourt, Pls. X, XI).

The blowing end of the Egyptian trumpet has attached round it a metal ring rather like a wedding ring, and this appears to have been the only mouthpiece provision. The same 'ring' mouthpiece is found still in Southern India, in brass trumpets about 75 cm. in length, sounded in pairs alternately at certain funerals with 'ear-splitting monotony without interruption to the end of the obsequies'. Other Indian trumpets have inserted mouthpieces but apparently not these, while an inserted mouthpiece would have given the Egyptian trumpet a different appearance in the pictures. Hickmann therefore tested Tutankhamen's bronze trumpet as it stood, avoiding a consciously modern embouchure and pressing hard against the lips in the manner implied by the two-handed grasp which in fact proved necessary. He obtained raucous and powerful sounds on two pitches, about c' (flat fundamental) and a sharp d''; he could also produce a falset sound, somewhere between the two main pitches. (Trials by Kirby also produced the next harmonic, about a sixth higher, but evidently by using a modern embouchure.)

Plutarch's story (*Morals* 150 and 362) that certain Egyptian delta towns detested the trumpet since it made a noise like a donkey, to them an ungodly animal deprived of fodder on days of sacrifice to the Sun, points on the face of it to a series of powerful blasts on a pitch roughly corresponding to the lower sound of this trumpet. The Louvre example may be from Plutarch's time, and the comparison may have arisen merely from degenerate methods of sounding the instrument in a temple summons, little reflecting signals of command given by military trumpeters in far greater days long before.

On the other hand the Jewish people, having adopted the Egyptian military trumpet on their return from exile (*Numbers* 10) may have handed down something of the ancient manner of sounding it through the tradition of calls delivered on the shofar. A shofar must be made from a ritually killed sheep or goat, and in its most usual form has the small end pierced with a long narrow passage which connects the elliptical mouthpiece cavity with the main cavity of the bore. The acoustic behaviour is strange. Two pitches are obtained, often but not always about a fifth apart, and apparently representing h2 and a falset below. Now when two pitches are employed on a small horn it seems to be a human instinct to commence a signal on the lower (cf. Ex. 3a from Africa) and then, if possible, to focus the interval to a consonance felt in the ear, particularly a fifth. This is what synogogue calls do in several ways: three of them are illustrated in Ex. 7.

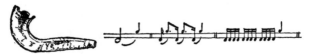

Ex. 7 Examples of shofar sounds. On left, a shofar.

David Wulstan has recently shown (*GSJ* XXVI) that there was much interchangeability through biblical times between functions of the Jewish horn and trumpet and that their calls might be identical. The long code of war signals laid down for the trumpet (*hatsotserah*) in the Dead Sea 'Scroll of the War of the Sons of Light and Darkness' shows a close parallel with the synagogue code for the shofar as known in written sources from the Middle Ages, notably in the Codex Adler in New York (see Sendrey, Wulstan). The argument cannot be summarized here save to notice that the first call in Ex. 7 corresponds to 'Assemble' in the Scroll, the next to 'Advance', and the third, described as 'like raindrops', to 'Pursue'. A fourth figure, like the first but more drawn out, meant 'Regroup'. Projecting this back to *Numbers* 10, and beyond to the Pharoahs, we can imagine a code of two-pitch military sounds rising to the upper note of the short trumpet, far more urgent and commanding than the hoarse monotone vaguely suggested by Plutarch and the donkey. A similar sound-picture may be kept in consideration when the short trumpet appears among other ancient peoples, the Hittites, Assyrians (a little larger, Fig. 5, c), and possibly the Macedonians. The classical Greeks were not themselves among the great trumpeters of the past; rather they were military singers and pipers. But Alexander's vast armies would hardly have been manageable without a trumpet of command, and though later times attributed to them some kind of hydraulic hooter, Macedonian 'victory' coins show a short trumpet. The shortness may however be partly due to the cramped space on a small coin.

Rome and the North. On the face of it the Roman trumpet, *tuba*, represents an enlargement of the older short trumpet: about two cubits long instead of one (Fig. 5, e). It is, all the same, one of several instruments employed by the Roman *aeneatores* ('brass players') which show features which seem to point to absorption of ideas from sources outside the old tradition of the short trumpet. Most of these instruments, for instance, have mouthpieces which foreshadow our own, with cup, choke and back-bore, cast in bronze separately from the instrument (Pl. II). The only known precedent for these, prior to Rome, is in those great bronze horns of Bronze-Age North Europe, today described as *lurs*, a word which normally in Scandinavia denotes horns or alphorns but which was bestowed upon the prehistoric instrument soon after the first specimens were exhumed from a bog in Brudevaelte moor, North Zealand, in 1797. Nearly fifty have been found, most in Denmark, some in South Norway and Sweden, and a few in North Germany (Broholm, 1949). They are difficult to date, not having been found in association with dateable pottery or metalware, but the period from the tenth to the sixth century B.C. is at present accepted for them, i.e. from the beginning of Etruscan civilization in Italy two centuries before the traditional foundation of Rome, and ending when the Iron Age changed the northern scene.

The body of a lur is cast in two detachable curved parts, expanding throughout and always laid separately in their lonely graves, possibly places of concealment between times when they were needed. The smaller section, practically semicircular, has the mouthpiece cast with it. A fringe of jingling plates hangs next to the mouthpiece on short chains. The larger part carries a bronze sun disc; there is no flare to the tube itself. When joined in the same plane the two parts make a curl like a capital 'G'. One of the lurs can be assembled only in this way, but with the rest the two parts lock together at right angles, bringing the disc above the blower's head and pointing forwards. Tube-length is from 160 to 225 cm. (6 to 7-foot G to D flat). Specimen mouthpiece dimensions are in Table 3.

Many lurs were found buried in unison pairs, one built as the mirror image of the other like a pair of animal's horns. An obvious model for them would be the tusks of the woolly mammoth, which the makers could not have known alive though probably well enough as half-buried remains in river banks, etc.; mammoth tusks were still plentiful enough to support a small trade in ivory up to a few centuries ago. Aurochs horns have also been suggested, but these cannot exceed a metre in length, or half a lur. The lur makers, presumably a proto-Germanic people, left no written

Table 3

Dimensions (mm.) of some ancient cup mouthpieces with others for comparison

	max. width	cup width	throat	depth
Wide				
Danish lur, 4th period	43	25	8	24
Danish lur, 5th period (cf. Pl. II)	35	25	6	16
Roman large *cornu* (Pl. II)	32	26	5·5	11
Roman small *cornu* (Brit. Mus.)	28	25	5·6	8
Roman small *cornu* (presumed, Pl. II)	30	25	6	5·5
Asiatic: Usbek *karnai* (Pl. III)	38	30	6·5	13
Asiatic: China, large *hao-tung*	60	27	3	10
European trombone (average)	38	25	6·5	21
Medium				
Roman *tuba* (presumed, from Behn)	27	21	5	14
Indian folded trumpet (Pl. IV)	31	22·5	5·5	4
Narrow				
Gallo-Roman *tuba* (Orleans)	16·5	16	3	5
Asiatic: Indian *sringa*	25	17	3	5
Asiatic: Indian folded trumpet, narrower type	23	17	3	5
Asiatic: China, *la-pa*	50	19	3	4
European trumpet (average)	27	17	3·7	10

history, nor do writers of the Ancient World mention the instruments. They were no doubt cultic embodiments of the protective, as blowing horns have tended to be particularly in the north of Europe where vision amid flat forests and misty swamps can be perilously restricted and a far-carrying horn could be a vital possession. In Scandinavian rock drawings at Kivik in Sweden and elsewhere, symbols include precious belongings like axe, ship and wheel, while a lur (or some smaller horn) is being blown as if to protect by its sound, rather than to symbolize fertility through horn shape as in the Bronze-Age Mediterranean. How lurs were sounded of course we do not know, but in those early times the entity of a cultic instrument might be compounded of its ritual formulae, its actual shape, the sound produced on it, and anything else, all in equal measure. If the shape were that of a great beast, mythical to the lur-makers, then perhaps it produced the mythical sound of that beast. The trombone-sized mouthpiece points to baritone pitch, and we may imagine a tremendous far-carrying lowing kept up by men blowing alternately—a threatening roar, as Horace said of the Roman horn *cornu*.

An existing instrument which has some resemblance to a lur though itself not attested before the second century A.D. is the Indian metal horn *rana-sringa* ('war horn') of sheet brass or copper, though sometimes cast in brass. The two main sections are each semicircular, lur-like in bore, and the wide end carries a disc, often like a rosette and hollow, filled with rattling seeds or lead shot, recalling the jingling plates of the lur. The tube-length varies around 150 cm. and when the instrument is held with the bell raised above the head a pair of village performers standing side by side at a religious festival can look unbelievably like two Danish musicologists demonstrating lurs (Pl. I). The sringa is also blown at sunset and at the hours of the night by village watchmen, and at weddings, processions, etc. Meadows Taylor recalled that a detachment of troops was seldom without one. But in contrast to the lur the mouthpiece is narrow and shallow—a high-note mouthpiece, and the sound, usually of two or three harmonics, lies high in the treble though in Nepal, slow and strikingly beautiful phrases are sounded up to h10 by the semi-professional *damaï* musicians when accompanying a wedding procession through the hills (recorded by M. Helffer for the Musée de l'Homme).

Cornu. It is an obvious thought that the Roman cup-mouthpiece, without known precedent in the South or East, may have had some connection with that of the lur by way of the Etruscans, themselves noted bronze-workers from the eighth century B.C. and traders to the North. They or their agents must certainly have brought reports of the lurs to Italy. The Etruscans were later credited by the Romans with the 'invention' of their horns and trumpets, and they produced a variety of horns in the shape of three-quarters of a circle, seen in tomb murals from about the fifth to the fourth century B.C. carried on the shoulder, some held by a cross bar, by white-robed officials at funeral processions. The Villa Giulia Museum in Rome possesses (Pl. II) a fairly small specimen about the size of the eighteenth-century European 'half-moon' bugle and said to be from an Etruscan tomb. In fact it looks very Roman, of a type seen in several representations, two of which are sketched in Fig. 6 (a, b) for comparison. The civilian gravestone (a) was found in a garden on the Capitoline Hill in the sixteenth century. It has since disappeared but the legend, 'member of the guild of *liticines* and *cornicines*' confirms the name of the horn and of the hook-belled *lituus* also.

A number of cast bronze mouthpieces for this type of *cornu* have survived, either still attached or found separately (Pl. II); inside one of three in the British Museum the end of the horn survives, having been broken off the tube. These last were purchased in Italy in 1839, and are all wide and very shallow (Table 3) with a narrow backbore which continues the throat dimension for about 5 cm. before opening out conically to be fitted on to (not into) the instrument—the obvious method with a conical tube before general use of reverse-taper sockets. Some Indian brass trumpets have an equally wide and shallow mouthpiece. With this, one particular harmonic can usually be produced very much more powerfully than any other, and this was probably the case with these Roman horns; their sound was mostly described as 'raucous', suggesting a main note of medium pitch which the player perhaps approached in divers ways facilitated by the constricted backbore.

By Imperial times the Romans had introduced another type of *cornu*, with a narrower tube formed into a '*G*' by prolonging the mouthpipe-end so that the bell points forwards beside or above the player's head. This is the military horn shown with marching troops on Trajan's Column (A.D. 113, Fig. 6, c); the *cornicines* look tired, as well they might since a Roman army had no drum to which men will march while almost asleep, and the hornists may have performed a corresponding function in some manner. The tube-length seems about 200 cm., an average for the lurs but still considerably shorter than that of the five great *cornua* in the Naples Museum from Pompeii (buried in A.D. 79). These are civilian instruments of the kind played in the gladiatorial arena; the players sat before the organ while a trumpeter summoned the crowd's attention (Fig. 6, d). With a tube of 330 cm. (11-foot G) they must represent the largest size made. Their mouthpieces are very much longer than those just mentioned, and have deeper and more rounded cups. They fit on to the tapered end of the instrument, which expands for about 40 cm. rather as in our French horn crooks and then more slowly up to a small flanged bell. Replicas produce a sound rather like a narrow-bore G trombone

M·IVLIVS·VICTOR·EX·COLLEGIO

LITICINVM·CORNICINVM

Fig. 6 a. From Bellori, *Le pitture antiche*, 1706; b. from a funeral procession, late 1st century A.D. (Aquila Museum); c. Trajan's Column, Rome, A.D. 113; d. Circus scene, mosaic of late 1st century A.D., Zliten, Tripolitania.

but do not seem to invite exploration of high harmonics. Amphi-theatre scenes certainly suggest that these large *cornua* in some way aided the organ in regulating the progress of events in the arena; yet at the same time one is bound to notice that acousticians of the Ancient World, who were interested in any instrument that could demonstrate musical intervals, pass over the horns and trumpets in silence. But in warfare, one can imagine the sheer tempest of sound which preluded a Roman army's assault. The *cornicines* close by the standards with their bell-front horns, blaring the traditional battle call, the *classicum*, while the trumpeters, *tubicines*, stood forward with the men, who are shouting. yelling, clashing shields with their javelins, roused by the blare to fearlessness in their sanguinary duty.

Tuba. Most revered of the Roman labrosones, symbol of power and achievement, and the only one to have left a real legacy to posterity. Yet its actual remains are peculiarly scarce and frag-mentary (the nearest to a complete specimen may be that in the Nemzeti Museum, Budapest). On the monuments the *tuba* (short 'u' as in 'wood') measures about 120 cm. (4-foot C; Fig. 5, e), expanding gradually to a narrow bell. It is held high, and like the other Roman instruments, was sounded with inflated cheeks. There is some doubt about the mouthpiece, but it was most likely of a type illustrated by Behn (1954, Plate 79) with several speci-mens of undeclared provenance: short, with a small tenon fitting *into* the main tube, and with rounded cup of medium size and depth (Table 3). This might suggest that the sound lay higher than with the horns. The usual word for it, *clangor*, was applied also to the noise of cranes, geese, coots and dogs; Pliny rather vaguely likens an elephant's trumpeting to it, and this rises well into the treble register. We know of course from the poet Ennius (second century B.C.) that its sound in battle was a terrifying *taratantara* (Fragment 143), indicating calls that were articulated by tongue. Tactical signals listed by Pollux (IV, 85) and mentioned many times by Dio Cassius tell nothing further of the sounds, but Aristides Quintilianus, writing in Greek (*De Musica*, II, 6) states that the trumpet had a particular *melos* for each contingency, which seems to suggest more than monotone.

For imperial funerals and other major state events in Rome the city's sacrificial *tubae* were produced. These resembled the army instrument. But there was also by Imperial times another model, seen in the amphitheatre (Fig. 6, d), longer and more slender, like earlier Greek trumpets shown on vases of the sixth century B.C.[1] Two splendid late examples are in France, excavated with various Gallo-Roman cult objects in the Loire region and now preserved in the Archaeological Museum at Orleans and the Castle at Saumur (Fig. 7). They are of fine sheet bronze in de-

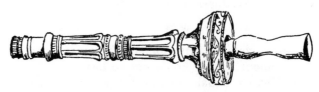

Fig. 7 The Saumur tuba, based on drawings of 1863. Below, detail of mouthpiece socket, with mouthpiece as in the Orleans tuba.

tachable sections, mostly cylindrical with 19 mm. outside diameter and meeting under thick cast ferrules decorated with annular motifs suggestive of cordage. The mouthpipe of the Orleans tuba is 20 cm. long and tapers down from 16 to 12·2 mm. (outside) to an ornamental socket resembling a Roman chandelier. Apparently found with it was the narrow bronze mouthpiece rather like that of our cornettino (Table 3). The Saumur bell, almost complete, expands with an almost modern 'exponential' profile, and the total length of each instrument seems to have been about 160 cm. (5-foot G) if it is assembled correctly.

It is possible that the Romans also made a folded trumpet: Behn shows two apparent examples seen on gravestones. He terms them *bucina*, an unusual interpretation of this word.

[1] No fully attested Greek trumpet survives. The 5-foot instrument in the Boston Museum of Fine Arts, made of short sections of ivory socketed together, was only said by a dealer to have come from Olympia. The bore is cylindrical, very narrow by any standards, with a plain evasement for a mouthpiece. The bronze bell has a Roman shape, not that of a ringing bell as seen on vases and in the contemporary bronze statuette sketched in Fig. 5, d—whence the Greek term for it, *kōdōn*, 'a bell'.

Lituus and buccina. '*Lituus*' is said to be an Etruscan cultic word concerned with sacrifice under favourable omens and denoting the stylized shepherd's crook with which the soothsayer ritually quartered the sky in his professional performances. Rome inherited this and also an Etruscan blowable version which appears to have been, at any rate at first, a composite trumpet of cane with a goat horn secured by ribbons (Fig. 6, a). It was also made in bronze: the fine example in the Vatican Etruscan Museum, from an Etruscan tomb of perhaps the late fourth century B.C., has a faintly tapered straight section of bronze sheet formed of two lengths longitudinally, the two seams being flanged over—a construction also employed in some Celtic trumpets. The blowing end is unfortunately incomplete. On Roman monuments the *lituus* is less conspicuous than *cornu* and *tuba*, but it had a place with these in funeral processions, always with a single player whereas the others are usually paired. The sound was described as 'strident'.

The word '*buccina*' (in classical Latin usually *bucina*) probably derives from *bucca* in the sense of a mouthful distending the cheeks, and had a general meaning of any small instrument on which people sounded calls, such as a conch or shepherd's horn. In the Imperial armies a *buccina* was one of the most-used instruments, to judge only from the numerous gravestones of a *Buccinator*, who held a position in his own right along with the *Cornicen* and the *Tubicen*, serving as a kind of camp bugler and also apparently associated with mounted troops. There is no adequate contemporary description of the military *buccina*. Vegetius (fourth century A.D.) mentions the horn of the wild ox as a prototype, but transposes the names '*buccina*' and '*cornu*', whence much confusion over these terms later (*Milit.* III 5). However another late source, once ascribed to Acro,[1] refers to the *lituus* as an instrument of the cavalry. No other literary source confirms this. But one of the best preserved of these military instruments is a horn about 72 cm. long (Pl. II) of sheet bronze soldered together down each side, found in the Rhine near Düsseldorf and now owned by the Saalburg Museum, Bad Homburg. It is conical, with mouthpiece attached and an upturned bell-mouth which gives a faintly lituite

---

[1] 'Litui acutus sonus est, tubae gravis. In antiquis scriptis lituus equitum est et incurvus, tuba vero peditum est et directa.' Commentary on Horace 'lituo tubae permixtus sonitus': see O. Keller, *Pseudacronis, Scholia in Horatium Vetustiora*, I, Leipzig, 1902, p. 18.

appearance. Two slinging eyes are unusual for a Roman instrument and might point to use by Celtic horsemen, rather than Roman, in late Imperial times. There are fragments of two more similar horns from the same region, while on a metal plaque from a Roman standard, in the Römisch-Germanisches Zentralmuseum in Mainz, there protrudes from a bunch of military trophies a bell of the same type beside the bell of a *tuba*. No representation shows a proper *lituus* in use with the Roman forces, to whom the Homburg species may have seemed a kind of *buccina* which some people, but probably not soldiers, called 'lituus'.

As for the rest of Western Antiquity, numerous and strange bronze instruments have been unearthed in Ireland, a few with hook bells, others with (apparently) vast blowing holes in the side. These remain problematic, and likewise some Celtic horns contemporary with the Roman Republic, built of riveted bronze tube in wide semicircles and somewhat recalling the Pergamum statue of the Dying Gaul. A more distinctive species is the *carnyx*, a wide cylindrical pipe with a glaring boar's head fixed atop. It is shown on many Gaulish coins, brandished by a galloping horseman (see, e.g., D. Allen, 1958), but for sounding it was held vertically and somehow 'blown upwards and into' as the Iliad Scholion, which records the name of the instrument, says of a similar but bull-headed 'Paphlagonian trumpet' of Asia Minor. Among the Etrusco-Roman instruments the closest to the *carnyx* is the *lituus* brandished by the augurs, while much of *carnyx* shape and decoration is preserved in early examples of Irish bishops' crook or crozier: the instrument evidently had some cultic background. The Iliad Scholion, p. 1139 (see bibliography, Eustathius) was compiled in late Antiquity from earlier material, some of it going back to about three centuries B.C. It describes several other 'national' kinds of *salpinx*, some of them very odd like the 'Egyptian' which was 'strongulate', and the 'Medic' with a cane (or cane-like?) tube and 'deep-sounding bell, and giving a swelling sound'.

THREE

The Middle Ages

The victorious incursions of Goth and Teuton introduced a fresh, if transitory, phase in the ancient history of war instruments, which western Christian art reflects mainly in consequence of the occurrence of the word *tuba* in passages of the Latin Bible which provided favourite subjects for illustration, such as the Psalms and the book of Revelation. Here, up to a good two centuries after Charlemagne, we see suprisingly little of the trumpet, but instead a plethora of curved instruments or horns of various shapes and sizes, some quite ordinary (oxhorn size), others very large yet quite different from the big Roman horns which had vanished entirely from Europe. The reason for this must be sought first in Italy, where artists set a style of allegorical illustration which was subsequently copied, with or without variation, in the monasteries of Germany, France and Britain. For example, it is possible that the early illustrators knew that in so many of the Old Testament texts 'tuba' in fact represents the Hebrew 'shofar', and that a shofar was recognized to have the form of a horn even if St. Jerome (who knew this perfectly well) had chosen 'tuba' as a more fitting verbal equivalent than the more commonplace 'buccina'. This explanation seems, however, far-fetched, and it is more likely that the prevalence of horns as 'tuba' symbols should be attributed to changes in the signal instruments observed in use, especially those of war.

One factor bearing upon this at the time was no doubt horn-blowing tradition among the barbarians themselves. But the Byzantine armies too employed some kind of horn, known by the Latin name adopted into military Greek as *boukina* (the trumpet similarly becoming *touba*), and the years round A.D. 540 offer some possible clues to its nature.

In Ravenna in 545 the church of S. Michaele in Affrisco was consecrated. Its showpiece, now in Berlin, was an apocalypse-like mosaic with six 'tuba angels' blowing peculiar dark-brown curved horns, long and rather slender (Fig. 8, left). The artist may have had a Byzantine military horn in mind. Of similar length though more substantial in build are some horns in northern iconography which is believed to be founded on earlier Italian or Italo-Byzantine originals, most notably in the celebrated Utrecht Psalter (Rheims *c.* 820; Fig. 8, right). Far too big to be animal horns, yet they were light enough to be held up by one hand.

Fig. 8 Left from mosaic, S. Michele in Affrisco, Ravenna, A.D. 545; **right** from the Utrecht Psalter, Rheims, *c.* 820 (*in sono tubae*).

Five years before the consecration of the Ravenna church, Belisarius was laying siege to a town nearby. Serving under him was the future historian Procopius, who describes how, during this siege, he had suggested to the great Byzantine commander a simple order by which to avoid useless loss of life through irregular and incautious sallies against the Gothic defenders. Since, Procopius said, the trumpeters did not know how to sound the clear and unmistakable tactical calls of the old days, why not designate the 'cavalry salpinx' for Advance and the 'infantry salpinx' for Retire, since no one could confuse their sounds, the first being made of 'leather and thin wood' and the second of 'thick bronze' (*History of the Wars*, VI, xxiii). The general agreed and the losses were cut down.

Just after this, in the same century, the Emperor Mauricius (or whoever it was who wrote the *Strategikon*) stated most emphatically that all calls were to be given correctly and the troops trained to obey them, both on *boukina* and on *touba*. Among these calls (all unfortunately described without details of the sounds), *Move* (*sic*, i.e. March) was given by the *boukina* and *Sta* (Halt) on the *touba*, which broadly correspond with the two commands proposed by Procopius. We are nowhere told that the *boukina* was particularly an instrument of the cavalry, which, armed with bows and arrows, had become the spearhead of the Byzantine forces. However, prior Roman association of a curved horn with mounted units, small though the evidence is on the matter, points in that direction. The 'cavalry salpinx' mentioned by Procopius ('*salpinx*' being applicable to a signal instrument of any form) may thus have been a large and sonorous *boukina*, made in wood by halved construction and covered with leather like our cornetts. Certainly the sound of such an instrument should have been unmistakable from that of a bronze tuba.

More large horns are seen in the series of tenth and elventh-century figures in Fig. 9, exhibiting a chain of copying by one French or English artist after another in illustration of a passage from the Christian poet Prudentius (*Psychomachia* 636): 'Kindly peace banishes war...the trumpeters' curved brass are silent, the sword returned to its scabbard' (*cornicinum curva aerea*, but in some manuscripts, *tubae*). Their styles, and the antique lyres drawn on other pages, still point back to earlier southern originals. But in other manuscripts of these times stringed instruments representing the *cithara* of the Vulgate have taken on forms which clearly belong to their immediate place and period. The instrument representing *tuba* should therefore do the same. In the great majority of cases it is still a curved horn, and generally quite small, ox-horn size and brightly coloured or garnished with precious metal. Many such horns were no doubt all-metal, some of copper alloys, sometimes gilded, like the king's 'golden horn' in Gottfried's *Tristan*.

Horns were distinguished according to their purpose. For example, medieval Welsh kings were entitled by the laws to three ox horns (*chorn buelyn*): for drinking, for mustering (war horn, probably large), and for hunting (carried by the chief huntsman, and certainly small). Was the horn ever employed in music? In many illustrations which apparently show lifelike scenes a horn is present among other instruments. One such scene, in a French miniature of *c.* 1060 (the Nevers Graduale), shows a horn-blower and a dancing fiddler on either side of a tree. Across each figure

Fig. 9 Prudentius, *Psychomachia* 636: four versions of the same picture, 10th to 11th cent. **Upper** Paris, Bibl. nat. lat. 8318 (the earliest of the four); Leyden, Cod, Voss. lat. oct. 15. **Lower** Brit. Mus. MS Cleop. C. VIII; do. Add. MS 24199 (the seated figure is here unclear).

is penned a row of neumes, those for the fiddler indicating a rising pattern of sounds and those for the horn-blower a slightly different pattern at a constant pitch (which makes a finger-hole horn unlikely here). Bachmann, reproducing the picture (*Origins of Bowing*, Pl. 27), may be right in seeing an intention of the artist monk to underscore the contrast between a melodic rebec and a monotone horn. From the tree, a May-tree, we can imagine a Spring festival and 'bringing home the May' to the noises of horn-blowing, as still observed till recently in parts of Britain. But had such horns participated in music itself one might have expected traces of the practice to have survived in European folk music. Nothing of the kind seems, however, to have been reported.

While horns were evidently the commonest summoning and war instruments of the early medieval warrior and feudal knight, the form of the straight trumpet nevertheless appears now and then in the iconography of the period (Fig. 10, a). Occasionally there is a mark of contemporary realism, as in Scotland, where two much-eroded stone slabs of the ninth or tenth century, carved by the Southern Picts rather in the style of the Irish stone crosses, show straight instruments blown at stag hunts (Allen, J. Romilly, fig. 59; here Fig. 10, b). They may be compared with the conical trumpet, banded in blue and gold, which represents *tuba* in the eighth-century St. Gall Gospel Book, held by saintly figures staring stiffly in Celtic style and executed no doubt by a monk from Ireland. From the stout shape and total lack of turned-out rim one may suspect that at least some of these instruments were of wood. The beech or yew tube, 107 cm. in length, from the ninth-century Oseberg Viking ship at Oslo has halved construction and,

Fig. 10 a. Trier Apocalypse, 8th or 9th cent.; **b.** stone slab, Hilton of Cadboll, Ross-shire (at Invergordon; after Romilly Allen); **c.** Exultet Roll from Sorrento, 11th cent. (Monte Cassino, 2); **d.** Capua, S. Angelo in Formis, painting, *c.* 1070; **e.** The Berlin Apocalypse, Italian, 2nd half 12th cent.; **f.** Psalter of S. Louis and Blanche of Castile, early 13th cent. (Paris, Arsenal).

if a sounding tube it is, provides tangible evidence of a chieftain's trumpet of such a kind (Brøgger, *Osebergfundet* II, fig. 165; also Crane, 1972, pp. 59–60). In *Beowulf* the hero's uncle calls his warriors to battle at the summons of his 'horn and bieme' (1.2943). This Anglo-Saxon word, *bieme* or *beme*, which glosses *tuba* in the psalms and is always translated 'trumpet', has a wooden ring about it and may have at first denoted a wooden instrument, perhaps one which some built straight, others in horn shape. (Behind *tuba* itself is the word *tubus*, 'tube', no doubt in the earliest times a wooden drain-pipe, like those large ones of halved wood bound with birch-bark which have been excavated from medieval Novgorod.)

The bell-less profile is also seen in Continental manuscripts from the eleventh century onwards, coloured white or red, often with a broad band of darker colour at the wide end (Fig. 10, c). Buhle, in his classic study of early medieval wind instruments (p. 26), considered these to have been of metal and that the old German word *trumba* may have been a name for them. This word glosses *tuba* in a number of texts from the eighth and ninth centuries, often with a prefix, as in *heritrumba* ('war trumpet') or, more rarely, *horntrumba*, as if the form of the instrument were immaterial so long as a sufficiently powerful signal could be drawn from it. Possibly such signals delivered mainly or entirely on one pitch were responsible for the adoption, about this time, of the term *tuba* for the reciting note in psalm singing. But one cannot be sure.

Full revival of the trumpet. Some remarkable tenth or eleventh-century illustrations to Isidore's *Etymologies* in a manuscript at Turin include a *tuba* which clearly has the conical tube, cup mouthpiece and distinct bell rim of the old Roman instrument. It is reproduced in *MGG* ('Isidor von Sevilla') and a further example is scuptured on the baptistry of Novara Cathedral, which dates from the beginning of the twelfth century. This is followed later in the century and the early part of the next, again in Italy, by a number of church frescoes depicting more trumpets with bells and probably of silver: Capua (in St. Angelo in Formis, Fig. 10, d), Nepi, near Rome, and Civate, by Lake Como. The Capua frescoes, praised by Pignatti as the *capolavoro* of Benedictine art, have attracted much attention from instrument historians, not merely for the size of the trumpets but in view of the proximity of influential Arab culture and crafts then thriving in Sicily under the Norman rule. The Capua trumpets have in fact been seen as first evidence of the impact of the Moslem on an older trumpet tradition in the West. Unfortunately the comparatively rich Western trumpet iconography of this period cannot be matched from the Arab side, which shows us little until the thirteenth century.

What had probably occurred was a genuine resurrection of the Roman *tuba* by the proud and prosperous free cities of North Italy, led by Milan, with their neo-Roman aspirations and great processions organized by the bishops, with the sacred battle-wagon consciously imitating a Roman Triumph. Through the twelfth century silver trumpets were regularly given and received by the Pope as presents, and played a part in such proceedings. Meanwhile the Arabs, whose battle sounds earlier in the Middle Ages had been given by drums and cymbals—their speciality, acknowledged at the time by the Byzantines—had almost certainly found their way to trumpets during the same period. This is not surprising in view of the long and continuous use of the *tuba* in Byzantium. But the fully-evolved Moslem trumpet was no simple copy of anything within the Western sphere, nor of an earlier Sassanian trumpet which was soon forgotten after the Arab conquest; but a product of subsequent Persian brass technology, with a very visible hallmark in the ornamentation of the trumpet with *pommels.* This is the cylindrical trumpet seen in Europe from about the time of the Third Crusade and which set the style for the Western trumpet for the remainder of the Middle Ages (Fig. 11).

Some evidence for the new Moslem trumpet comes from Western sources. In the earliest manuscript of the *Chanson de Roland,* written in the twelfth-century, the French word *buisine* (*buzine, bosine,* etc.) is encountered for the first time. Considered to derive from *buccina* (like *cuisine* from *cocino*) and likewise possessing a verbal form (*buisiner* or in Fig. 11, a, *bosiner*) it had obviously already been a spoken word for a long time and most likely with the fairly wide meaning of any powerful labrosone employed among the knightly caste; thus even in the thirteenth century it can be attached to a large ornamental curved metal horn, as in the figure. It is curious, however, that in *Roland* it denotes solely the instrument by which the Moorish Sultan of Saragossa roused his troops, the Franks sounding only *cors* (including the ivory *cor d'olifant*) and smaller horns, *graisles*. Evidently those monks who had been elaborating the legend up to the time of the manuscript—over two centuries after the actual events commemorated—had retained in their narrative the horns traditionally associated with Roland and his men while introducing the grandiose term *buisine* for something rather special that had latterly come to attract notice in the armies of the Moslems.

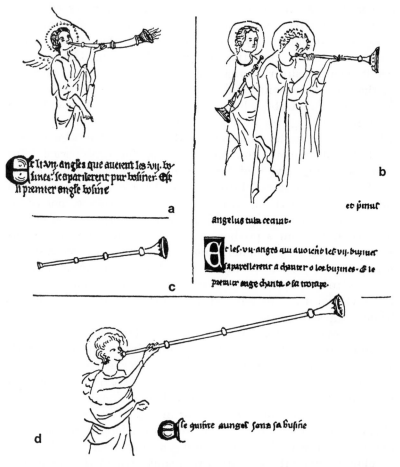

Fig. 11 a. Paris, Bibl. nat. fr. 403, (13th cent., '*Et li uns angles que aveient les vii bosines se aparilerent pur bosiner . . .*'); b. Brit. Mus. Add. MS 17333, beginning of 14th cent. ('*. . . et le premier ange chanta o sa trompe*'); c. The Douce Apocalypse, Oxford, Bodl., *c.* 1265; d. Lincoln College, MS 16, early 14th cent.

Then the First Crusade itself. The Christian knights took with them various kinds of military instrument: all four of the old Latin names are profusely scattered through the first-hand accounts of Fulcher of Chartres and others (*Recueil des Historiens*, occid. III etc.) often in most confusing ways, as when Fulcher writes 'buccina' but another author describing the same event writes 'lituus'. Yet the use of the terms can hardly be totally haphazard, considering the vivid realism otherwise (how the scorching sand was always in one's eyes and ears; how the meat went bad and one had to eat eggs). Up to a point Roman precepts seem to have been followed: 'buccina', 'cornu' and (or) 'lituus' were sounded for things like Reveille and other camp calls, also for commands like Retire; the Latin names overlap too much to be positively equated with spoken French words unless 'cornu' was the small slung *cor*. 'Tuba' on the other hand was a battle trumpet, also associated with royalty, with the Venetian fleet, and with formal occasions, as when in 1099 a thanksgiving procession was led up the Mount of Olives by chanting priests bearing holy relics followed by the soldiers barefoot, carrying their banners and *tubae*. Meanwhile the narratives refer to the Moslem instruments by the same Latin names, plus *tympanisti*. But at one point Fulcher is curiously specific, relating how in 1123 the Moslems leaped ashore from the Egyptian ships with tremendous yelling and the immense sound of their *aereae tubae*—'brass trumpets'. Some of the Christians' trumpets must have been of brass by this time, but what struck Fulcher was perhaps the particularly brazen look of the powerful Asiatic trumpets as the sun glinted on their pommels.

A possible early representation of an oriental trumpet with pommel is in India among the sculptures on the temples of Khajuraho (of erotica fame). They were built about the time when the local Hindu state was fighting off fresh Moslem raiders, and sounding the war conch and also the trumpet, as described in the early twelfth-century *Manasollasa*. The sculpture in question (reproduced in A. Danielou's *Inde du Nord* in the series *Les Traditions musicales*, 1966, Pl. 15) appears to show a small-sized *karna*. In the West a pommel is seen a century later in a sculpture at Santiago de Compostela, and thenceforth one, two or even three are always present. In construction a pommel may be beaten from one piece of brass (as when making a door-knob) or of two cups soldered edge to edge. Its purpose is less for holding a banner than to give the plain tube a look of grandeur which is distinctly oriental in character, and Indo-Persian especially, for it is less prominent in Arab trumpets.

The trumpet was no doubt taken westwards by the Seljuk Turks, to be added, just before the First Crusade, to the band of drums, cymbals and shawm which the more powerful emirs took with them on campaigns; it bivouacked close by the commander's tent. Indeed right up to the beginning of the present century Moslem rulers in Persia and Afghanistan still took such a band on military expeditions, while its peacetime duties lay principally in performing at regular hours of the day and night from a gallery over the palace gateway, whence the band's traditional title *nakkara khana*, musicians of 'the drum tower'. Their traditions are musically most precious, since the irksome omission in brass history up to this point has been description of actual sounds. The drum-tower and other band traditions outside Europe can give us an inkling of these; for oriental trumpets in general have never been truly integrated into literate musical art, but continue to be employed on pre-literate levels (as in the West up into the Middle Ages), and quite possibly with no small inheritance from Romano-Byzantine times.

Oriental trumpets. As they are today these may be summed up in three structural groups. (1) In North and West Africa they are long cylindrical instruments of brass, copper, or tinplate from old petrol cans, and made in sections which are taken apart after use (Pl. III). The tube is wide by subsequent European standards, in bore 16 mm. or more. The mouthpiece, which in almost all oriental trumpets is built up from sheet metal, here amounts merely to a slight funnelling out of the main tube with no choke whatever (Fig. 12, a). With the *kakaki* of West Africa a wide rim-plate is soldered to the end. Pommels are small, sometimes absent. Length of instruments: 150 to 250 cm. (5 to 8 feet).

(2) In Persia, and Uzbekistan in Soviet Central Asia, the trumpets are outwardly somewhat similar (Pl. III) though the tube is wider—c. 33 mm. in the *karnai* and over 50 mm. in a Persian *karna*—and the bell is also wider. But while appearing cylindrical to the eye, the first section of the tube, which may be up to 3 feet long, has concealed within it a conical mouthpipe, the narrow end of which is soldered to the throat-orifice of the wide, shallow mouthpiece cup, as can just be seen in the photograph. The visible cylindrical pipe protects this and is soldered to the rim of the

mouthpiece, thus strengthening an otherwise weak construction (Fig. 12, c). It looks as if brass workers in the past had sought to replace a cast mouthpiece of the Roman type by a stable construction in sheet metal. Pommels number two or three and are frequently big. The largest (14 cm. diameter) pommel of the Khiva instrument contains rattling pellets. The bell garland frequently carries the dog-tooth border which is so commonly seen in Western medieval illustrations (Fig. 11, c, d).

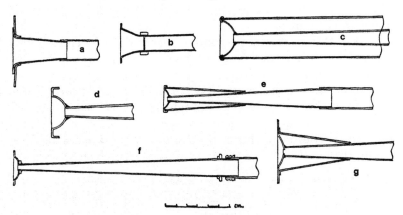

Fig. 12 Mouthpieces: **a.** *kakaki*; **b.** *nafīr* (Morocco); **c.** *karnai* (Pl. III); **d.** Tibet, lama trumpet; **e.** India, folded trumpet (small cup); **f.** do. (wider cup, Pl. IV); **g.** China, large *hao-tung*.

(3) East of the main Moslem area, trumpets of the Himalayan states and the Far East are conical; the sections are not detached after use but are telescoped, an idea perhaps of Indian origin. If partial extension is required for setting the trumpet to a higher pitch, the interstices at the joints may have to be packed with cloth. The best pommels are in China. Mouthpieces are exceedingly shallow and are mostly soldered to the narrow end of the tube without further support.

In India trumpets of all kinds are met, some of them over the entire country. The *karna* here varies from long and thin to short and fat, with the concealed mouthpipe and bell as wide as 40 cm. Small straight trumpets are both conical and cylindrical. Folded models are common, with cylindrical tube usually in the form of the European trumpet (Pl. IV) though also undulating or coiled like a snake. In India these have wide tubes, around 16 to 20 mm. externally. The mouthpieces are again shallow, and the cup is

attached to a conical mouthpipe about 20 cm. long. In most cases
an external tube supports the rim but does not always cover the
total length of the mouthpipe (Fig. 12, e). In their general proportions such mouthpieces have a remarkable resemblance to the
cast mouthpieces of the Roman *cornua*, and examples can be
found in India where they similarly fit *over* the main tube, though
usually they fit into it.

Sounds of oriental trumpets may for the moment be considered
under two headings:

(1) LONG MONOTONE, the most widespread. In Morocco it may
still be heard when the man with the *nafir* daily climbs his mina-
ret through Ramadan, dispatching 'long mournful blasts' after
the cannon shot to announce the prayer hour. Monotone is also
the role of the *karna* in the traditional *nakkara khana* band of
Persian cities as that in Plate III which Sykes (p. 163) photo-
graphed in Meshed, where the hereditary posts were held by
locksmiths. In Ex. 8 the trumpet enters below the shawms at

Ex. 8 Persian town band, extract from an old recording. The 2nd *surna*
sustains *a'* throughout. (Place of the performance not known.)

vague pitches higher than his main one which thereafter he keeps
to during his periodic interruptions of the shawm melody. These
interjections by the *karna* were not unnaturally to early European
visitors 'a most unpleasant sound like the bellowing of a bull', but
Poullet wrote in 1668 that the Persians were so charmed by it that
the Shah had to call upon an English trumpeter to cease, as he
could not bear the *rudesse* of his playing. In India too, the monotone of the *karna* was 'esteemed by all Brahmins to be especially
pleasing to the gods'.

Such instruments are in fact hardly capable of anything else
than monotone. Another is in China, where funerals formerly demanded a band of shawms, percussion and two trumpets, all laid

[1] In shadow plays recorded in South Taiwan by Prof. Piet van der Loon,
the trumpet, pitched in *a*, starts the show with a slow, strong alternation of
h3 and 4 (*e'* and *a'*), then touching h5 on reversing the sequence to end

on by the undertaker. The peculiar trumpet here used has a vast tubular bell, sometimes formerly of wood, which merely imparts a booming quality to the note given by the conical section (inevitably inviting comparison with the trumpet-tubes of South American Indians). In a recording taken by Dr. Laurence Picken of what has survived of ancient military music in Korea, reed instruments play the tune while brass trumpet and conch again sound in monotone, the former on a pitch about *a*.

(2) RHYTHMICALLY ON TWO PITCHES, starting, following the usual instinct, on the lower, h2, and rising to h3, which may sound around a sixth higher. A player may now and then strike h4, but higher harmonics are seldom practicable even with tube-lengths exceeding 7 feet. Working back from the Far East, the Chinese flare-belled *la-pa*, recognized as a former military instrument, today sounds h3 and h4 while announcing acts during theatrical performances.[1] The Tibetan lama trumpet, though in most recorded examples one hears only a drawn-out h2, also produces a full-sounding fundamental (as low as G') and evidently an articulated h3, to judge from Vandor's transcriptions of monastery notations (1973; perhaps unique trumpet notations east of Europe). But methods in Moslem countries concern us more. Here may be heard strongly rhythmic playing with marked flavour of military

Ex. 9 *Karnai* with *nagara* (kettledrums), Uzbekistan, USSR (from a recording by F. Karomatov). The two notes of the *karnai* sound approximately *a* flat and *e'*.

taratantara. In Soviet Central Asia among the Uzbeks and Tajiks, the shawm, drum and trumpet band performs on festive occasions and to announce fairs. The *karnai* may be waved from side to side from a roof to draw the people's attention (Fig. 13, a). For such

with. The fiddler (*er-hu*) then takes over, always repeating the same two notes before proceeding to the actual tunes. (From field recording.)

uses the instrument is ideal: of all trumpets the *karnai* is the best built for producing immense volume without excessive physical effort. Ex. 9 is from a recording by Professor Karomatov of Tashkent, kindly sent from there by Dr. Picken. Trumpet and kettledrums are here performing alone. The principal sound is h2, while h3 is uttered as a kind of 'end sound' or whoop. Articulation is with the breath—the instrument responds poorly to the tongue —and the drum-roll effect at the end of the second excerpt is made by this means also. In the last century the *karnai* still had a place as a royal and military instrument. Some calls sounded at the Khan's palace in Khiva, quoted by Sadokov (1971) appear on paper as reiterations of h2, though this is much as Ex. 9 might sound at a distance.

In West Africa, Moslem emirs of the Hausa and neighbouring peoples maintain mounted bands also of shawm, drums and trumpets, which perform at regular times like the eve of the Moslem sabbath, and special occasions. The trumpet's name *kakaki*, presumably deriving from the abrupt style of the playing (Ex. 10) was already in use in the fifteenth century when the Hausa adopted the instrument along with other prestigious items like

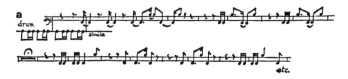

Ex. 10 *Kakaki*, West Africa, two excerpts from feast music. **a.** Agades, Niger, **b.** Maroua, Cameroons. The two notes sound approximately *e* flat and *b*.

ostrich-feather fans and large harems from the Bornu Empire around Lake Chad, which had accepted Islam in the eleventh century from the direction of the Fezzan. Any question of European colonial influence is thus ruled out: *kakaki* players sound **what** they sounded in the late Middle Ages and what other **Moslems** had no doubt sounded earlier. Connections with the shawm melodies in the band's performance seem to be absent, save for a tuning of the trumpets—as often in Asia too—to the shawm keynote in a lower octave. There is no doubt much yet to be learned about this from the musicians themselves; but the impression with the trumpets is one of sounds brought in from another context and superimposed on an already-existing shawm and drum nucleus, and this other context must have been that of palace fanfares and war calls.

In this last connection the trumpet of Ethiopia might be mentioned, though its sounds are on one note only and the instrument itself has only recently been made of metal, being traditionally one of those 'composite' trumpets made of a long cane with gourd (or metal) bell affixed, noticed in the last chapter. It is end-blown, is royal and military, and must surely be derived directly from the metal trumpet of some ancient neighbour to the north, possibly long before the Middle Ages notwithstanding the very African decoration with cowrie shells. To quote James Bruce (1790) 'it sounds only one note, in a loud, hoarse and terrible tone. It is played slow when on a march or before an enemy appears in sight; but afterwards it is repeated very quick and with great violence, and has the effect upon the Abyssinian soldiers of transporting them absolutely to fury and madness, and of making them so regardless of life as to throw themselves in the middle of the enemy, which they do with great gallantry'.

Alas, nothing whatever is known about how the trumpets were played in the famous Janissary bands of the Ottoman Empire. European bandmasters took over in the last century; and now all that can be found for the trumpet-players to play in the revived *mehter* (band) in Istanbul, with its shawms, correct drums, singers with their crescent staffs, and full seventeenth century costume, is to double the shawms in feeble unison on European B flat valve trumpets.

Trumpet sounds of the High Middle Ages and Early Renaissance. The first Europeans to patronize the Moslem band music were probably those who remained in the East between the Second and Third Crusades as residents or on permanent garrison duty. Richard I was accordingly greeted outside Acre in 1191 with sounds of *trumpae* and *tubae* on every side, the piercing airs of the *tibiae* (shawms) and the thunder of the *tympana*. On European territory, an early record is the town band of Siena in 1257, with three *tubatores*, one *tamburello*, one *ciaramella*; all players named and with duties (described somewhat later) after the oriental fashion, for instance performing at certain hours every evening up to 3 a.m. Their appearance is probably well conveyed in Fig. 13, b, from a courtly German manuscript of 1334 in which the adjacent text names the instruments: *bosunen* (trumpets, a pair as usual), *tambur*, and *schalemin*; elsewhere the poem alludes to the great snarl and crackle made by the first (*Casseler Willehalm Codex*, see Freyhan, Pl. 43).

Fig. 13 a. Uzbek band performing on roof at fair (after *Atlas*); b. Casseler Willehalm Codex, 1334.

Ꝟ œ ꝺꝛ kuṁigın ḣup ꝼid epn ꝼ꜂ḁl
Ʒ velꝼ voꝼuṅꝰ bluꝼen ꝟꝼ
Ʒ u ꝺœme ꝼꜩꝺꝛ waꝛꝛ epn miꜩꝺꝛ lôꝼ
Ƈ ꜳmbuꝛ man ꝼlukꝟñ blıs ꝼdꜳlcṁ

No medieval trumpet survives to show whether, for instance, any of them contained a concealed mouthpipe.[1] Nor does any source describe the manner in which these groups played. Contemporary bagpipes frequently appear to have a brass drone shaped like the trumpet, as if the intention had been to reproduce the effect of a shawm-trumpet combination in which the trumpets were sounded on one pitch beneath the shawm or gave an overall impression of monotone (as Ex. 9 might be said to give); a bagpipe drone, sounding its fundamental, would of course be shorter than a trumpet sounding h2. Often cited is the instrumental tune in Bodleian MS Douce 139, with its refrain in which an f', thirty times reiterated, is written above the melody and is largely dis-

---

[1] *Note to the Dover Edition.* The year 1984 saw the discovery in the City of London of a late fourteenth-century straight trumpet (the 'Billingsgate Trumpet') now preserved in the Museum of London: see G. Lawson, *Galpin Society Journal*, 1988. It is *c.* 145 cm. long, in four cylindrical sections

cordant with it. Has its writer tried to jot down an impression of what must have been among the most familiar sounds of the time? Against this, the melody itself (with odd suggestions of the later tune 'Goddesses') looks more like a harp tune. But a further pointer to trumpet sounds on one pitch, or mainly so, may be those occasional early fourteenth-century depictions of one man sounding two trumpets at once, even on horseback (Brit. Mus. MS Stowe 17, f. 126). The feat has been recorded from Ancient Greece to modern India (here in monotone) and was presumably resorted to in medieval Europe on occasions when only one man was available for sounding the customary pair of trumpets. It is unlikely that such players were able to produce in this fashion more than two at most of the deeper harmonics.

By the end of the thirteenth century the trumpet had become the regular instrument of the knightly class in war, in tournaments (practice for war), in cavalcades and at banquets, and here it becomes possible to form a glimmering of its early sounds. A basic code of cavalry calls must have been in existence, with names for the calls and likewise for the different notes of the trumpet as the men spoke together and taught their sons. Some of these note names, as we know of them later, must go back at least to the time of the Crusades. They formed a kind of trumpeters' *lingua franca* compounded of French, German, and later Italian elements, and include the archaic names for the two lowest harmonics that calls use, h2 and h3: 'bass' (or 'gross') and 'folgent' (later corrupted 'volgan', 'vurgano' etc.), terms of high antiquity in German and signifying in this sense the 'boss' or master (or simply 'the fat one') and the 'follower' (or 'attendant').

The names of the calls have mainly French origin; thus *Ughetto* (Italian), *Auged* (German), *Auquet* (Jacobean English), all from the French *Au guet*, 'Set the watch'. For the calls themselves, written versions come not until the late sixteenth century, in German and Italian manuscripts to be mentioned later. The calls are not quite consistent throughout, varying even in the two sources from Italy; they represent versions known to the men on the spot. But the striking feature among these calls is a motif, different for each call, composed of two low harmonics. This is the essential part which might alone be sounded in stress of emergency, i.e. omitting the formal string of varied sections and the flourish to higher notes which could end and sometimes precede a call. And in four of the principal calls these two notes are the 'bass'

(no concealed mouthpipe), has two pommels and an integral mouthpiece which is a simple *évasement* of the tube with a narrow rim added to it. Tube outer diameter *c.* 12 mm.; of bell rim *c.* 8 cm.

and the 'folgent': in the *Bouteselle* ('Saddle', in England corrupted
to 'Boot and Saddle'), the first command of the day; *Monte-cheval*
or *A cheval* ('Mount'); *A l'estendart* ('Retire to the standards');
and *Au guet* itself, whose opening low C and G are still remembered in the Last Post.

Through this characteristic, the general nature of the calls can
be traced back before the sixteenth century through imitations or
parodies in vocal works. There is a rapidly syncopated figure on
c and *g* which occurs fleetingly in the fourteenth century in contratenor parts of Machaut's rondeaux and other part-songs. No
declared reference to trumpet calls is here. But when similar
figures appear in the next century, worked out at greater length
in pieces which have the word *Tuba* in their title, a connection
need hardly be doubted. First are the two three-part compositions
in the lost Strasbourg MS from which pieces were copied by De
Coussemaker before the fire of 1870 destroyed it (see Borren, van
den, 1925, pp. 96ff.). In the longer piece, entitled 'Tuba Henrici
de Libero Castro' ('Tuba of Henry of Freiburg', whom some have
tentatively identified with Henry of Lauffenberg) the top part has
a sacred text while the lower two, marked respectively *Contratenor tubae* and *Laudate eum in sono tubae*, lie between *c* and *e'*
in sections of vigorous trumpet imitation (Ex. 11) separated by
diatonic sections. While no literal imitation, being too compressed
and containing some non-trumpet notes, allusion to trumpet calls

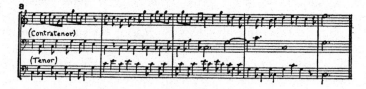

Ex. 11 a. Part of *Tuba Henrici* (Strasbourg MS, No. 15); **b.** *Bouteselle*
('Boot and Saddle') after Mersenne.

seems clear (cf. Ex. 11b though this is from a considerably later
source) and likewise a family relationship with the *kakaki* sounds
in Ex. 10 though these do not rise above the folgent.

Some have taken the view that these parts were intended for a trumpet with a slide. Against this, two contemporary treatises, likewise from beyond the Rhine, point to vocalization. The earlier, at Breslau (Wolf, 1918), briefly states how the style of music called *Trumpetum* is composed with parts which keep moving to the fifth and octave in the manner of trumpets.[1] The later treatise, by Paulirinus of Prague, *c.* 1460 (Reiss, 1925), adds that Trumpetum may be done in a rather raucous voice 'like *tubae gallicanae*' though without making discords and cacophony.[2] The second piece from the Strasbourg manuscript is in fact entitled *Tuba gallicalis* ('tuba, French style'): a vivacious composition without text but with only one of the parts truly 'trumpet'. This amounts to five variations of a strongly rhythmic figure across implied h2–5, somewhat resembling later Retreats or terminations of *Bouteselle*, etc.

Both these pieces are fairly boisterous and show more lapses from strict euphony than Paulirinus might have approved. Quite

Ex. 12 **a.** Dufay, *Et in Terra*, excerpts from Tenor and Contratenor parts; **b.** Fantini, start of the *Battaglia*; **c.** Bendinelli, Toccata to *Butasella*, first part; **d.** Thomsen, ending of 9th Toccata; **e.** Bendinelli, *Butasella*, first two sections (the two notes on *dran* appear as crotchet and minim in other versions).

[1] Sed trumpetum et stampania possunt habere duas vel tres partes et delyrant frequenter ad quintam notam vel ad dyapason idest ad octavam ad modum tubae vel lyrae.

[2] Trumpetum est cantus mensuralis per quatuor choros procedens, in quo quilibet suo fungens officio in cantando, via sua cantacionis directa progreditur, sed quartus obviat omnibus voce sonora aliquantulum rauca in modum tubae gallicanae sine hoc, quod alicui faciat suo occursus caccofoniam seu malam et dissidentem sonoritatem.

different is the neat moulding of trumpet-derived figures in Dufay's *Et in Terra* '*ad modum tubae*', indexed in one of the manuscripts as '*quod dicitur Trompeta*'. The figures, shared out between two lower voices, form a musical tenor below two upper voices in canon (*DTÖ*, VII, p. 145; also *Corpus mensurabilis musicae*, 1. IV, p. 79). Through most of the piece the lower line swings see-saw fashion between c' and g; the cavalry call 'Charge' may have been one of the things floating in the composer's mind (Ex. 12, b). Then, precisely as the upper voices land upon the long-held chord of the 'Amen' (x in Ex. 12) the lower parts accelerate their pace with a brief nod to *Monte cheval* and end with a reference to the customary terminal flourish, here rising to an implied h6. Some thirty years later, however, in Cousin's *Missa tubae* (*DTÖ* 120, p. 3), triadic 'trumpet' figures have become fully absorbed into the compositional process and one can no longer smell the stables.

To bridge the gap up to the time of the first actual trumpet manuscripts, Jannequin's well-known part-song *La Guerre* (1528) accurately quotes the essential kernels of several calls including *Bouteselle*, writing them both across a fourth and across a fifth, following the principles of imitative counterpoint and sounding recognizably the same either way. In the trumpet sources, too, certain calls appear on both intervals, firstly on h2 and h3, then in a 'high', 'second', or 'Italian' form on h3 and h4 (Thomsen, Mersenne, Bendinelli). Dufay's brief quotation of the higher and evidently newer version of *Monte cheval* seems to confirm the supposition that the deeper and more usual forms were heard before his time, and probably long before.

Clarion. This Anglo-Norman word and its equivalents in Continental languages introduce problems. But it may be said at once that, through a succession of various meanings which the words had over nearly three centuries, one may detect certain particular threads in the development of the trumpet as a tuneful musical instrument; that is, up to the application of 'clarino' in Germany and Italy to melodic playing in the high register of the normal trumpet.

Passages in thirteenth and fourteenth century official documents indicate that two categories of trumpet (i.e. of instruments, not only players) were employed by municipal and baronial establishments, though not necessarily always for simultaneous use.

Once more we must start in Italy, where in about 1240 the Emperor Frederick II presented the town of Arezzo with four *tubae* and a *tubecta,* all of silver. '*Tubecta*' (with the Latin diminutive ending) stands for the vernacular *trombetta,* as in the *trombetta et tubatores* of Lucca seventy years later. A corresponding French use of the diminutive is in the payrolls of the Count of Poitou, 1313/14: *menestrel de cor sarrasinois* (probably shawm, not horn), two *trompours, menestrel de naquaires* (small kettle drums) and *menestrel de trompette.* In Spain the King of Castile's musicians in 1293 included: one *anafil,* four *tromperos,* five *tamboreros;* the first term (from Arabic *nafir*) is described in dictionaries as having been a short trumpet, or in an Old Provençal glossary quoted by Marcuse as *parva tuba cum voce alta.* A length of 80 cm. is later mentioned in Castile (Donostia, *An. Mus. II,* p. 134).

In many of the earlier references like these where two trumpet terms appear together, *trompours* (or *tubae,* etc.) outnumber *trompette* (etc.) which is often single. An observer of the time would therefore have been likely to notice the instrument of the former more than the instrument denoted by the latter. The 5–6 foot long trumpets which are so much in evidence in pictures, on their own or with other instruments, are therefore those of the *trompours* (as in Fig. 13b). That the *trompette* was something special is further suggested in a French text of 1319 quoted by R. Wright (1941, p. 177): sums were made in payment to '2 *trompeurs* and to the one who plays the *trompette*', and each trompeur received only a third of the fee paid to the trompette.[1]

In fourteenth-century England a corresponding distinction may be seen between the words 'trompe' or 'trompette' on the one hand (these two terms having apparently coalesced) and 'clarion' on the other. In 1348 Edward III had five trompettes and two clarions. Attached to a fleet in 1377 were one claryoner, two trumpeters and four pipers. Again, these proportions in numbers must have some significance relating either to duties or to technique.

[1] A thirteenth-century French illustration showing trumpets of two sizes in action together, though without naming them, is a tournament scene in Brit. Mus. MS Royal 14 E.iii, where the long trumpet (as in Figs, 11d and 13) stands beside a taborer opposite a short trumpet (as Fig. 11 b, c) stationed beside a bagpiper. The scene is reproduced in Strutt's *Sports and Pastimes* (Hone's edition, 1868, p. 136).

In the Romance languages of France and Spain *clarin* had a meaning of something sounding high and clear, as the smallest of a set of sheep bells. In Low Latin, *claro* occurs in a charter of 1220 quoted in Marca's *Histoire de Bearn* (1640, p. 337) referring to the public cryer's use of *tuba* or *claro* as the custom may be; not that the second term here necessarily denoted a brass instrument. But as for the fourteenth-century English clarion, Maurice Byrne's searches in the records of the Goldsmiths' Company of London (*GSJ* XXIV, p. 63) prove definitely that in 1391 this was an instrument which was lighter in weight than a 'trompe' in the ratio of 7 to 10. A later entry, in 1420, notes that a 'trompe' came in seven pieces and a clarion in eight. This is a mystery. But the gilt pommels, entered separately, seem to have numbered two for each instrument, which suggests that both were straight-built, since folded models seldom have more than one. Unfortunately the second half of the fourteenth century is rather a weak time in trumpet iconography, and it is impossible yet to check directly whether a clarion was lighter in weight because shorter, or because narrower in tubing, or from a combination of factors.

Among oriental trumpet customs there is sometimes a feature which has not yet been mentioned. Some of the old *nakkara khana* employed trumpets of two sorts, one large like the *karna*, sounding its bellowing monotone; the other shorter or shriller, referred to in Persia and India as *nafir*, and often made in folded shape. In India during the last century it was heard in religious ceremonies accompanying the karna at intervals with 'a wild, shrill effect', though 'no calls or modulations are blown upon it'. Dr. N. A. Jairazbhoy has most kindly made available his recording and photograph (Pl. IV) of musicians of the Paidi tribe, Araku Valley, Andhra Pradesh, Central India, in 1963. The player of the folded trumpet, here named *baqa*, now and then bursts in above the shawm with exactly this effect, virtually what is now known in jazz as 'squealer trumpet' (Ex. 13a). In Egypt under Napoleon's occupation, Villoteau found the folded trumpet, *nafir*, to be the only trumpet of the Mameluke bands, with an excruciating sound on a few high notes above the tumult of shawms, drums and cymbals. Within the last few years, squealer trumpets, straight-built and not very long, have been heard leading circumcision processions in Tunisia. In Europe there is a tradition something like it in Andalusia, where the wars of Christian and Moor are still enacted in religious folklore. These are the *saeta* trumpets of Holy Week, with their high, wild flourishes between strains of a solemn dirge of a military band. The players reach h12 or higher, with an effect of the fastest baroque *clarino* done

Ex. 13 a. Trumpet, *baqa*, Paidi tribe, Central India (from a recording by N. A. Jairazbhoy, 1963); b. trumpet phrases from a *saeta* at Seville.

entirely without tonguing (Ex. 13b) on a five-foot straight trumpet. For another example, from Cadiz, see Larrea, 1949, Ex. 11. The phrases may show some affinity with Hispano-Moorish vocal preludes, but their interest here lies in their execution on trumpets, and trumpets which, whatever their length, are always special ones.

In none of these cases is the high register employed for a distinct melody, any more than are the deep notes of a *karna*. A purely speculative possibility is that high blowing on trumpets in the medieval West at first had a similar wildness of character, executed on the short trumpet (the *tubecta*, *cf.* Fig. 11b), sounding it soloistically in piercing warblings as high as possible at moments when the long trumpets fell silent. The shorter trumpet appears also in Moslem art, while the Castilian *anafiler* of 1293 was a Moor (Lamaña, 1969); he marched ahead of the *tromperos*, whose names were Christian. Perhaps already he could reach h10. It is anyway worth noticing a strange little melisma on h8, h9 and h10, which occurs late in the sixteenth century in Bendinelli's work in a fanfare of a kind whose name, *Sarassineta*, presumably recalls the ancient antagonist. It is quite unlike any specimen of 'clarino' music, while the corresponding place in Thomsen's manuscript has an isolated high E (*e″*) with a pause over it, as if a shorthand indication of something idiomatic which was difficult or pointless to write down.

During the fourteenth century the short trumpet becomes

rarer in both East and West as players no doubt came to appreciate the higher range of harmonics which a rather longer instrument brings within reach, and to execute passages as those in Ex. 13. Certainly each world knew what the other was doing. Thus the trumpet folded in 'S' form was in both areas about the end of the fourteenth century: in Europe in the Worcester choirstall carving of *c.* 1394, illustrated by Galpin (1910, Pl. 49); in Persia in the treatise written about ten years later by Ibn Ghaibi, one of Tamerlane's favourite minstrels (the *karrahnay* [karna] 'with the middle of the tube turned back on itself', to quote Farmer's translation).

But whereas oriental trumpeting methods thereafter stood more or less still, in Europe the clarioner, as we may now call him, was swept ahead by the Western urge to integrate diverse instrumental elements into unified musical schemes. By degrees he proceeded, by methods still non-literate but much thrashed out among the men themselves both at home and as they travelled abroad in the retinues of kings, to achieve a coherent distinctness of effect whereby the music of trumpets became so articulate that royalty danced to it, as in 1393 when the Duchess of Burgundy and her court danced to *trompettes* in the cloth hall at Ypres (though without mention of clarions: Van der Straeten, IV). How they played, we still do not know. But pictures of the first third of the fifteenth century show trumpets of two main and markedly distinct types: the straight instrument some 5 feet long; and the trumpet of greater tube-length and deeper pitch, usually in folded format and on the whole seen more frequently. To these conspicuously different types the terms clarion and trumpet must have respectively been applied, and again it is the reasonable hypothesis that the former denoted the shorter-tubed instrument, or at any rate the common form of it: we can ignore schoolmaster Horman's free translation of the Latin of Vegetius where he interprets a description of *buccina* as 'clarion wound in a hoop'.

The two types appear in battle scenes, both together (Pl. IV) and separately. So too French and English descriptions of war and ceremonies mention the two terms, often together and sometimes with shawms. But in France and Italy, official records now show no sign of a distinction, so that evidently men from a corps of *trompettes de guerre* (who also performed at feasts) or from ducal *trombetti* were selected by aptitude to handle the clarion, much as a court trumpeter would become a clarinist in Germany later on.

There then comes, later in the fifteenth century, a time when the conception of 'clarion' underwent a change. Everywhere the straight trumpet begins to recede into the background to become eventually an antique model reserved for certain ecclesiastical, state or mayoral processions and pageants; those of the Doge of Venice in the seventeenth century, for instance, were of silver, supported on the shoulders of youths.[1] Meanwhile the name itself, where it was preserved, gained a different physical meaning. In Nicot's *Trésor* it is said under 'Clarion' that this anciently served as a treble to *trompetes* which sounded tenor and bass, adding that it had a *tuyau plus estroit* than the trumpets of the tournaments etc. The instruments were otherwise the same. If Nicot really meant 'narrower tubing' he may be historically recalling a development which other evidence can associate with Germany at the time of the rise of the Nuremberg makers in the mid fifteenth century. In that country a *clareta* was then, or could be, a full-length folded trumpet (perhaps sometimes with a pull-out mouthpiece as noticed in the next chapter) and, if one can trust the accuracy of the illustration in Virdung's work of 1511, with narrower tubing than the common trumpet. All the instruments then sounded in the same tonality, bringing the possibility of a big musical advance for a trumpet ensemble and one which Germans—whom we later acknowledge as great high-note experts—were by nature disposed to make full use of. Thus at a ducal wedding in 1474 in Amberg, Virdung's home town in the Upper Palatinate, the bride was escorted by the two Dukes of Saxony who brought their trumpeters with them. They danced 'not to the musicians but to the music of trumpeters, which the Dukes have of top quality and are very unusual in respect of *clareten stimmen*, which go higher than one could imagine possible' (Pietzsch, 1960, p. 31).[2] It seems safe to suppose that all these trumpeters played at once with a foreshadowing, on the *clareta*, of the future clarino parts.

Finally, during the sixteenth century, the tube of the cavalry trumpet itself, if up to then it had preserved something of an

[1] For an illustration of a Nuremburg example by H. Hainlein, 1658, see Baines, 1966, Fig. 730. A few specimens have earlier dates on the bell even back to 'Siena 1406' (listed in Crane, 1972, p. 65). Some are certainly not in original state and all of them merit close scrutiny.

[2] Sy tanzten nach kainem saitenspiel dan nach den trumpten; die haben die herzogen von Sachsen guet und gar frembd von clareten stimmen also hoch einer denken mag.

ex-oriental width, was narrowed, first perhaps in Nuremberg, until there were no longer two species of instrument but only one—the 'baroque' model in fact, with the front bow brought forward to the bell rim, superseding the protruding bell of previous times; (an ancient cavalry-trumpet tradition may be preserved in an instrument of 1623 by J. Sander, Hanover, in the Nuremberg Collection: outside diameter of tubing, 13·5 cm., the sound big and clear, with h2 rich and comfortably in tune). The assimilation would have brought some sacrifice of sheer power in military calls, with the gain of a better-blended and more graceful sound in the full ensemble. But to follow the musical development to high-register playing through allusions in songs and keyboard works is difficult because clarettists would now themselves have obtained ideas from prevailing melody elsewhere. A little light is thrown on this by the manuscripts which are to be mentioned again when the subject is resumed in Chapter 5.

One of these manuscripts, by the German trumpeter Thomsen, includes a number of examples of another and very charming kind of trumpet music which is based on ordinary melodies but without going high: the notes which are not normally on the trumpet in the octave h4–8 are changed to those which are. The carol in Ex. 14 tells clearly what it is if one hums it through without looking at the solution below, and it is possible that something of a similar kind may be perceived in certain songs in the fifteenth-century Spörl Liederbuch (*Acta Germanica*, 1896, pp. 164 etc.). 'Das Küehorn' ('cowhorn', i.e. herdsman's song) is given, with the words which the scribe says were usually sung to it, in two versions, one of them diatonic within the octave, the other keeping to the notes of a major arpeggio save for an occasional fourth degree which remains unchanged. 'Das Nachthorn'

Ex. 14 Thomsen MS, 3rd and 4th sections of 'Sonnada Jossoph' (in the original most minims appear as semibreves); below, the carol.

in the same manuscript is in the minor, on the notes D, F, A plus the C below; but in another manuscript (Munich Cgm 4997) it is transposed into the major and altered to fall on a simple triad throughout save at the first and last lines of the song. The title 'Cowhorn' suggests a herdsman's alphorn (sometimes called *Kuh-horn* in more recent times) but the 'natural' version of the tune is not of a kind which one associates with that instrument. The other tune, in its major version, is not unlike certain village night-watchman's songs still sung upon the hour eighty years ago in the Salzburg area, with which region the Spörl book is associated. Some enterprising palace trumpeter of the years around 1400 may have been responsible for both of these 'natural note' versions. Another player to adopt the same course may have been the *trompette* who, at a royal wedding at Stuttgart in 1454 (Marix, p. 73) was not content to sound a fanfare but played 'chansons a sa trompette'—though right through the Renaissance period one can never keep out of mind the possibility of mechanical assistance through a slide.

FOUR

Renaissance Slides

It has long been inferred by historians that trumpets must have existed in Europe from the early fifteenth century which could be played diatonically in the middle and lower parts of their range; and that if this were so, then it must have been by means of a slide in the form of a long telescopic mouthpipe, the trumpet being pushed to and fro along the inner pipe to which the mouthpiece was securely attached. That no such instrument survives from the period need not be wondered at, considering the exceedingly few musical instruments of any kind which have done so: the only known trumpet which acts in this way dates from a good two hundred years later (Chap. 7). And though there is no contemporary description of the device it must certainly have formed a stage in the evolution of the trombone during the same century. The initial reasons for supposing its existence are to be found in various Franco-Flemish religious compositions dating from between about 1410 and 1440 in which the lowest of three parts is, or includes sections which are, textless and marked *Trompetta*, *Tuba* or suchlike, yet diatonic and lacking military-call flavour. Next there is the manner in which the trumpet is held in many pictures, at first mostly French and Italian, where a shawm band is depicted (Fig. 14). It is usually a trumpet in folded format, either an open '*S*' or with the bell bow turned to drop the bell section into a position close to the mouthpiece, and in some pictures, though by no means all, the mouthpiece seems to be pressed to the mouth between the first and second fingers of one hand, usually the left, while the other hand grasps the mouthpipe branch with the arm extended, in some instances as far as it can go. Motion is then clearly implied. So too in the *Hausbuch*, where opposite the musicians sketched in Fig. 14, d a playful young trumpeter shoots the instrument downwards to tease a dog.

In French-speaking courts the title of this band was *haut*

Fig. 14 a. Giovanni di Paolo, Asciano, *c.* 1425: **b.** from the Bible of Duke Borso, 1455–61 (after Besseler, 1950); **c.** Dance of Death, Basel, late 15th cent.; **d.** *Mittel-alterliches Hausbuch, c.* 1475; **e.** cavalry trumpeter from the same, for comparison.

menestrels, 'loud minstrels', a title which shawms earn particularly well. The band is normally seen with players of one or two treble shawms, tenor shawm (*bombarde*), and the trumpet who is placed at the end of the row. Through the 1422–1462 records of the Burgundian court, resident mostly in Brussels and Lille, this trumpeter is listed as *trompette des menestrels* in distinction from the men of the corps of *trompettes de guerre*; the post was held first by Everart Janson, then by another Janson, and finally by Adrien de Rechter, all presumably Flemings. Just earlier, in 1418, one Hermen was in service with Charles VI of France as *trompette pour menestrier*, probably a post of the same kind. The

Burgundian instruments were bought, as far as the records show, from Flanders: thus in 1425 a set of shawms was obtained for the *menestrels* from a maker in Bruges (2 *bombardes à clef*, 1 *contre* and 2 *chalemies*) together with 'a *trompette* serving with the said minstrels'; the shawms cost 14 *livres* the lot and the trumpet 10 (Marix, p. 102). This would be the postulated slide trumpet, today often referred to as 'minstrel's trumpet'. Also in Spain, the shawm-band personnel at the Aragonese court included a '*trompeta* of the said minstrels' (1423, see Lamaña; the instrument is later named there *trompeta bastarda*).

Its diatonic capacity would in theory depend upon the proportionate length of slide in relation to the total tube-length of the trumpet in the closed position. From pictures, the maximum sliding distance can be estimated from the visible length of the mouthpipe branch between the player's face and the start of the outer bow, deducting, say, 8 cm. (about three inches) at the mouthpiece for the grasp of the left hand, and 5 cm. as the smallest permissible overrun of inner and outer tubes at fullest extension, i.e. about 13 cm. in all. For argument's sake, let us take a 6-foot trumpet (Fig. 15, top) and fold it into shapes (i) which are fairly typical in French and Burgundian pictures of the first half of the fifteenth century (and in Germany from just afterwards), either in open S-form or as shown to the right. The three branches measure about 64 cm. (bell), 38 cm. and 63 cm., which with 25 cm. added for the two bows makes 190 cm. in all, about modern E. Assuming the trumpet to be fully retracted, its slide would offer a maximum extension of 63 minus 13 = 50 cm. or over a quarter of the closed total and good for lowering by two tones—provided that the two hands were initially placed near together (L and R). The two-tone extension then comes just within arm's reach.

Yet it may be incorrect to analyse the capabilities wholly in theoretical terms, especially in the lower register, with which suspected uses of the instrument are very largely concerned. With the small and abrupt bell expansion which is usually seen, with the wide mouthpiece which pictures hint at, and at an early period in embouchure history, it may well have been the practice to employ 'short' positions on h3. Experiments with replicas do in fact allow one to imagine that men who were using the instrument every day of their lives may have produced strong, clear sounds, well in tune, with extensions very considerably shorter than those expected by theory, e.g. with as little as 18 cm. for the whole tone. They may then have attained, though practically in falset, the lowering of a perfect fourth which supplies the note above the closed-position h2, and completes the diatonic scale down to that harmonic.

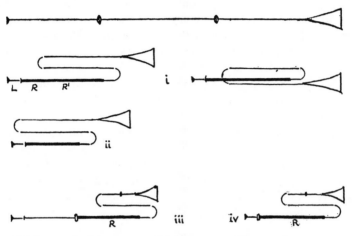

Fig. 15 Scheme of 15th century slide trumpets. (See text.)

Use of short positions is perhaps borne out by the curious fact that in the great majority of pictures the right hand is placed somewhere near R' (Fig. 15, i). Still assuming the instrument to be retracted, this attitude, which looks comfortable for balance and which seems to have caught the eye of observing artists so constantly, puts the theoretical extension for two tones well beyond arm's reach. But perhaps these trumpets are depicted in a partly extended position. It must then have been a position which players were constantly using, and this could only have been a whole tone out from the closed position, since the retracted instrument presumably gave notes which formed part of the regular scale, and a semitone down from these would in most cases merely lead to little-needed sharps. Let us therefore draw back the instrument figured at i until the bow almost hits the face, i.e. back by about 18 cm. (ii). The total tube-length becomes reduced to 172 cm. and the lower branch to 45 cm., allowing an extension of 32 cm.: just good for a tone and a half in theory, but with 'short' positions two tones—not however the perfect fourth unless by the most drastic falset.

Possible slide trumpets of the period also show other proportions than those in (*i*). For instance there are small instruments in S-form with the bell rim brought back level with or even behind the outer bow, by which the proportionate length of slide can become much increased. This is seen particularly in the earlier Italian paintings, from (possibly) Giovanni di Paolo's angels at Asciano, *c*. 1425 (Fig. 14, a) to Fra Angelico, and especially in the dance band of a miniature in the Bible of Duke Borso of Ferrara, *c*. 1455, reproduced by Besseler in his article of 1950 and sketched here in Fig. 14, b and 15, *iii*. The player is very obviously stretching for the biggest possible extension, while a small boss or collar on the slide branch evidently marks the near end of the outer sliding tube. If we close this trumpet up (*iv*) we find a little instrument (type of slide clarion?) with some 4-foot tube (modern B) and maximum shift of 27 per cent, theoretically two tones but probably allowing a good perfect fourth in semi-falset. The object of the short bell and middle branches may thus have been to secure this shift within arm's reach through using a model of short tube-length and high tonality.

The religious compositions. These include: Arnold de Lantins, *Et in terra* (lowest part marked *tuba*); Estienne de Grossim, *Kyrie* (*trompetta, trompet*); Richard de Loqueville, *Et in terra* (similarly); and Johannes Franchos, *Ave Virgo* (*trumpetta*).[1] A section of the work by Grossim, organist of Notre Dame in Paris, may serve as an example (Ex. 15).

The first question is whether any trumpet would have been admitted in church music at that period. Affirmative evidence is not wholly lacking. Gerson, canon of Notre Dame, who died in 1429, wrote that only the organ was normally used in church, yet sometimes one added the trumpet though very rarely reed instruments.[2] The Duke of Savoy's chapel at the mid-century, when Dufay was cantor there, lists a trumpeter with the singers

[1] Transcribed or in facsimile in, respectively, Van den Borren, *Polyphonia sacra*, pp. 10, 15; De Van, *Mus. Disciplina*, 1948, p. 5ff; von Fischer, *Acta Musicol.*, 1964, p. 95; *DTÖ*, XL, p. 19.

[2] After a brief note on the 'modern' organ Gerson continues: 'Hoc [the organ] solum vel praecipuum retinuit Ecclesiastica consuetudo musicum genus instrumenti, cui vidimus aliquam jungi tubam, rarissime vero bombardas, seu chalemias, seu cornamusas grandes, aut parves, vel alia si qua sint, quae nominaverimus instrumenta' (*De Canticis*, Du Pin, III, col. 628).

(Bouquet, 1968, p. 251 and cf. Marix, p. 117). This is getting rather late, but *one* trumpeter, and with the choristers, perhaps indicates participation in music inside the church. Some historians maintain that such evidence is insufficient, and that these

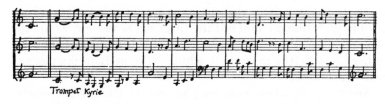

Ex. 15 Part of *Kyrie* by Grossim (Aosta Codex 53v, 54, after a transcription by Frank Ll. Harrison).

'trumpet' parts were vocalized after the *Trumpetum* manner noticed in the last chapter. But on the whole, the truth of performance of these parts on a slide trumpet is agreed, and with use of an instrument of the same cumbersome nature as that which the *haut menestrels* used in their bands. For its pitch, many modern authorities have opted for a nominal D series when closed, the awkward note a whole tone above h2 here being *e*. In the Grossim (lowest note *f*) and the two short pieces by Lantins and Loqueville (lowest note *c*) this *e* is touched only in one of two versions of the Lantins and there only once. It can be seen in Ex. 15 how well the Grossim part lies for a D trumpet poised in a tone-out position which gives the C major triad, and drawn back for *d'* and *a*. Two-tone lowering is needed for *f*, however, so that if this note were produced with its correct extension the closed format would have resembled Fig. 15, *i* or *iv*, with the hands placed near together. But in the Franchos, *e* occurs as frequently as the two notes above it. Below this, the tonic *d* is most frequent of all and so rules out a trumpet in C (though this would supply a low *A* which here occurs once). Again D seems most likely. But if the actual size of the instrument corresponded with those of the *haut menestrels*, the D would have been higher than our D by at least a tone. Grossim's treble part might then lie rather high for the voice unless the composition were performed a fifth lower (at our pitch nearer a fourth lower than written). This may have been so, because the scarcest note in its *trompetta* part is *b*, which would then become the falset *e* of the D trumpet—though equally it could be the falset note of a small 'slide clarion' in A.

Most problematic is the one known secular composition of the period with a 'trumpet' part: the *rondeau* of *c.* 1440 ascribed to Pierre Fontaine (*Documenta Musicol.*, 1958) with a *Contratenor trompette* part descending below *c* to *A G F* and *D*. It would all lie on a trombone pitched in the G of the time, but the date seems too early for this. On a slide trumpet in D the low *D* could have been a good fundamental but the three notes above it would have demanded falset with a vengeance. The other parts lie, however, rather low also (the top only touching *f'*) so perhaps the piece was read a fifth higher.

Assuming that the trumpet was used in these works—which themselves are copies or versions of compositions, mostly written down in Italy or Austria—a reasonable notion is that the instrument may have served also, on suitable occasions, in other sacred or ceremonial pieces of the same period which have lower parts similar in configuration but not marked 'trompette'. An attempt to enlarge on this question would have to begin with a discussion of the known 'trompette' works in their full musicological context. For this there is no space here. But some of our practical musicians today have experimented with a more extensive use of the slide trumpet, and indeed they have some authority to go further. At the Council of Constance three trumpeters of the Earl of Warwick gathered attention in 1415 by performing together, in the procession on the feast of St. Thomas of Canterbury, 'in three parts as one customarily sings' (Schuler, 1966, p. 165). The German word in this text of the chronicle, *prusunen* (with this odd interpolation of 'r'), still denoted trumpets —not yet trombones. The almost inevitable conclusion that they must have been slide trumpets opens a wealth of possibilities which, perhaps, should be viewed cautiously while hoping that more historical evidence will come to light.

Basse danse. Duties of *haut menestrels* included, among many things, marching at the head of processions and playing at dinner.

At this period the use of three different diatonic instruments
certainly suggests polyphonic playing; but each instrument
possessed limitations and nothing has yet disclosed the exact
methods which these no doubt exceedingly capable musicians
employed on such occasions in favourite compositions of the day.
The loud minstrels also provided the music for court dances,
where a favourite dance from around 1440 to the end of the
century was the *basse danse*, and with this it becomes possible to
reconstruct a partial picture of how the band performed. The
music for this dance was constructed upon a *cantus firmus* tenor,
many examples of which are preserved in late fifteenth-century
sources, written in long notes of equal duration with signs above
them indicating the complex steps of the dance. The speed of
these long notes may have been between 10 and 17 per minute
(Crane, 1965, p. 186). A big collection at Brussels, from the
Burgundian court library (Closson, 1912), contains over fifty of
these tenors, some of which have been shown to derive from
earlier *chansons*, in two cases by Binchois. The notes are written
over the range *c* to *e'* (Ex. 16, a).

Ex. 16 a. *Basse danse* tenor, 'Le petit roysin' (Brussels MS 28); b. start
of same with treble above it (Perugia MS, after Bukofzer, 1951);
c. start of '*Alta*', Fernando de la Torre (Cancionero musical de Palacio,
Madrid).

To make, from these tenors, live dance music in parts the
minstrels, though they performed without music, would naturally
have prepared and rehearsed their arrangements beforehand,
broadly observing appropriate polyphonic conventions of other

music of the time. The tenor itself seems to have been taken care of by the powerful bombarde: in 1439, Burgundy bought from Bruges *trois teneurs à clef* (cf. *bombardes à clef* quoted on p. 96); and in 1456 one of the players there who is named in neighbouring years simply as *menestrel*, as all the shawmists normally were, is listed as *teneur des menestrels*. We can however see from pictures that the bombarde could not have descended to *c*, while the sixteenth century evidence from both books and surviving instruments is that its lowest note was *g*. The basse danse tenors were therefore played at a considerably higher pitch than their notation suggests.

After the tenor the next part to be coped with was the treble, performed by the treble shawm. The known three-part arrangements of basses danses at the heyday of the dance are in German collections of organ music, notably the Buxheim book (*c*. 1460–70, see E. Southern, 1963). The treble parts here follow a common pattern in contemporary composition: an active, florid part elaborating a simpler underlying melodic idea which keeps consonance with the tenor on the main beats, i.e. in normal cases on three subdivisions of each long note of the written tenor. In a manuscript from Italy, slightly later, one of the favourite basse danses is written down in these two parts alone—tenor and florid treble—conceivably an actual minstrel's arrangement (Perugia MS, transcribed and discussed in Bukofzer, *Studies*, 1951, p. 199). Ex. 16, b gives a few bars of this. The lowest note of the treble is written *g*; but again, we know that the lowest note of the treble shawm was about *d'*, confirming an upwards transposition which would certainly make brighter dance music (in one of the organ arrangements the tenor is in fact raised by a fourth). No doubt the shawmist, having once thought out his part for a given dance, would vary it by improvisation while playing it day after day.

This leaves us with the third part, contratenor, and with the third instrument, the trumpet. The one must have been the occupation of the other. The contratenor, which a composer normally supplied after writing the other two parts, fills out the harmony, keeping consonant with these and proceeding at much the same pace as the tenor, sometimes inserting passing notes. For a player utterly familiar with the idiom this should not have been difficult to improvise once he knew fairly well what his colleague on the treble was going to play. In the Buxheim versions it is largely sandwiched between tenor and treble, though as with most contratenor parts it frequently crosses the former especially at cadences, to avoid landing on the same note. At the raised performing pitch of the band such a part would lie quite high where a slide trumpet, played up to h7 or h8, would have been least hampered by its primitive mechanism. Also, it may cease from time to time: by its nature it is a part that can be left off without the hearer losing the thread of the music, and this is how a brass-player may have preferred things to be in the puffed-cheek days. Later on the part lies lower, mainly below the tenor. An example probably from the end of the century is a Spanish arrangement of the same dance as that shown in Ex. 16a (Davison & Apel No. 102; see Ex. 16c). Entitled '*Alta*' ('haut'), it is either for keyboard or possibly a work of the minstrels themselves. The contratenor descends to *F*, therefore nearer *c* in the band. The lower pitch many reflect the introduction of the trombone. Tinctoris, describing the *haut menestrels* of this time (though he does not specifically mention dances) tells how the trombone's purpose was to play contratenor parts including the deepest of such parts, as distinct from the part played by the 'tenor commonly called bombarde'.

The contratenor may seem a curious part to have been given to the solitary brass-player; but we have to remember that he was there principally because trumpets—formerly two or more—had been associated with shawms by long tradition. As these musicians proceeded to embrace regular polyphony (a bombarde already existed by the 1350s) it must have been a problem at first to fit the trumpet in, but whether the slide was originally introduced in aid of this is impossible to say in the absence of particulars of band methods prior to the basse danse period. We have seen that the instruments bought from Bruges in 1425 included a *contre*. If this were a shawm suited to the kind of contratenor which lay mainly above the tenor, then the trumpeter may have had some other duty. His instrument was, after all, still a trumpet, and fanfares may have had some place in the proceedings—and again perhaps in processions, sounded where required whilst the music of the shawms went on.

Claret. A short slide just feasible with a not-too-long straight trumpet might conceivably account for the extra piece belonging to the London Goldsmiths' clarions in 1420. Certainly the Venetian painter A. Vivarini's 'Adoration of the Magi' (in the Dahlem galleries, Berlin) seems actually to depict the device twenty years later. Seventeen heralds carry 5-foot, nafir-like brass trumpets at the slope (straight trumpets were still popular among Italian *trombetti*) and one of the men holds separately in the same hand a short mouthpipe with small mouthpiece attached (the painting is reproduced in Bryan's *Dictionary of Painters*, 1905, and the interesting detail by Smithers, 1973, Pl. 1). Assuming this to be a slide, it would be good for a whole tone and make possible diatonic melody across the treble stave. (An instrument apparently of this kind was still known in Italy in the eighteenth century, described by Bonanni (1722) as '*Altra Tromba spezzata*', used by country people; he may be referring to those annual pageants held in provincial towns, but he does not mention the kind of music played on the instrument.)

The question next takes us to Germany. The word '*Claret*' occurs early in Flemish (town minstrels at Furnes, near Dunkirk, in 1451) apparently as equivalent to French *clairon*: '*trompetten* and *claretten*'. The terms here denote the players. But in Germany, rather later, a cryptic entry in the Frankfurt-am-Main town records for 1490/91 notes sums paid for six trumpets ordered from Nuremberg, namely 3 *Feldtrompten* at two florins each, and to each one a *claret montstücke* (mouthpiece) at one *ort* apiece; and 3 *mitlean* (middle or 'mean') *trompten* at 2½ florins each, and to each one a *quint mondstücke* at 5 *albus* apiece (Valentin, 1906). To translate these sums into approximate modern equivalents is difficult since the relative values, especially of the *albus* ('white penny') varied, but if a field trumpet cost £10 and a 'mean' trumpet £15, then a claret mouthpiece cost about £1·25 and a quint mouthpiece between £1 and 70 pence. The question then is why a claret mouthpiece should have cost around a third more than that for the 'mean' trumpet, which may have been an instrument of older and wider proportions and played with the others somewhat as the later 'principal', for which 'quint' was a synonym.

The quint mouthpiece may have been of a type which seems historically primitive and known, for example, by a mouthpiece preserved with the Basel trumpets of 1578, the earliest-known dated specimens of folded trumpet, made by the city's trumpeter and trumpet-maker Jacob Steiger. Rather like an oriental mouthpiece it is built up from sheet metal, here silvered brass, in five pieces so far as can be ascertained without dissection (Fig. 16;

also Table 5, p. 125). The stem is internally cylindrical and the throat of the cup just overlaps it. It works well enough for what it no doubt had to do, giving the trumpet a rich, powerful sound in the fanfare register and well in tune down to the fundamental itself. The more expensive 'claret' mouthpiece could have been simply of more advanced form and better for high notes, turned from a casting with integral stem, or with a short spigot fixed to a cylindrical stem of sheet metal, internally also cylindrical—a construction noticed by Halfpenny (*GSJ* XX p. 78, XXII pp. 53, 55) among English and Scottish trumpets of the 1660s and also met in some more ancient German mouthpieces including one for trombone (Fig. 16, right).

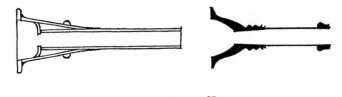

cm.

Fig. 16 Left Mouthpiece of Basel trumpet, 1578 (Basel 30); **right** mouthpiece of trombone by Anton Schnitzer, 1579 (Verona, Accademia Filarmonica).

On the other hand the claret mouthpiece may have been something like that held by Vivarini's herald, though now with a folded trumpet. Fifty years after the Frankfurt document, some correspondence of the Nuremberg maker Georg Neuschel (Eitner, 1877, p. 149ff) mentions '12 *deutsche trommeten* complete with *mundstücken* and *claret-stücken*'. Some thirty years later (1573) a Cassel court inventory lists '3 *teutschen Trromptten* together with Zugen and mouthpieces' (*GSJ* IV, p. 31) and in 1601 the same court lists two *Zugk-Trometten* (*ibid.* p. 34), which is from then onwards the normal German term for the slide trumpet, a classic instrument of the town musician and tower player up to the eighteenth century (Chap. 7). In Fig. 17 it is being played at dinner, with singers and other instruments.

The term *Zug* had already appeared in Neuschel's letters with the evident meaning of a trombone slide. With trumpets, we may ask whether it next came to replace '*claret stück*' and thus explain the greater cost of a 'claret mouthpiece' in 1490: i.e. a cup attached to a cylindrical stem as described above, but with this stem accurately prolonged and employed regularly or optionally as a slide to give the player a diatonic compass below h8. Returning to 1474, the year when a wedding party at Amberg was so struck by very high *claret-stimmen* (p. 91)—which no doubt signified performance well above h8 quite apart from any question of a

Fig. 17 From Ammerbach's *Orgel oder Instrument Tabulatur*, Leipzig, 1571.

slide—the tower player at Lübeck had his duties defined, namely 'to blow and play every evening of the year on the *claritte* as the custom has been' (Menke, p. 36). If 'blow' refers to the time-signal fanfare and 'play' means a tune afterwards, this trumpeter cannot be imagined standing up there alone in the bitter night venturing the skills of the natural clarino register. Either he adapted popular melodies to the harmonics of the medium octave as in Ex. 14, or like his baroque successors in Germany he had a slide.

The slide trumpets in long S-shape which are modelled in Pacher's altarpieces (one of them illustrated in Sachs, 1950, also in Bate, Pl. 14) probably represent this *claritte* or, as Virdung names it, *clareta*. It certainly looks as if to Virdung, and to Agricola shortly afterwards, slide trumpets were so familiar that they were taken for granted, calling for no detailed remarks on their mechanism. Virdung's *Thurnerhorn* ('tower player's trumpet') is described as that which ushers in the day and the night, and must be another, while many German illustrations also show a slide trumpet in use with shawms for dance music after the earlier fashion (Fig. 14, d). But upon such freedom the voice of the old aristocracy, spoken through the Imperial Guild of Trumpeters and Kettledrummers from its headquarters in Dresden, were to drop the gate, prohibiting its fraternity from what were viewed as debasements of the historic war trumpet and so preparing the ground for that intensive development of pure natural-trumpet music which we know today as 'baroque'.

TROMBONE

This, with the two-legged slide which reduces the previous shifts by a half, could bring a new nimbleness as well as the power to lower a harmonic correctly by a fourth or more. When and where it was first made has not yet been pin-pointed.

The present word is recorded in 1439 in the Este archives at Modena, but as the nickname of one of the trumpeters: a special banner was issued for the 'tuba-ductilis played by the tubicen whom they call trumbonus' (Valdrighi, 1884, p. 439). At this date he must have been the slide-trumpeter. But an account of some festivities at Florence in 1459 notices that the pifferi (shawmists) and the trombone played a saltarello (a dance which was performed after a basse danse; Heartz, 1967, Appendix D). That the instrument here may have been a trombone can be supported by pictorial evidence, provided that one concedes a point in the matter of artists' observation.

Two paintings come into question. First, the ballroom scene in the series of paintings, well-known as 'The Wedding of the Adimari', on a Florentine chest, undated but probably not much later than the mid-century. Second, an altar painting done for a church in Cologne by the anonymous Master of Marienleben between 1460 and 1480 (Munich, Alte Pinatothek; Sauerlandt, Pl. 9). In both representations the rear bow lies over the player's shoulder, as it does in a trombone to counterbalance the slide. More essential to a trombone is a provision by which the hand at the mouthpiece keeps the bell stationary while the slide is moved. This is the cross-stay which joins mouthpiece socket to bell tenon. The other stays are basically extras; for example, the slide was first moved by one of its branches. The German painting shows no stay at all. With the Italian example it is hard to say, the painting having been restored, but a dark scratch *might* have indicated the stay.

More to the point, however, is the position of the bell mouth. In these pictures it lies close up to or beyond the outer bow, which is not where one expects to find it in a trombone. But if, on the other hand, the two instruments were simply enlarged slide trumpets with the rear bow taken back over the shoulder for balance, then the bell-mouth position would bring a length of bell which would reduce the proportionate slide length by an amount that would absurdly deprive the slide of much of its anyhow limited musical value. The two depictions must surely represent trombones of early models and roughly contemporary with the Italian written account of 1459 mentioned above.

The French name *sacqueboute* is known from 1468 if Olivier de la Marche faithfully reports the wedding of the Duke of Burgundy to Margaret of York at Bruges in that year; the music included a motet (unfortunately not named in the *Mémoires*, p. 369) played by the *haut menestrels* with *trompette-saicqueboute* and three shawms, disguised as goats.[1] Ferdinand of Spain employed a player of the *saccabuche* from 1474, named Gassó (Madurell, p. 223). In Germany, *Posaune* seems to have its new meaning in an account of a Corpus Christi procession at Heidelberg in 1469, 'with the bells pealing, and *Pusaunen*, *trumetten* and many *pfiffen* (shawms)'. In all these instances the trombone has taken over the old brass role in the shawm band, with which it maintains a close connection well into the seventeenth century. But the late years of the fifteenth century saw over much of Europe an explosion in the use of instruments in church, and in this the transformed minstrel's trumpet was quickly allotted a share.[2] At a

---

[1] *Sacqueboute*: perhaps from Old French *sacquer*, 'to draw out', e.g. to unsheath a sword (Nicot, *Dictionnaire*, 1573), whence Engl. Seykebud or Sakbudd (with Shalmes in royal events of 1509: Lafontaine, pp. 3, 4) and Shakbush (1495). The last comes closer to the Spanish word *sacabuche* ('to draw out the innards') which some have held to be the parent word. French and English both adopted the Italian name *trombone* when the instrument was revived in the later eighteenth century.

[2] A hostile reaction to this came from Erasmus, who describes how the *tubae*, *litui*, *fistulae* and *sambucae* were everywhere battling with the voices within the churches. By *litui* he probably meant trombones. (*Opera omnia*, 1703 etc., VI, 731C–732C; see also Miller, 'Erasmus on Music', *MQ* 1966, pp. 339–340.)

wedding at Torgau (Saxony) in 1500 two masses were sung 'with the help of the organ, three *Posaun* and one *Zinken* [cornett]' (Pietzsch, 1960, p. 14 note). In the monumental engravings of 'The Triumph of Maximilian', begun by Burgkmair in 1516, one waggon bears the Emperor's Hofkapelle, with cornett, trombone, and twelve men and boy singers, all reading from a large music desk under the watchful eyes of the Capellmeister with the composer Senfl seated beside him (well reproduced in Besseler, 1931, Pl. XVII). It can therefore be safely assumed that works by Isaac and his contemporaries were frequently performed by such combinations.

For trombones as a group, Corteccia's Florentine *Intermedii* of 1539 concludes with a five-part motet played by four of them, with one part sung for the sake of the words (the music is printed in Minor & Mitchell, *A Renaissance Entertainment*, 1968). In Germany, a set of Rhaw's part-books of 1533, *Symphoniae Jucundae*, contains an early manuscript note in the tenor book which observes that certain of the pieces are 'good on trombones etc.'; in one of these, Brumel's *Sicut Lilium*, part of which is given in Ex. 17, the treble rises to f'', suggesting perhaps a cornett

Ex. 17 Brumel, 'Sicut lilium', bars 10–19. (Rhaw, *Symphoniae jucundae*, 1533.)

unless the piece were played a fourth lower using the three sizes of trombone. The existence of these about that time may be inferred from Neuschel's correspondence of 1541–45 (Eitner, 1877): *gemeine* (ordinary) and *mittel Posaune* would signify tenor; and *quart* (a fourth below) and *grosse Posaune* are bass. 'Mittel' may then imply existence of a *klein* or alto. The terms 'alto', 'tenor' and 'bass' are rarely employed for trombones before the end of the century.

The instrument. Surviving sixteenth-century trombones are with one exception German, built by the makers of Nuremberg,

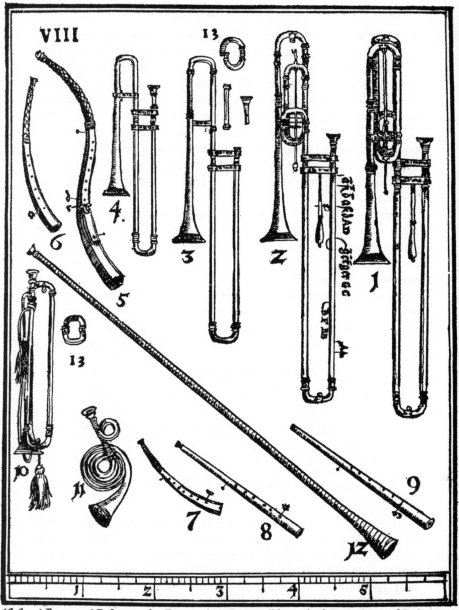

Fig. 18 Praetorius, De Organographia (*Syntagma* II), 1618, Pl. VIII (six inches on scale approx. equivalent to 5½ English inches).

[1] *Note to the Dover Edition.* The two trombones bearing the earliest dates (1551, 1557) have been judged not wholly acceptable, the Erasmus Schnitzer

among them dynasties celebrated until past the mid-eighteenth century (listed at the end of this chapter). Not all the instruments are wholly in original condition.[1] The oldest are of tenor pitch, by Erasmus Schnitzer, 1551 (Nuremberg Collection), Georg Neuschel, 1557 (Vienna), Anton Schnitzer, 1579 (Verona), Conrad Linczer, 1587 (Hamburg), Anton Drewelwecz, 1595 (Nuremberg; Pl. VI), and the only early French instrument, a bass by Pierre Colbert of Rheims, 1593 (The Hague). These are followed by a rich patrimony of baroque trombones which may also be considered here. Indeed from 1607 to the end of the seventeenth century there exists a dated Nuremberg trombone for about every three or four years, including at least seventeen in the tenor range, five basses (mostly pre-1650) and five altos (post-1660). Thereafter, as horns become more numerous, trombones tail off.

They are made, as trombones still are, in two separate parts, the slide and the bell. The inner branches of the slide supply a fixed amount of cylindrical tubing while the outer branches introduce a proportion of wider tubing which increases as the slide is moved—an automatic compensation in bore to total length, thanks to which the sonority over the different positions of the slide is so effectively balanced (better so than in our valved instruments over the different valve-combinations).

The old trombone slides are without stockings (which came in after the mid-nineteenth century) and the inner and outer tubes differ in width by about 2 mm. In the earliest period free motion is assisted by soft leather packing in the clasps of the flat stays (Pl. VI) which are removable (in this period all joints of a brass instrument were normally detachable). The flat stay is not comfortable to hold, but we have seen that the slide was at first grasped by one of the branches (much as the hand had previously grasped the slide trumpet). During the seventeenth century the flat stay, though often retained on the bell (with a pin through the clasp), became replaced on the slide by more comfortable tubular stays, the moving stay made in two telescopic sections, and this is still found well into the nineteenth century in all countries. Slide bores for alto and tenor are usually very narrow, between 9 and 10 mm. For bass, on which positions given by h2 were constantly required in music, bores are considerably wider, between 11 and 12 mm. The Neuschel tenor of 1557, however, which has much of its original slide, has a bore of nearly 12 mm.;

partly an original trumpet and the Neuschel partly a bass trombone (Henry G. Fischer, *Historic Brass Society Journal*, 1989).

this may have been conservative for its time and possibly some indication of the kind of bore which a slide trumpet had in earlier times.

The bell joint is cylindrical up to and including the bow. The ascending branch is shorter than today and the descending branch with the flare is longer, thus bringing the bell rim further forward. Because of this the length of the expanding section has the same proportion to the whole as on a trumpet. Actual profiles of the expansion undergo a marked change across the period from the sixteenth to the eighteenth centuries, matching changes in the German trumpets and probably following them. The earlier bells expand from the bow considerably faster than later bells, which, however, flare out about an inch from the end to a rim 2 to 3 cm. wider than in the early bells (cf. Chap. 1, p. 21). Fig. 19 is an

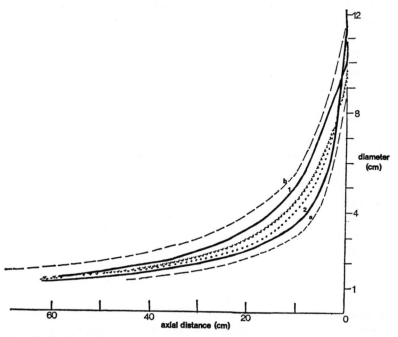

Fig. 19 Bell profiles of Nuremberg trombones, 1557–1783, diameters enlarged five times. (See text.)

attempt to illustrate this point, showing outside diameters enlarged five times. The thick lines enclose profiles: upper thick line (1), Neuschel; below it, tenors (toothed line), Drewelwecz; (dotted) Paul Hainlein, 1684 (Berlin Collection); and (lower thick line), Schmied of Pfaffendorf, 1783 (*ibid.*). In broken line above and below are (b) the bass by I. Ehe, 1612 (a most beautiful trombone), and (a) an alto by H. Starck, 1670 (also in the Nuremberg Collection). The alto bells match contemporary trumpets closely and for tenors and basses the diameters are scaled up by steps approximately of 3 : 4.

Table 4 shows dimensions of some mouthpieces which are judged to be contemporary, naming the instrument with which each is associated. That with the 1579 Schnitzer is engraved NURNBERG and matches the instrument in decoration. Total length can seldom be given, most examples being well jammed in. This also interferes with examination of the stem, which in some early instances takes the form of a cylindrical shank as shown above in Fig. 16. The cups (Pl. V) have sharp, wide throats and flat rims very much like contemporary trumpet mouthpieces. Also the general dimensions for tenor mouthpieces, while not markedly different from those of today, are interestingly close to those of the earliest cavalry trumpet mouthpieces (Table 5 in the next chapter), from which we might suspect that similar dimensions had been used among the fifteenth-century slide trumpets also.

Table 4 (mm.)

| | Diameters | | | Depth | |
	max.	cup	throat	of cup	
Alto					
Birckholtz, 1695 (Nuremberg Coll.)	33	21	8	12·5	
Tenor					
A. Schnitzer, 1579	37	23·2	8·2	13·9	(Fig. 16)
I. Ehe, 1612 (Nuremberg Coll.; bass trombone but tenor mouthpiece?)	37·5	24	8	21	
Bass					
Colbert, 1593	41	25	—	18·3	(Pl. V)
Reichard, 1607 (Nuremberg Coll.)	43	28	9	20·5	
I. Ehe, 1616 (Munich, Bayer. Nat. Mus.)	43	28	8	20	(Pl. V)

The playing qualities of well-preserved examples has often been judged by modern players to be excellent: harmonics in tune, and good even tone over the compass required by the parts. Altos and tenors have effortless high notes, basses are full and resonant. One can readily understand how these full-compass and intonation-perfect instruments were rated so high among the wind instruments of the time, and the massive reliance upon them by the Gabrielis in Venice and their pupils in Germany. At the same time they also became curiously cast in roles of death and lament, and by extension the Shades of Hades, which has endured from Monteverdi and Schütz up to funeral marches in Belgian villages today, and must have arisen through subconscious atavism for brass instruments had not been very noticeably associated with funerals since Rome.

The stocking-less slide, while imperfect by the best modern standards of slide-making, did not unduly hamper technique. Mersenne noted that good trombonists could execute divisions in semiquavers. A Venetian book of divisions which mentions the trombone is Francesco Rognone's *Selva di varii passaggi* (1620); this includes a division for violone or trombone which has semi-quavers and descends to *C*—though among the deep wind instruments the *fagotto* (curtal) was on the whole preferred in Italy and Germany for low-register divisions at that time. Another matter of technique, the eternal question of trombone articulation—whether or not always to tongue the notes—is already raised by Speer (p. 223). Some, he says, slur 'with the breath', but it is better and brighter to attack cleanly with the tongue.

Positions and pitch. In Germany and France slide positions were numbered diatonically, as would be natural before players became concerned with the chromatic scale as such. Speer (1697) describes the first *Zug* ('pull') as 'by the mouthpiece' and giving the series of A. Moving out 'two *Querfinger*' gives *c'* and *g* sharp (misprinted *f* sharp). One 'Querfinger' must here be understood as two fingers placed together, so that twice this, about 7 to 7·5 cm., accounts for a semitone shift and is about right for a German tenor trombone of the period. The 2nd *Zug*, 'by the bell', gives the G series and two fingers further out, *b* flat. The 3rd *Zug* gives the F series and the 4th, 'as far as the arm can reach' the E series plus, 'a little further out' the note *B* flat, 'which enables a bass part to be played on tenor trombone', i.e. to play the scale of F from *F* upwards (the actual slides in fact appear to be long enough to provide the 40 per cent extension theoretically needed for the tritone).[1]

Thus the two B flats are taken in, by modern reckoning, 4th and 7th positions, neither of them in 1st. The old German tenor trombone was in A, but a very sharp A. The instruments had no tuning slide and were built with a considerable sharp tolerance whereby town musicians could where necessary match old high organ pitches, a tone or so above modern, which Praetorius hoped to see disappear but were still met even in the eighteenth century, described by some as Cornett-ton. To find the correct Chorton (Choir-pitch), a fraction lower, Praetorius (II, 232) recommends extending the slide of a Nuremberg tenor trombone by two fingers' breadth, i.e. approximately a quarter-tone. Thus the instruments, or most of them, had a floating 1st position, 'by' the mouthpiece but not necessarily right up to the stop, the player deciding it according to the local needs (or inserting a shank between slide and bell if this were better). In early nineteenth-century Germany, Fröhlich, the first writer to describe the modern system of seven chromatic positions with B flat the first, adds that some players using the older instruments were still reckoning their positions diatonically, their first 'by the mouthpiece' corresponding (he says, 'Von der Posaune', p. 30) to the second of the seven chromatic and giving the series of A as these players knew it at their old sharp pitch.

The corresponding alto trombones were in E or D, with an interesting series of Austrian solo parts from Vejvanovsky to Michael Haydn (whose *Larghetto* in F is described by Donley Thomas in *BQ* VI, 1). Basses were *quart* in E or *quint* in D. From the point of view of slide technique, all these A, E and D pitches mean that the old German music, including those excellent *Stadtpfeifer* compositions of Pezel and Reiche, should, now that the trombone is in B flat, today be performed a semitone higher, which would also bring them closer to their original pitch in sound—though this would require cornetts built a semitone above

---

[1] 'A' pitch seems confirmed in *Il Dolcemilo* by Aurelio Virgiliano, a manuscript of around 1600 in the Museo Civico, Bologna, published in facsimile by Studio per Edizioni Scelte (Florence, 1971, with a preface by M. Castellani). Scales are laid out in four parts for cornett (with fingerings) and three equal trombones (positions following the series of A, G, F, E).

the ordinary since one cannot play this instrument in the key of G flat.

Among other countries, Italy procured her trombones from Germany, and France may have largely done so too. Mersenne's dimensions for the very German-looking tenor which he illustrates work out at 260 cm., corresponding to the tenors at German high A pitch (e.g. the 1557 Neuschel, 262 cm.). In England, Talbot's measurements of a 'Bass Sackbut', allowing for obvious confusion at one point, come to 360 cm. (between modern F and F sharp), matching a German *Quartposaune*. He did not measure a tenor but he observed that this seemed 'to bear the proportion of 8 : 11' to the bass, which comes also to 262 cm., a fourth higher. A space for 'Treble' (alto?) he leaves blank. Mersenne describes the scale on a basis of C in the closed position, probably in order to pursue an analogy with the harmonics of the trumpet. It could hardly indicate any performing pitch of French wind music a minor third below that in Germany since the sizes of Mersenne's shawms also equal the German sizes (in Praetorius) and the French treble likewise had to go down to the note written *d'*.

The old sources also mention crooks, inserted between slide and bell and very commonly used with trombones. They are in fact the first brass-instrument crooks of which we have knowledge: Neuschel's letters name 'two pairs of *Bogen* for the *Quartposaune*'. He means literally two pairs of 'bows' or, as English and American makers once used to say, 'crooks' in the sense of U-bends. A pair of these bows put together made up a whole-tone crook (about one eighth of the whole, Fig. 18). Such crooks of loose components are preserved with the 1579 Schnitzer and with the Colbert. A pair of them could be put in series side by side as Mersenne shows, to make a bass trombone, or end to end as seen in Jan Breughel's 'Allegory of Hearing', gingerly inspected by a toucan (Prado). As well as for playing a deeper part crooks could be used when transposing music down. With fingerhole instruments like cornetts, different-sized instruments could serve this purpose up to a point without the player having to change the fingering for the written notes, and in the prosperous days of the later sixteenth century complete trombones on the same lines, partially dispensing with crooks, are listed in German inventories. Thus in the Stuttgart *Hofkapelle*, 1589 (Bossert 1912), the trombones included a *Terzposaune*, three *Secund-posaunen*, as well as a fine new ordinary *Posaune* which one could crook to use as a

Secund and *Quart-posaune*. '*Secund*', a tone lower than ordinary, should signify a trombone on which you played *a* and it came out *g* and so on. An additional reason for using such instruments (and crooks) may have been to avoid having to use h2 on the tenor when transposing downwards, lest its rather different density of tone upset the balance of weight and colour between low tenor parts and the bass. Among stranger terms from the same period, a Dresden inventory lists a Quint-terz-tenor: it would be hard to say what this was. But a few of the surviving 17th-century instruments have tube-lengths between 300 and 330 cm., still with tenor bore, and may be 'secund' or 'terz' trombones: e.g. G. Ehe, 1619 (Paris), and Birckholtz, 1650 (Leipzig).

Nuremberg Bass Trombones. These mostly have a short extra slide in the bell, amounting to a crook which can be actuated by means of a long rod for the left hand (Fig. 18 and Pl. VI). In seventeenth-century examples it will lower by a whole tone, but since it can be moved whilst playing only when the slide is closed its purpose was probably for a transposition which was frequently needed. A band led by shawms played a whole tone higher than the written notes (according to Praetorius) and here a plain *Quart-posaune* could have dealt with the bass part comfortably, the awkward low F (fullest extension of the normal slide) becoming G. With a chapel choir on the other hand, the bell slide could be pushed out to make a *Quint-posaune*, on which an untransposed bass lies better, and the bell remains secure without the interposition of a crook. On an instrument built as a *Quint* the bell slide helps with very low notes down to *G'* occasionally written, as in Schütz's setting of Psalm 24, and desirable in those transpositions of music down a fourth, on which Praetorius has much to say (*Syntagma*, III).

Some late sixteenth-century inventories mention an *Octav-posaune*. Dresden, about 1593, had one which was kept 'as a rarity'. Praetorius alludes rather obscurely to two constructions of this, one of them possibly indicating a double slide (four legs). The double slide with an early trombone in the Leipzig Collection appears to be a later replacement, but Nuremberg town in 1576 listed a 'short double trombone' which belonged to Anton Schnitzer and was returned to him (Nickel, p. 338). Evidently the players did not like it. The other construction, in normal trombone format, is represented by an instrument by Oller, Stockholm, 1639, from the Swedish royal chapel (Musikhistoriska Museet). With tube-length 550 cm. (modern B'' flat) and heavy slide 132 cm. long externally the latter has to be pushed along the ground or moved by a co-performer. The *Discant* trombone is mentioned in Chapter 7. It belongs to the eighteenth century, a rather sad time on the whole for the trombone outside a few royal chapels (notably Vienna) and German town bands. This must have been partly due to the decline of the cornett with which trombones had been so closely associated through the seventeenth century. One of the latest survivals of the combination was the *Concerto Capitolino* of two cornetts and three trombones which led Papal processions through Rome up to the French occupation of 1798, after which a military band was substituted. Attempts to locate its music have so far failed (Vessella, pp. 174ff.).

List of some of the leading Nuremberg trumpet and trombone makers known by extant examples, the data largely from Wörthmüller, 1955. *Surnames appearing on only one instrument* are omitted, though in several cases the instrument has been noticed in the preceding pages. The last column names the *kinds* of instrument made.

Birckholtz, Wolfgang	d. 1701	trumpet, trombone
Ehe, Isaac	1586–1632	trombone
— Georg	1595–1668	trombone, 1619
— Johann Leonhard (I)	1638–1707	trumpet, trombone
— Johann Leonhard (II)	1664–1724	trumpet, trombone
— Friedrich	1669–1743	trumpet, trombone, horn
— Johann Leonhard (III)	1700–1771	trumpet, trombone
— Martin Friedrich	1714–1779	trumpet
— Wolf Magnus (I)	1690–1722 ⎫	marks indistinguishable;
— Wolf Magnus (II)	d. 1794 ⎭	trumpet, trombone
Haas, Johann Wilhelm	1649–1723	mark: hare looking forwards; no less than 40 trumpets, also trombone and horn
— Wolf Wilhelm	1681–1760	mark: hare looking backwards; trumpet, trombone, horn
— Ernst Johann Conrad	1723–1792	mark: hare looking forwards, all four feet off ground; trumpet and horn

Hainlein, Sebastian (I)	d. 1631	trombone, 1627
— Sebastian (II)	1594–1655	trumpet, trombone
— Hans	1596–1671	straight trumpet, trombone
— Paul	1626–1686	trumpet, trombone
— Michael	1659, d. before 1725	trumpet, trombone, horn
Kodisch, Johann Carl	1654–1721	trumpet, trombone
— Daniel	1686–1747	horn
Nagel, Michael	1621–1664	trumpet, trombone
Schmidt, Jakob	1642–1720	trumpet, trombone
— Johann Jakob	1686, d. after 1756	trumpet
— Paulus	b. 1719	trumpet
Schnitzer, Erasmus	d. 1566	trombone
— Anton (I)	d. 1608	trumpet, trombone
— Anton (II)	b. 1564	trumpet, trombone
— Jobst	1576, d. before 1616	trombone
Starck, Hieronimus	1640–1693	trumpet, trombone, horn
Steinmetz, Georg Friedrich	1668, d. after 1740	trumpet, horn
— Cornelius	1720–1780	trumpet
Wittmann, Christian	d. after 1807	trumpet, trombone

FIVE

Natural Trumpet

Before touching upon this august subject a word should be said about its main documentary sources. These include the works by trumpeters themselves. First, the two manuscript volumes in the Copenhagen Royal Library (Nos. 1847, 1875), one signed by Hendrich Lübeck and dated 1598; the other, signed 'M.T.', identified with Magnus Thomsen, who was killed in action in 1612; his volume is undated. Both were German trumpeters in service with the Danish king. Their works contain every kind of trumpet call and fanfare, and since these were not normally committed to paper, Lübeck and Thomsen have felt free to employ the musical stave in various *ad hoc* ways, using the lines alone or the spaces alone in order to indicate the lower harmonics of the instrument and so they are not always decipherable with certainty—as Schünemann points out in his publication of the two volumes in 1936 (*Das Erbe deutscher Musik*, series I, vol. 7).

In contrast, the contemporary and equally copious manuscript of Cesare Bendinelli, *Tutta l'arte della Tromba*, is written clearly in normal notation. Having held the position of chief trumpeter at Munich, Bendinelli presented his work in 1614 to the celebrated academy of Verona, his home town (Bibl. dell'Accademia Filarmonica, Mus. 238); a page from it is reproduced in Turrini (1941) while the whole has been published in facsimile edited by Edward Tarr (Kassel, 1973). There is much resemblance with Thomsen in arrangement of the contents, both men being mainly occupied with toccatas and sonatas in the low register. Both include the 'carol' sonata in Ex. 14 (Chap. 3), rather vaguely entitled by Bendinelli 'Christmas Day'. Both reserve until near the end some illustrations of making a high clarino part on the natural harmonics.

In the *Modo per imparare a sonare di tromba*, 1638, by Girolamo Fantini, Trumpet-major to the Grand Duke of Tuscany, the emphasis is dramatically reversed. Fantini disposes of the cavalry register in seven pages, then to be concerned wholly with the 'clarino'—*balletti, ricercate*, dances and high sonatas, many provided with a bass part for performing with the organ, which shows his elevated intentions and looks ahead to the Italian trumpet sonatas of the full Baroque. Before him, Praetorius is important particularly for instructions on using trumpets with voices and other instruments. These he gives in Vol. III of the *Syntagma* (pp. 169ff.). Mersenne meanwhile contents himself with the military calls and a long disquisition into trumpet acoustics. Among the little German books on instruments published from the late seventeenth century, Speer's is the earliest and tells most. Then, by far the greatest literary work on the trumpet is the *Versuch* of Johann Ernst Altenburg, two years Haydn's junior, who wrote with the object of setting on record the grand old art fostered by the Imperial Guild. Altenburg's father had been a distinguished court-trumpeter in Saxony (Weissenfels) and of course a member of the fraternity, in which young Altenburg duly graduated and served as trumpeter in the Seven Years' War as his father had previously served at Malplaquet. He then pursued a career as a lawyer. He writes nostalgically of the proud lore of the Guild, and though the work appeared in 1795, part of it was announced in Hiller's *Nachtrichten* of 1770, and much of his precious information and judgements refer back to nearer the times of his service. His biographical notes on players cease with 1774, and he describes the clarinet as having lowest note *f*, which the most aloof of German trumpeters could hardly have believed even then. After Altenburg, the trumpet section in Fröhlich, a man of Beethoven's generation, is, like everything that he wrote on wind instruments, of great value. A number of tutors then follow dealing primarily with the natural trumpet, notably that of Dauverné (Paris, pre-1848) while Kastner's *Manuel générale* appends the past and present military calls of every European state.

The instrument. The baroque trumpet is built in one loop, from 55 to 80 cm. long and reaching right to the bell rim. It is grasped in one hand, the other placed on the hip. The tube is cylindrical from the mouthpiece socket to the bell branch, through which expansion starts slowly and flares to a rim 10–11 cm. wide. Midway along this branch a pommel (in English of the period 'boss') is mounted on a ferrule slid over the branch. The great majority of surviving instruments are German, nearly all by the Nuremberg makers and including some sixty by the Haas family alone (Pl. V). Their most comprehensive description is by Wörthmüller (1955) while a list of Haas trumpets is by Smithers in *GSJ* XVIII (p. 34ff.). The Nuremberg trumpets are rarely dated save for the earliest group, which includes late-sixteenth-century examples by A. Schnitzer, among them beautiful instruments of silver or silvered brass (brass dipped in molten silver) in the Vienna Collection. Two are built in the fancy knotted shape based on a figure-of-eight. Austrian trumpet-making is represented by fine Viennese instruments of Geyer and of the Leichamschneider brothers, dated between 1684 and 1738.

Next in number are English trumpets dating from just before the Restoration and onwards (Pl. V), described by Halfpenny in *GSJ* XV, XVI and XXII. They differ from the German particularly in the disposition of mouthpipe and bell, which in Germany run parallel at a small distance apart, held together by tasselled cordage over a wooden spacing block, but in England usually run close together at a small angle, the mouthpipe passing through a hole or slot in the pommel, which is often enormous. In both countries the branches meet under decorated ferrules or 'garnishes', alternately long and short, and often detachable, presumably for cleaning the branches. Worn joints could be kept airtight with wax; in most cases posterity has failed to resist the temptation to solder them up. Italy, though contributing much to trumpet music, relied mainly on the Nuremberg makers and no Italian-made baroque trumpet has yet come to light. The virtual absence of French instruments is more remarkable. The Versailles establishment listed two makers of *cors et trompettes* from 1674 but only one of them, Crétien, is known by surviving instruments and these are all horns of some kind. The Paris Collection has the much-altered remains of a large C trumpet with fleur-de-lis embossed on the bell and on the huge 11 cm. pommel. It is said to date from the time of Henri IV (so *c.* 1600) but after this, although trumpet-making is seen in the illustration in the *Encyclopédie*, there seem to be no survivors before the Revolution when manufacture of short-model cavalry trumpets was instituted. The few seventeenth- and eighteenth-century regimental trumpets preserved in the Musée de l'Armée in Paris are all Nuremberg-built.

Bore dimensions vary even among instruments by the same

maker, whether Bull in London or Haas in Nuremberg. The London trumpets are the narrower, 9·3 to 10 mm. Nuremberg bores are mostly around 10·5 mm. Altenburg (p. 10) notices particularly thickness of the metal: thick, good for military calls and *Principal* but too breath-consuming for the high-register *Clarin*, whereas thin makes for an easy-blowing and pleasant-sounding high register but lacks power and penetration for the former uses; so for general use, choose a trumpet of medium weight and preferably made by Haas, he says. The change in bell profile over the period, mentioned in the last chapter, may be concerned with range and intonation, though this has not been shown to be the case by trial. Alternatively it could reflect a change towards a brighter, more translucent tone-quality, comparable with tonal changes among woodwind instruments over the same span of time.

Trumpet mouthpieces have flat rims, sometimes very wide and made separately from the cup. Cups are generally segments of a hemisphere, but Menke also shows (Appendix) some flat-bottomed cups resembling that in Fig. 16. The throats are usually sharp (Pl. IV) and except with the 'primitive' examples with internally cylindrical stem, the long stem provides up to 9 cm. of tapered backbore, the only conicity in the instrument until the bell.

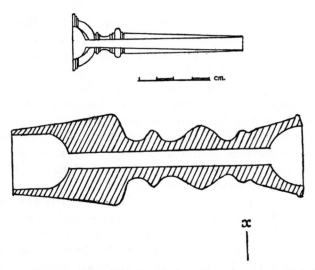

Fig. 20 Trumpet mouthpiece, Fröhlich, 1811, showing recommended depths for 1st and 2nd Trumpet. **Below** Baroque wooden trumpet mute (Basel, Hist. Mus.): *x* marks approx. position of Steiger bell rim when mute is inserted. Length 152 mm.

Dimensions vary as always and Altenburg (p. 81) speaks of them as players have done since, for instance advising against a narrow cup and throat for the sake of getting very high notes. His drawing of a mouthpiece which his father, a clarinist, had always used and comfortably reached e''' with, unfortunately seems over-scaled and shows neither the depth nor the width of throat. Fröhlich ('Von der Trompete', p. 21), though over forty years younger and writing too late to bear strictly upon the practice of the greatest days, is nevertheless deeply concerned with maintaining proper distinction of the clarino and principal styles and shows a smaller depth for 1st Trumpet than for 2nd Trumpet (Fig. 20): rim 52, cup 19, and throat 4·5 for both; but depth 7·5 and 9·5 mm. respectively. Some specimens are tabulated opposite, though of course we do not know who used them or in which species of trumpet music, save for the two oldest which are certainly cavalry or fanfare mouthpieces. The instrument named is in each case that with which the mouthpiece is associated. The German examples are all from the Nuremberg Collection save for the last five which are from Copenhagen, Munich, Berlin, Vienna, and (Swiss) Basel. The English are from The Queen's College, Oxford (1666), the London Museum, and the Ashmolean Museum, Oxford.

Pitches of trumpets. In the sixteenth century these were mostly built to fairly high pitches. Praetorius says D, and his drawing indicates a tube-length of seven Brunswick feet or about 200 cm., modern E flat, still the pitch of most cavalry trumpets today. But some were certainly higher. Bendinelli, while he writes the notes of the trumpet in C as normally, on his first page puts the harmonic series in F a fifth lower, evidently a mistake for 'a fourth higher', giving an impression of the actual sounds. He himself would have played constantly, perhaps always, on Schnitzer trumpets, and the 1581 Schnitzer has a tube-length of 166 cm., corresponding to a pitch of modern F if not higher.

Praetorius adds that some of the German courts had recently lengthened their trumpets or given them a crook in order to be played in C in music with other instruments and voices, and he writes for them so in his setting of *In Dulci Jubilo* (in *Polyhymnia caduceatrix*, 1619). The trumpet so lengthened would have a tube of approximately 225 cm., corresponding with Mersenne's size of 'around seven feet', by the larger French foot about 227 cm. This is nearly matched later in England in the information extracted

Table 5 (mm.)

Maker of trumpet	max. diam.	cup diam.	throat diam.	depth	total length	end bore
GERMAN						
shallow cup						
W. M. Ehe	29·8	18	4·5	7·5		
M. Leichamschneider, 1725	21	16	4	7·8	94	
J. L. Ehe, set of three, 1746	27·6	18·5	3·8	8	87	10
medium depth						
Wittmann	31·2	17·5	4	9·5	95	
E. J. C. Haas (Pl. V)	29·4	19·5	4	9·8	92	9
Schöller, 1753	26·8	18	4·5	10·7	100	7·7
deep cup						
W. W. Haas	28·4	18	3·8	12		
M. Hainlein (F trumpet)	28	18	4·5	13	95	
very deep and wide						
A. Schnitzer, 1581 (Pl. IV)	39	23	7	17		
Steiger (Basel), 1578 (Fig. 16)	37·5	25·5	8	12·5	100	9·2
ENGLISH						
anon., 1666	35	20·5	7·2	13·2	117	10
			(length of backbore 11·8)			
Bull	32·5	20	4·6	8·5	89	8·2
Bull	35	19	5·5	11·5	108	9·5

by Talbot from the player John Shore (*GSJ* I, p. 20): 'the natural pitch of the Trumpet is a ♭E', by Talbot's measurements 215 cm. This pitch would have been inherited from earlier times and require lowering to concert pitch for musical purposes by crooks: with the D crook it became 231 cm. and with the C crook 250 cm. This is fairly confirmed in extant trumpets by Bull, 218–220 cm. as they stand, and indicating a concert pitch some three-quarters of a tone below modern.

During the late seventeenth century this low pitch had entered Germany along with the new French woodwind and was adopted there as Cammerton ('chamber' or concert pitch, or as Majer calls it in 1732, p. 32 'Cammer or French pitch'). With this a German trumpet in old C now came in D and a crook could put it in Cammerton C. But during the first half of the eighteenth century this pitch became slighly raised in order to come a clean wholetone

below the still prevalent Chorton of German organs. About A =
422 seems a likely central value for this 'high' Cammerton, and
agrees with tuning forks associated with Handel and Mozart cited
by Ellis. Chorton would then fall around A = 474, or 130 cents
(over a semitone) above modern. At this high Cammerton a D
trumpet might be expected to measure about 220 cm. Some trumpets do. But instruments were often built on the sharp side to
allow players in those days before tuning slides a sharp tolerance
and to adjust downwards with tuning bits or with paper round the
mouthpiece.[1]

The court-trumpeters' D trumpet, of baroque music, was not,
however, everything. Many instruments were required for regimental cavalry, in which the Germans seem to have preferred a
higher pitch, though not as high as that which trumpets could
have in Bendinelli's day. Cavalry trumpets 'are in a deep Dis'
(S. Halle, 1764), or 'many are in E♭' (Altenburg, p. 11, also
reckoning at Cammerton). There was also the trumpet used by
infantry. This is already alluded to by von Fleming (*Vollkommene
Teutsche Soldat*, 1726). He writes that military bands (*Hautboisten*, primarily an infantry institution) had in England and
Prussia one trumpeter on foot along with the customary oboes
and bassoon instead of the pair of horns which he was used to in
Saxony. Some sets of parts for oboes with trumpet exist from
that period. They appear all of them to be written in the keys of
E flat or D. Not until the end of the Seven Years' War do we
read of 'the shorter E or F trumpets used by the infantry, provided with crooks and with tuning bits for ⅛, ¼ and ½ tones' (S.
Halle again).

Something of all this is reflected in Fig. 21, on the left of which
tube-length is set against modern pitch on a basis of 212 cm. for
D. The triangles on the right mark tentative assessments of
German pitch-zones—Chorton being peaked a little to take in the
vaguely-defined Cornett-ton. In the centre, each horizontal line
represents a German trumpet, nearly all of these made in
Nuremberg at some time and, one hopes, excluding specimens

---

[1] A tuning bit is a short tube made in a reverse taper matched to the
external taper of a mouthpiece stem. An example preserved with the
second instrument in Table 5 (in Cammerton D) is 84 mm. long, tapering
from (outside diameter) 12·3 mm. to 9·5 mm. A ferrule at the wider end
bears two small wings to facilitate removal from the instrument.

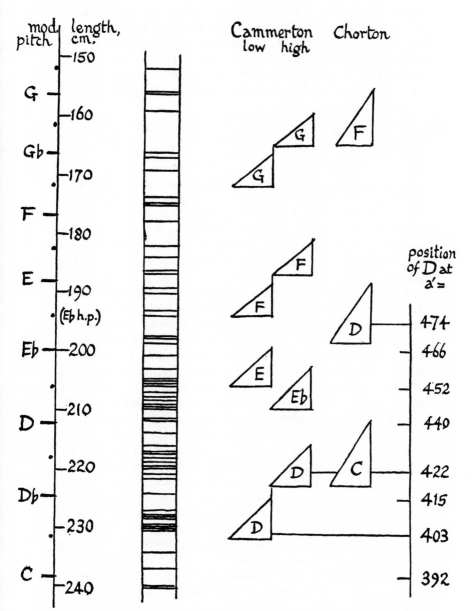

Fig. 21 Chart of German baroque trumpets in terms of tube-length against pitch. (See text.)

that have been subsequently very much shortened to suit later playing pitches. Not shown, at 277 cm., is a trumpet in Cammerton B flat by Fr. Ehe (Nuremberg Colln.) but not originally built in this deep tonality. At the bottom are a few instruments built to Cammerton C by J. W. Haas and some of the Ehe dynasty. Concentrations around 230 and 220 cm. represent low and high Cammerton D. The high density in the E flat region around 205 cm. may be explained partly by sharp building but probably more by military usages.

Further ascending the chart the specimens become fewer. Some half dozen in the Cammerton F region include Nagel (Vienna Colln.), J. W. Haas (Brussels), M. Hainlein (Berlin). There would anyhow have been fewer infantry trumpets than cavalry and court-establishment instruments, and an echo of this may be the scant orchestral use of an F trumpet before the classical era, as by Bach in his one celebrated example, the second Brandenburg Concerto. In normal format an F trumpet looks to the eye some 18 cm. (7 inches) shorter than a D, which may be one explanation of the name 'short trumpet', occasionally met in music.

England shows much the same picture. After the time of Talbot's data the E flat of the trumpet rose with the general rise in pitch through the eighteenth century, while as the baroque era receded the F trumpet with crooks became known with the infantry band. The crooks normally ran down to C; B flat was reached by coupling the C and D crooks together. In France by 1780 the plain trumpet had a pitch described by La Borde as E, which would come near the English and German E flat. The orchestral trumpet playable from F down to B flat was also in use there by that year (Marcuse, in *GSJ* XIV, p. 36).

Returning to Germany, Walther (*Lexikon*, 1732, 'Clarino') says that there were trumpets in all keys from B flat up to F. He is probably reckoning at Cammerton. There are however at the top of Fig. 21 a few trumpets with tube 170 cm. or less, as by M. Hainlein, 1689 (Vienna), J. J. Schmidt (Munich, Städt. Museum), and from Austria, Geyer, 1684 (Copenhagen, Claudius Colln.). None of these are described as having been shortened, so that one could equate them with Chorton F or with Cammerton G, the former being more likely for the two dates given. However, the existence of a trumpet pitched a third or so above an 'ordinary' instrument is indicated at the end of the seventeenth century in

Christoph Weigel's *Abbildung* of 1698 (p. 232). The passage, which occurs again some ten years later in a Saxon treatise on the Guild, *Ceremoniel und Privilegia* by Friese, and again in Zedler's *Lexicon* ('Trompete', 1745), runs in translation thus: 'brass and copper trumpets are rarely better than when made in Nuremberg, and these are of various kinds: German or so-called ordinary trumpet; French, a tone higher; and English, a whole third higher'; (also 'wound Italian', considered later in this chapter). Various explanations have been suggested but still the namings make no clear sense. Nuremberg makers had used such terms from the sixteenth century, but at no early period are the pitches stated. Nor does Altenburg help, as far as one can see, in giving a version of the list in which he positively relates the terms to the peoples named, also stating specific tonalities, thus (p. 11) after D for the 'German': 'Field trumpet otherwise called French' in F and 'introduced by the French'; 'English or *tromba piccola*' in G, 'customary among the English'. Altenburg should have known English military trumpets well enough and certainly none were ever, as far as we know, then in G, even late trumpets with a full set of crooks.

Trumpet-corps sounds. The first two of the trumpeters' note names, perhaps as old as the brass trumpet itself, were mentioned in chapter 3: the *basso* or *grosso* (c, h2) and the *folgent* (*vulgano* etc., *g*, h3). Above these Fantini continues with the *striano* (*c'*, h4), *toccata* (*e'*, h5), and *quinta* (*g'*, the fifth sound, h6). A dance is named *striana*, Istrian, in Prudenzani's poems *c*. 1420 but the trumpeters' term may derive from Old French *estreindre* in the sense of 'to press' or 'tighten', and in that case reveal something about the war-trumpeter's technical 'feel' of the instrument in early times. *Toccata* no doubt seemed apt enough for h5 in an old Italian sense of a touch of the spur or whip, as in Ex. 18, where the *e'* is 'flicked' between *c*'s—as it is still in the British 'Flourish on the March'. The term must have originated however as the top note of the early flourish of the same name, the Toccata or Tucket, itself a word born out of Spanish *tocar*, 'to play', just as the longer kind of flourish, Sonata or Sennet, got its name from Italian *sonare*, also 'to play'. It does not necessarily follow from these internationally-adopted names that the flourishes themselves were invented respectively by Spanish and Italian trumpeters. An early mention of 'toccata' as an independent fanfare is from

1494, when the coronation cavalcade of Alfonso II of Naples left the castle to 'una toccata de trombette' and returned from the cathedral to another (Gombosi, p. 52). But French royalty had been greeted with 'battures' long before this, and with the fast

Ex. 18 Fantini: the cavalry March (1638).

speed in professional contact between European nations a fanfare of trumpets probably always varied more in accordance with the nature of the circumstances than with the nationality of the men's employer, very much as was the case with the military calls also.

Many toccatas are written out (monophonically) in the trumpet manuscripts, some ending with a rise to higher notes (Ex. 19,b). Basically they usually amount to a motif stated with variation three times—the ancient ritual number going back on the war trumpet at least to the Byzantine army's call to Church Parade on

Ex. 19 Toccatas: **a.** Thomsen, 3rd toccata as it appears in the original notation of the manuscript; **b.** Bendinelli, toccata No. 16.

the *touba,* and to the three sounds before a single combat. A Sonata rose to *c"* and had seven or more sections. Bendinelli's concentrate on quick and difficult tonguing. Those of the two German trumpeters do this too, but yet, despite limitation to the notes of an arpeggio, often possess an irresistibly tuneful character, quite apart from the comparative few which are founded on popular melodies as noticed earlier in Ex. 14.

The number is observed too in Monteverdi's *Orfeo* (1607) in the Toccata which opens the work. This is the earliest written example of a fanfare fully filled out for performance by a trumpet corps in parts or, as Fantini says, 'per sonare in concerto'. For this, two drone-like parts were supplied by the folgent and the bass and were so named. The Folgent part kept to its *g*, slowly reiterated (whence another German term, *Faulstimme*, 'lazy part'). The Basso kept to *c* until later times when it might swing to *g* to match dominant harmony in the upper parts and the *G* of the kettledrums which properly supplied the ensemble with a true bass. Below the Basso might be added, though unimportant, a Sotto-basso on *C*, the fundamental, best done, says Speer, with a trombone mouthpiece, but it ends some of Fantini's fanfares which include high notes and was therefore obtainable with the ordinary mouthpiece.

Above this primitive and no doubt ancient mode of accompaniment came the part named Toccata (a third sense of the word; it appears as *Dughetto* or, in France, *Douquet*) lying in the chief register of a Toccata flourish, *g* to *e'*. Above again could lie a Quint or Principal, up to *c"* in the range of a Sonata and sometimes called by this name (Praetorius, III, p. 171). Lastly, at the top of the ensemble, came the diatonic Clarino, up to *a"*, or two Clarini of which the second shows a fairly natural tendency to follow the first in close imitation or in thirds. Another term to be mentioned is 'Alto e basso' or 'Alto basso', signifying 'up and down'. Bendinelli and Praetorius (*'Alterbass'*) apply it to a part above the Folgent which moved homophonically below another part, keeping for the most part one harmonic below. Thus to accompany a Toccata, an Alto basso required mainly h2, h3 and h4. Under a higher part, a Quint or Principal, it fell in the toccata range and became equivalent to a Toccata part.

All the performers would normally have constructed the five- or six-part edifice on patterns taught aurally, and with a good deal of beat-by-beat homophony. Yet apparently not always, unless Monteverdi's Toccata is quite exceptional. Too well known to quote here, we see that the part modestly labelled 'Alto e basso' is no filling-in part but the toccata itself, apparently an abridgement of Toccata No. 16 in Bendinelli. It may be compared with those shown in Ex. 19, especially if the three notes in Thomsen's notation are read as E, C, G. But if Schünemann's reading one harmonic higher is correct, then the likeness here is to 'The Trumpetts' in *My Lady Nevell's Book*. Meanwhile Monteverdi's part above it, Quinta, is similarly extracted from a 'Quinta o Intrada' in Bendinelli, and has echoes in the 'Imperial Intrada' in Fantini. The two parts proceed quite independently, re-stating their themes at different points while the Clarino meanders freely above them in its contribution to one of the most extraordinary musical miniatures ever set down on paper.

Bendinelli's examples for sounding a Clarino above a 'Sonata', though not all as elementary as Ex. 20b, seem rather mechanical. Thomsen, however, gives some examples in which the *Clarin* takes the lead, as it does in later trumpet-corps music. Sometimes he uses a popular tune for it: one is 'Brother Martin' (*alias* 'Frère Jacques', Ex. 20a); another foreshadows the opening of the 'Hallali sur pied' of the future French hunting-horn code. A comparable transcontinental adaptation in the eighteenth century is of 'Lilliburlero' in a Prussian *Aufzüge* (fanfare) quoted by Titcomb in *GSJ* IX (p. 77, No. 3). But Fantini shows no interest in any of this. His toccatas are reduced to mere tonguing exercises, while his splendid sonatas, dedicated to various noble families, are promoted to the Clarino register and reach c'''.

Ex. 20 a. Thomsen, 1st *Aufzug* with *clarin* (after Schünemann); b. Bendinelli, 'Il modo corretto di sonare il clarino sopra la sonata', 1st example.

Monteverdi notes in his score that the instruments of the orchestra, when joining in the Toccata, must play a tone higher should it be desired that the trumpets be muted. The old trumpet mute was a hollow wooden affair and a 'transposing mute' raising the pitch by a whole tone. This it does very well: the mute preserved at Basel (Fig. 20) produces a most effective sound, distant but not stifled, and no wonder that muted trumpets, if originally intended for special purposes in war, became quite popular among composers of the Baroque. Another mute is preserved at Prague and a good illustration is in Mersenne.

Principale. On the special art of the baroque Quint or Principal, rooted in the old trumpet-corps Quint or Sonata, every German writer speaks with special affection. 'A beautiful part' says Speer, if properly done, powerfully but not over-forced. Tonguings formed an important ingredient. The cavalry calls had been learnt with speech-like syllables whereby to aid the memory, though also so that they might be expressed with an eloquence as close to verbal command as an instrument is capable (especially Ex. 18, where adjacent vowels are in most cases elided; *teghe* is the modern *tu-ku*) .In course of time they became stylized, in Germany particularly in a semi-quaver triplet called *Doppelzunge*, or as we might now say, triple-tonguing. This was delivered with the famous *schmetternd* effect which made the metal vibrate (Fröhlich) and was adored in Germany and Austria while regarded by French and English trumpeters with qualified admiration. In written parts it often appears as a duplet, but Altenburg (p. 92) and Fröhlich both show how it should be executed as a triplet.

Ex. 21 Fröhlich (1811): examples of double-tonguing for *Principal*: above, part as written; below, as executed.

Exactly how far back this goes is not clear, but Handel's 'Trumpets Flourish' in *Joshua* should no doubt be thus treated. Fröhlich gives examples ('Von der Trompete', pp. 22–3), some shown here in Ex. 21, to illustrate ways in which a principalist should add tonguings to a plain written part—but not on a strong beat—and evidently with reference to the 2nd Trumpet of an orchestra since it is with this that his treatise is primarily concerned. The player, he says, should better do it sparingly rather than the reverse lest he destroys the composer's intentions. And in a small establishment, where the 2nd Trumpet for the orchestra has to be brought from the trumpet corps, he will be a principalist and bring a danger of overpowering the 1st Trumpet played by a clarinist. Fröhlich does not link these two considerations in so many words; but he makes one wonder what may sometimes have gone on in performances of symphonies and concertos during his period.

Another tonguing is briefly mentioned by Altenburg (p. 93) as the *Haue*: *to-ho-to*, e.g. in quick *c' g c'*, the first two slurred. But is was only for the end of a field or dinner call and not when playing *Principal*.

Clarino. In contrast to the *principale*, robust, *schmetternd* and commanding, the *clarino*, clear, singing and without double-tonguing, is baroque trumpet music as most people understand it. As an independent voice detached from the trumpet corps, Schütz writes a rather experimental part for *Trombetta o cornetto* with key signature of one flat, rising to h16 of the trumpet, with cadences on h11 and h13, in his setting of 'Buccinate in neomenia tuba' (*Symphoniae Sacrae* of 1629). But it has often been the case that developments in the music of wind instruments on a multinational scale have followed times severely marred by wars, and it is the period after 1650 that witnessed both the beginning of the obsolescence of cornett and trombone in every country and the rise of the clarino trumpet as a major and idiomatic voice of the baroque orchestra. In Moravia appeared the sonatas of Vejvanovsky in the 1660s, in Vienna the productions of Cesti and then Schmeltzer, in Bologna Cazzati's sonatas of 1665, and in France Lully's trumpet parts from 1662. A hundred years later, following the heights attained in the works of Handel and Bach, technical limits are reached in the concertos of Molter, von Reutter (1757, *DTÖ* XV, 2), Hertel and Michael Haydn (taking the D trumpet up to *g'''*, h24) capping a magnificent heritage which lies too far outside the present scope to enter upon, though some general technical points may be remarked on.

The stylistic distinction between principale and clarino is to some degree inherent in the long-tubed natural trumpet itself, and is one of the hardest things to do justice to with valved substitutes, on which the registers are colourfully and technically much less sharply differentiated. True, in France and England the distinction was stressed less than in the German lands, yet the natural registers inevitably possessed the same inherent differences in sound-quality and in player's approach.

An overriding problem for a clarinist playing with voices, violins or other instruments is, of course, the intonation of his scale. In music for trumpet corps alone, from which the solo and orchestral clarino originally emerged, the matter of h11 and h13 would have been less pressing. One was taught to recognize a close on the dominant and then try to drive h11 upwards to f'' sharp. The flatness of a'', h13, is dismissed by Altenburg as of no great significance; it was almost always a passing note, usually between two Gs. But in other music, especially after about 1700 when trumpets became more to be written in unison with other instruments instead of antiphonally, one would have thought that clarinists as a body must have been able to tune these harmonics. Indeed, to achieve it, 'long note' practice was advocated in German sources. Yet it is curious that Walther should conclude his short article 'Clarino' with the remark that f'' sharp gives a purer effect than f''. In theory, at Mean-tone the sharp is indeed only 29 cents above h11 while the natural is 47 cents below. But is the implication that f''—at least as Walther heard it in Weimar, etc.—was usually out of tune?

In England too the evidence is conflicting. The intonation of h11 can vary between different instruments, and some players today have felt that English trumpets of the period favour the F natural. This might help to explain how Handel, with his predilection for climaxes on the dominant seventh, was able to give this note the immense prominence that he does, notably where *Messiah* is brought to its highest point in sound in the 'Hallelujah' Chorus with a g'' (h11 on the D trumpet) sustained by the trumpet and the sopranos in unison. On the other hand, Burney later on complained of the distress which this note caused, and not only to himself, in the obbligato in the same work. The player then concerned, Sargant, was a leading player of the time and Burney otherwise admired his 'extremely sweet and clear' playing in this number. No technical secrets should have been lost since earlier times. Sargant would have learnt his profession not only while Valentine Snow was playing in Handel's first performances, but while John Shore, who had played for Purcell, was still with the King's Band. Either Sargant's strong point was not intonation; or perhaps he had lost some control over h11 through attempting to balance gigantic festival choirs in Handel choruses. For the evidence is that clarino-playing was normally fairly soft, i.e. produced at its natural volume, without intention to dominate, though in ordinary circumstances of the time it would always have come through. Shore sounded 'as sweet as an hautboy.' In Salzburg, Köstler was said by Leopold Mozart in 1757 to have a most refined and agreeable singing tone (the concerto of 1762, rising to f''', may have been written for him or a colleague there). A clarinist, Altenburg says, must imitate the cantabile of other instruments 'as far as possible' (p. 96), which sounds as though the instrument were played with a cautious concentration which militated to some extent against volume range in *espressivo*. It will be remembered too that this clarino period was on the whole one of small orchestras, with eight violins on the average, sometimes more but often fewer.

In our own times the trumpet parts in oratorios have usually been expected to dominate. Further, it is a modern trumpeter's training and skill exactly to centre every note as he produces it, which must make it more difficult to 'uncentre' notes on a natural trumpet. Moreover, players are on the whole reluctant to commit themselves to prolonged study of this instrument using a mouthpiece which has genuinely baroque rim, internal gradients and backbore; for it may prove that with such a mouthpiece the problem of baroque trumpet intonation can best be conquered by the modern artist—and indeed its full musical quality revealed also.

A secondary question is over notes like b', c'' sharp and e'' flat which, especially the first, are by no means uncommon in clarino parts of all countries, particularly through the middle of the period. They usually occur in fast passages and at cadences, especially dotted cadences where the short note was anyhow further shortened in performance. Efforts to produce them as full sounds could, Eisel says in 1738, only be to give even an unmusical listener an 'ear-Zwang', and indeed the experience of many present-day players is that these notes could scarcely have been more than 'suggested'. Yet Vejvanovsky, himself a noted trumpet-player, is one who must have mastered them more effectively to be able to write and play passages like those in

Ex. 22 (the first of which has a national flavour truly foreshadowing Dvořák). Nevertheless, that e'' flat should be on the whole the least common of these notes may indicate that, with the general run of clarinists, leading notes sounded at pitches fractionally below the main note were judged more acceptable than a sharp minor third made when attempting to lower h10 by 75 cents.

Ex. 22 From Vejvanovsky: **a.** Sonata à 4; **b.** Sonata à 7 (1666). (Musica Antiqua Bohemica, vols. 36, 47.)

In Ex. 22, h7 is required as a main note on b' flat, as it is also by other composers, for instance among the festival sonatas preserved in the archives of Bologna Cathedral, in Franceschini's sonata for two trumpets (1680); also in Handel's obbligato in *Judas Maccabeus*. Fantini, on the other hand, uses this harmonic as a' between two Gs. In four of his flourishes he also writes low f' and d': twice in the triplet sequence GAG, EFE, CDC, and once in a sequence GFG, EDE, (low) CBC (each group here a quaver and two semiquavers). This was evidently his own stunt: a story in fact got round that he could sound every note from top to bottom of the compass with no gaps (Mersenne, quoted by Hawkins, p. 612 of the 1875 edition). Not necessarily a 'story', however. In our own time the brilliant American player and historian Don L. Smithers has, using a mouthpiece of a genuinely baroque pattern, demonstrated the full possibility of producing on the natural trumpet, loud or soft, all pitches outside the harmonic series, acquired by a practice technique of forced glissando over the whole compass—an ability which he has passed on to many pupils.

Spiral instruments. For more than a century historians have pondered over the question whether at least some trumpeters of the· Baroque Age had obtained pitches up to a semitone below a natural harmonic by inserting fingers into the bell mouth or partially covering this with the hand, as players are known to have done to some extent during the Classical period (Chap. 7). Obviously the older trumpeters were aware of the possibility. Nothing is more natural than that a military signal may now and then have been sounded softly by placing the hand over the bell —the action is instinctive. But did they use it in music? There is absolutely no positive evidence for hand-stopping on a trumpet before the 1770s. Nevertheless the instruments invoked in support of its earlier employment must once more be briefly noticed. These include the circular or 'wound' trumpets.

The problem of these little instruments, about 20 cm. across, built in three or more coils wound spirally in one plane, is difficult to examine without also considering hunting horns of similar shape and size. Both are therefore noticed here together. For consistent terminology, 'three-coil' (for example) denotes the presence of three *complete* circles, though in fact the bell and mouthpipe can add the best part of another circle. Indeed, if one traces in the air, with the hand, the form of a single-coil instrument, it feels like making two turns though there is only one by this definition.

1. Virdung, 1511. The earliest illustration, see Fig. 22. Two-coil, with the mouthpipe placed for holding the instrument in the ordinary way of other small horns, namely with the bell pointed somewhat forwards and somewhat upwards. At first glance a thoroughly bad drawing. But Virdung's woodcuts, though not of the highest quality, try to portray instruments accurately, as can be appreciated among the other objects in the figure. This comes late in the book and shows a selection of popular, or as we might now say, folk instruments, which at once disposes of the idea that this gross spiral represents a hunting horn of a kind intended to serve the higher classes of society. To its right is an ordinary curved horn of the time, complete with baldric. Following the order of names in the line of text, this would be the *Acher horn*, meaning 'farmer's horn', or by another interpretation (Crane, 1972, p. 60) a pottery *'Aach-horn'* sold to pilgrims to Aachen; Crane notices specimens made by potters around Düren which have this curved shape and slinging eyes. However, the woodcut almost reverses the order of the text, so that this curved horn is

probably the *Jeger horn* (as one would anyway have supposed without the text) and the fat spiral an *Acher horn* made to the fancy of a local potter. It has every appearance of a horn of crude earthenware or rough porcelain, while a metal prototype is not necessarily implicit.[1]

Trumpeln/Schelle/Jeger horn/Acher horn/küschellen·Britsche/pff dem hafen

Fig. 22 Virdung, some popular instruments; text runs: Jew's harp, jingle bell, huntsman's horn, *Acher horn*, cowbell, clapper, 'on the pot'.

2. Dresden. The two little horns which Blandford examined in the hunting equipment section of the State Historical Museum in 1934; one still exists there, perhaps both. Four-coil, tapered tube, funnel mouthpiece (Pl. VII), and evidently the work of a late sixteenth- or early seventeenth-century maker (the smaller horn is engraved in German 'made in Dresden') and clearly very fine work too. The smaller horn, judged to be the earlier (though without any firm reason) and pitched, as Blandford tested it, in about modern A♭ (cornet pitch), is for holding bell-forwards. The larger (illustrated), in about 7-foot D, has a backwards-pointing bell (11 cm.) as have most that follow and is 21 cm. across the coils. Each has a slinging ring at the bell. (For further particulars see *The New Grove Dictionary*, Horn §3, Vol. 8, p. 703.)

The bell-forwards pattern is reproduced in wood and bark in one of the 'Allgäu' alphorns from Ambras now at Vienna (A.281): three-coil and evidently matching the entry *'allgewisch khrumbs*

[1] Neither for the drawing of a small bell-front circular horn in the contemporary Strassburg Virgil (1502); also in this a large three-coil horn in an open spiral carried round the neck in an unplayable position: the artist's interpretations of the instruments in Virgil—though of course one cannot be absolutely sure that they represent no more than this. Another puzzle well-known to horn historians is from a good century earlier: the object (horn?) in a Worcester choir-stall; see Galpin, 1910, p. 185.

waldthorn' in an Ambras inventory of 1613 (Schlosser, p. 96). In this instance a metal horn must have been the model.

3. Early seventeenth-century pictures of hunting horns: (i) in Breughel's 'Hearing', Flanders, *c.* 1618. Five-coil, funnel mouthpiece, etc.; also, on the draped table above it a minute 'snail' horn resembling Virdung's but with backwards bell. (ii) Mersenne: crude drawing of a spiral *cor* of a type 'not used as much' as a large metal horn of the curved kind. (iii) Hollar: two engravings which have not been precisely dated but may have been made before this Bohemian artist came to England in 1636, and are thus contemporary with Mersenne. Fig. 23 shows one engraving, Morley-Pegge reproduces the other. The five-coil horn, with backwards-pointing bell, funnel mouthpiece etc. as in Breughel, must have had a pitch of 8-foot C or lower.

4. Praetorius, 1619: 'some make the trumpet like a post-horn or wound like a snake, but not giving a sound like a normal trumpet'. This description is reasonably taken to match the *Jäger Trommet* ('huntsman's trumpet') shown among his illustrations (see Fig. 18). Four-coil, bell forward or nearly so, crook and trumpet-like mouthpiece. Estimated tube-length less crook, 180 cm., about modern 6-foot F. The drawing shows no taper though the remark about the sound might imply one (and even in Hollar's careful drawing the taper is very slight); Altenburg (p. 6) saw this *Trommet* as a horn.

A gap of fifty years after Mersenne brings us to the next item.

5. Haas, 1688: horn or trumpet in the private Fürstlich Hohenzollernsches Museum, Sigmaringen, in S. W. Germany and now in the Trompetenmuseum, Bad Säckingen (Pl. VII). Three-coil, 20 cm. across, slinging rings, some kind of conical mouthpiece, and a hunting scene engraved on the 13·3 cm. bell; tube-length 239 cm. including mouthpiece. In addition, one might perhaps mention a Haas instrument of the same width but much altered and now one-coil (Basel No. 15); though dated 1682 it bears the device of W. W. Haas, the son, which does not tally. It is suggested that the father made it in honour of the birth of his son.

6. Pfeifer, 1697, Leipzig: famous three-coil trumpet, with mouthpipe axis 60 degrees to the bell, slinging ring, and a trumpet-like mouthpiece (Pl. VII). Tube-length according to Menke (p. 200)

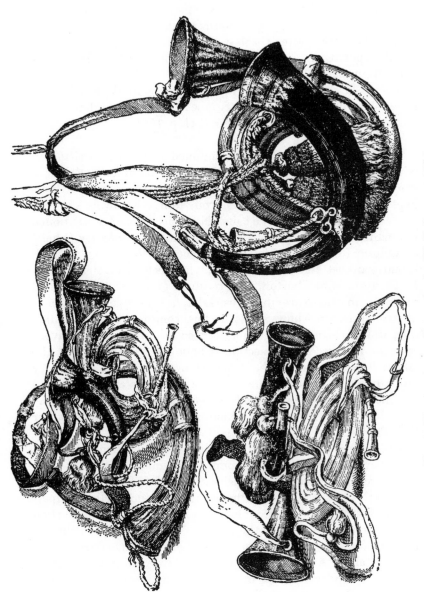

Fig. 23 Hunting horns. Engraving by W. Hollar, pre-1636.

235 cm., which probably includes the mouthpiece since he gives the pitch as D–D flat. The only known instrument by Pfeifer, who was also the Thomaskirche tower player. Found in the village church at Karlsfeld, sixty miles to the south, it was stolen from the Leipzig Collection after the last war and is replaced by a copy. Another photograph of the original is reproduced in *Grove*, 5th edn., 'Trumpet'.

Thomaskirche scenes of 1710 (reproduced in *Bach-Jahrbuch*, 1919) show only the ordinary trumpet and horn, the latter held up high (and apparently with a crook; cf. p. 156).

7. Weigel, 1698, the already-mentioned *Abbildung*, written in Nuremberg: fourth category in the list of trumpets: 'a class of wound trumpets, the Italian or *Welsche*, six-times wound' (perhaps what we have termed five-coil, unless it means six 180-degree bends, making three coils). No relative pitch is mentioned but Smithers (1973, p. 150) cites a manuscript *Salve* by Schelle of Leipzig (d. 1701) which has instructions for using a 'small Italian trumpet' for the Clarin part, which is for an instrument in D, presumably at Chorton. This confirms that the term was used not only in the Nuremberg workshops. No evidence of spiral instruments seems however to be forthcoming from the Italian side, unless perhaps in a trophy carved on an anonymous ivory recorder in the Paris Collection (Chouquet 395) bought at the sale of Rossini's effects. The trophy shows a three-coil spiral very much like the one at Sigmaringen, with tassels and wide horn-like mouthpiece. Below it are lute, baroque recorder, tambourine and triangle—an assemblage which suggests Italy possibly, rather than France.

The more significant word in Weigel's enumeration may, however, be *Welsche*. 'Welsche' trumpets are mentioned in the sixteenth century, and in Neuschel's letters of 1541 (Eitner, 1877, p. 150) the term has its other meaning of 'French'. His trumpets of this description were troublesome to tune and cost more than his 'German' trumpets in the ratio 4:3. What they were is not known. But the four extant Nuremberg trumpets from that century, all by A. Schnitzer, include the two which are made in the luxury model wound in a knotted figure-of-eight (one of them was presented to the Verona Academy by Bendinelli). This model must have had its name among the craftsmen. No one says that it was 'Welsche'; but had it been so it may have persisted as

a term for other wound shapes and for some reason become
equated with the name of Germany's other great Latin neighbour.

Whatever the true explanation of the terms may be, it seems
as if the spiral instruments were all spoken of in Germany as
'trumpets' qualified by 'Italian', 'hunting', etc., while the word
'horn' retained its ancient and usual meaning of a simple curved
horn until special forms like '*Waldhorn*' came to denote the horn
made in an open hoop. This would explain 'hunting to the
sounds of trumpets and horns' at Weissenfels in 1671 (Karstädt,
1964, p. 76). After all, the old rule was not that a hunting instrument should never be called, or sound like, a trumpet, but simply
that it should never look like one.

Trumpeters meanwhile began to employ the spiral in con-
certed music, partly perhaps because the bell faced backwards.
They would use their own kind of mouthpiece, so that the mouthpipe would be modified accordingly and perhaps the bell to match
it, as represented by the Pfeifer instrument of 1697. This need
not have greatly changed the sound on the high harmonics.
Vejvanovsky may have played it where he wrote for (or alternatively for) '*Trombae brevae*', notably in his 'Sonata venatoria'
of 1684 (*Mus. Antiqu. Bohem.* 36). The instruments are in D and
play mainly in Clarino style, but the opening phrase shows a
certain likeness to some French hunting-horn calls and this, with
the title of the piece, could suggest that 'short' here denotes a
spiral.[1]

Ex. 2 2 a.

8. Reiche's portrait by Haussmann, Leipzig, 1727. Four-coil,
silver (or silvered), Haas-like ornament on bell, mouthpipe axis
parallel with bell as in the Haas of 1688 etc. Large trumpet

---

[1] For an anonymous, probably earlier 'Sonata da caccia con un cornu',
also from Kremsier in Moravia, see Meyer, 1956, p. 388ff. The piece, for
'corno da caccia' with strings, is for an instrument in 8–foot C over the
range h3–h12 and is said to date from the 1670s. A few bars are quoted
(Ex. 22a) from a copy of the manuscript by Robert Minter, who saw in it
the hand of Schmeltzer (d. 1680).

mouthpiece. Pitch estimated as D without the crook. (Pl. VII; note the grasp, hardly one for hand-stopping).

9. Telemann and others, 1730s, Hamburg, Dresden: parts for *Trombe di caccia*, the best known being Telemann's violin concerto in F (*DDT* 29), with natural parts in Cammerton F reaching h18 like the part in the Second Brandenburg Concerto. The question is whether to equate the expression with *Jäger Trommet* or with French *trompe de chasse* (i.e. horn, sounding an octave lower). Among points in favour of the former, (a) Hasse's opera *Cleofide*, 1732, is said by Kleefeld in his article in *SIMG*, 1900, to contain parts for *Trombe di caccia* in D and also for horns in F; and (b) the French themselves at that period used '*cor*' very much more than '*trompe*' for the full-sized horn; even if, as is possible, *Tromba* could have this meaning in Naples or Rome (Kirkendale, *J. Amer. Mus. Soc.*, 1967), it would seem strange for a German composer to recall it in these rare cases only, though it would be an obvious word for the small 'Italian *Trumpet*' in a score. The same question arises over Telemann's difficult parts for *Tromba selvatica* in E flat in *Musique de Table* (1733; *DDT* 62), again up to h18. The 'hunting' finale in $\frac{12}{8}$ time would suit the 'Waldtrompete' (if this is what 'selvatic' means) and the contour of melodic interplay with the violins may be felt to point to the higher octave as the composer's intention. The prevailing opinion today is that horns are meant.

Inventions trumpet. Altenburg's version of the fourth category says (p. 12): 'the so-called *Inventions* or Italian trumpet... more convenient through having more coils[1]... used particularly in Italy', adding that such trumpets were not used by cavalry but only by infantry bandsmen. He is here eliding the old text (whence 'Italy') with his own experience at home (whence the rest), having in mind the *Inventionstrompete* in the sense of a short-model (two loop) F trumpet with crooks. A specimen of his time is by Schmied of Pfaffendorf in Silesia, dated 1772 (Leipzig Colln. No. 1824) but there are earlier examples, though with no crooks. Four of these are also in the Leipzig Collection, including a pair (Nos. 1820/21, destroyed in the war) by J. N. John of Breslau, dated 1735 and bearing the dedication of the Cloth-

[1] '*öftern Windung*'.

croppers Guild to a church in Schweidnitz not far away. Their tube-length is 171 to 177 cm. (about modern F) and the model length 37 cm. (Pl. V). The other two, and another example at Brussels, are by the Ehe family, with dates 1735 and 1741 (one of them illustrated in Menke, p. 101).

In these same years the Imperial Guild Mandates (of 1736; see Zedler, 'Trompete' col. 1121, also Altenburg p. 49) mention the 'so-called *Inventions-trompete*' along with the *Waldhorn* as instruments barred to members of the fraternity, and it has often been surmised on the basis of Altenburg's remarks that this instrument was an 'Italian' spiral—which, however, could hardly have been regarded at that time as something novel ('*Inventions*'). The short model was perhaps introduced partly to be used in towns or smaller churches where Guild restrictions forbade use of the normal trumpet. But whether also for convenience in hand-stopping now and then remains an open question.

Not all the mysteries come from Germany. From France, Mary Rasmussen notices (*BQ* VI, 1) the 'Pièce a double trompette et de different ton... de Philidor' in which an instrument written in C appears to have been convertible to low G (which would entail some 30 inches of extra tube-length on a trumpet) and back again without hiatus in the part. Possibly the instrument was a two-stringed *trompette marine*. This brings to mind some Austrian concertos of a hundred years later for '*Tromb.*', preserved at Budapest and argued by some scholars to be intended for a Jew's harp (in Central European languages *trombila* etc.) played in a well-known manner by holding to the mouth, back to back, two instruments tuned to tonic and dominant; or a single instrument furnished with two tongues. A virtuoso was thus performing before the Emperor in 1764. On the other hand, Rasmussen, quoting passages from one such concerto in E flat by Albrechtsberger, 1771 (*BQ* V, 3), suggests some kind of keyed trumpet. The question is complicated by the evident relish of Austrian soloists on both instruments for accompaniment on the mandolin.

SIX

The Horns

===

Hunting signals of the kind executed all over the world on conches and small horns by long-and-short on one note have a fair-sized European literature beginning with the fourteenth century *Livre du Roy Modus et de la Reine Ratio* ('King Manner and Queen Method') by H. de Ferrières, Lord of Gisors, who hunted the stag with horse and hounds in the Forest of Breteuil, between Rouen and Paris. By coincidence his call when the stag is taken, a long note followed by ten as short as possible, is also a 'good hunting' call on the conch among the Doboduro tribe of North Papua.

Small curved horns, bovine and metal, remained in use in most countries well after larger instruments had been introduced. Some

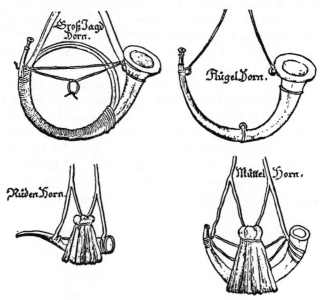

Fig. 24 Hunting horns (after H. F. von Fleming, 1719).

are shown in Figs. 23 and 24; the distinctive horn mouthpiece will be observed throughout. German youthful hunt servants used to earn the right to carry the smallest *Hifthorn* after passing an examination in sounding it. In England the straight model came into use in the 1670s (Fig. 25) in order, it was said, to give a more

Fig. 25 'The Death of a Hart'. R. Blome, 1686. Detail from plate dedicated to Henry, Duke of Worcester.

penetrating note from the coverts. It was then rather longer than the 25 cm. copper horn of today's fox hunt and remained so up to the early nineteenth century. Cameron (1905) describes how to sound the latter in time-honoured terms: 'almost close the lips, pressing them back upon the teeth, and half blow, half spit into the mouthpiece'. He gives the signals in crotchets and quavers, as Turberville did in 1575; Hardouin in 1394 gave them in black and white squares. No variations in pitch are indicated. The note of a small horn can however be made to express much by special methods of blowing, for example quaverings, and particularly by striking the note well below and at once whooping up to the true pitch with the effect of a rise of a fourth or fifth. This has been noticed with the shofar (Ex. 7, second part), while in some seventeenth- and eighteenth-century English versions of the hunting code (one of them reproduced by Cameron) syllabic 'names of the notes' like 'ton tavern' have been interpreted by Halfpenny (1954) as instructions to produce a similar effect. Moreover, resemblances in implied rhythmic pattern between many of these 'taverns' and the corresponding crotchet-and-quaver calls in the earlier work of Turberville would then indicate that the same mode of execution was employed here.

The subject of pre-musical hunting signals is one which cannot be dwelt on here, but some allusions to them in vocal and keyboard works are worth noticing. These may take the form of plain reiterations of one note, as in Gombert's 'The Hare Hunt'. Earlier than this, however, are allusions in some Italian *caccia* part-songs of the late fourteenth century which show lively figures on two notes a fourth apart. One is by Ghirardello da Firenze (Davison & Apel No. 52, after the words 'suo corno sonava'). Another, by Niccolò da Perugia (No. IX in Marrocco's edition) is sung to the syllables *don don don*, which would seem to portray clear lingual articulation on the horn. Taken literally, this would then imply h3 and h4, and so a tube-length of at least 75 cm. or that of our present post-horn. Curved and semicircular metal horns of this size were certainly made in later centuries but must have always been awkward to carry at the hip in the active conditions of the chase. A small curl or loop circumvents this: a 12 cm. diameter loop is all that is needed to reduce a 75 cm. tube to an overall size of about 30 cm. Looped horns are seen shortly after the period of the *caccie* in a French mid fifteenth-century scene of a hunt ball, for which two huntsmen have joined the *haut menestrels* who are seated on their right (Fig. 26a); the spiralled appearance of the horns may represent overwinding with velvet, or perhaps a writhen construction from strips of metal somewhat as gun barrels were once made. Looped horns are seen in the 'Dance of Death' woodcuts from Basel and more again through the sixteenth century and much of the seventeenth, usually quite small, up to about 35 cm. in overall size. Curiously, no such hunting horns seem to have survived in any collection although Mersenne said that they were the most used. He also distinguishes a superior manner of sounding the horn with lingual articulation (cf. *don don*) from ordinary ways which employed labial articulation (cf. 'tavern'). The alternation of two notes a fourth apart in 'The King's Hunt' in the Fitzwilliam Virginal Book (II) recalls the *caccie* as it stands on paper, but does not necessarily refer to a hunt call. In any case, pictures like those in Drayton's *Poly-olbion* (1622) show that the horn then commonly used in England was of the small curved kind.

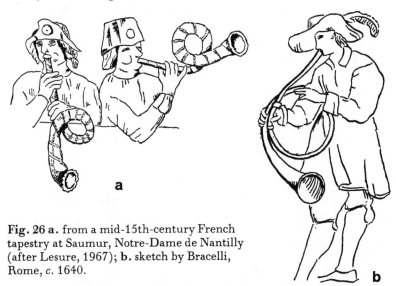

Fig. 26 a. from a mid-15th-century French tapestry at Saumur, Notre-Dame de Nantilly (after Lesure, 1967); b. sketch by Bracelli, Rome, c. 1640.

Beyond this there is the faint possibility that certain triadic figures in late sixteenth-century compositions may parody a fresh kind of courtly hunting fanfare containing h5, thus introducing the major third, which at one stroke intensifies the spirit of a brass-instrument call and raises the mere signal to the fringe of melody, and for this the spiral horns mentioned in the last chapter would have offered more than ample tube-length. The first decisive evidence of such a fanfare is not, however, until the 'Call to the Hunt' in Cavalli's first opera, *Le nozze di Teti e di Peleo* (Venice, 1639; see Morley-Pegge, p. 81). This short fanfare, discussed in every history of the horn, is written in C major for five-part string orchestra, the lower parts following the top part (Ex. 23a) in block triads except for the bass always on C. At first sight it looks rather military, and in fact there are a few passages not unlike it in Fantini. One might well imagine that to noblemen's huntsmen the sounds of the court trumpeters daily in their ears inevitably suggested ideas for expanding their own repertory, being encouraged to do so as the declining role of cavalry in warfare brought a deflection of some of its traditional display and trappings into an increasingly grandiose and formal hunt.

This may be partly true. But the purely rhythmic figurations of Cavalli's piece can be matched in contemporary horn codes written in notes without pitch, in France by Duffouilloux (1561 and onwards) and by Mersenne, e.g. upon sighting a stag: three shorts followed by a long. Anyhow, their apparent transformation in the opera into a melodic triad clearly depicts realism. The block harmony in triplets recurs fifty years later below hunting-scene arpeggi in Purcell's *Dido and Aeneas*: perhaps this feature is a realistic effect too. It might be going too far, though, to see in the repetition of each strain in the adjacent octave a portrayal of mingled huntsmen answering each other on different-sized horns; Cavalli no doubt did this to make good violin music.

Ex. 23 Horn calls and fanfares: **a.** Cavalli, *Le nozze di Teti e di Peleo*, top part; **b.** Lully, *Isis* (part books, Christ Church, Mus. 114–9); **c.** Philidor l'aîné, 'Pour la voye', (Bibl. Versailles MS 1163); **d.** 'Le Rapprocher', from an early version (cf. Karstädt, 1964).

After this, no 'realistic' horn fanfares have come to light until Lully's five-part 'Air des valets de chien et des chasseurs avec Cors de chasse' in his comédie-ballet *La Princesse d'Elide* (Paris, 1664). Says the stage direction: 'several *cors et trompes* were heard and in concert with the violins began the entrance air, upon which six *valets* danced, resuming at certain cadences the sound of their *cors* and *trompes*'. Opinions have since differed over what actually went on. The valets may not have been rehearsed to sound exactly what the violins played, but the themes certainly mirror habitual French hunting sounds of the day. Morley-Pegge reproduces the score in full (p. 83). Ex. 23b is the start of a very similar hunting music in Lully's *Isis*, produced thirteen years later in 1677. Again for normal five-part strings but in C instead of B flat, it utilizes identical motifs arranged a little differently. The slight resemblance to the fanfare of Cavalli no doubt reflects a general character of horn-blowing over Europe (rather than a previous re-staging of *Le nozze di Teti* in Paris). More interesting are the motifs themselves, for they recur deeply implanted in the *trompe-de-chasse* code of the future. We first see them again, written an octave lower in normal horn notation, in the earliest French collection of calls, a page in a Philidor manuscript of 1705 (Versailles Town Library No. 1163) entitled 'Tous les appels de trompe pour la chasse' (Ex. 23c).

It is extremely doubtful whether the spiral horn took part in any of this. We have seen from Mersenne that it had not been popular in France, and we are soon to learn from Furetière's Dictionary that by the date of this, 1690, it was virtually extinct. There are, however, indications that by the time of Lully's earlier fanfare the instrument built in the historic model for the future had already come into use by the mounted piqueur while other huntsmen were continuing to sound horns of simple types. This is, of course, the hooped horn, in which the open coil, initially a single coil, dominates the whole and brings the bell to point backwards as it had already done in many spiral horns. A germ of the idea is perhaps to be seen in an unusually large looped horn (Fig. 26b) shown among some very deft sketches of musicians made by the Florence artist Bracelli about 1640 (reproduced in full in Heinitz, p. 81). Unlike the common looped horn this larger one is being played upside down, the bell somewhat backwards.[1]

Then there is a short gap. The earliest example of the true hooped horn comes over twenty years later, just three years after Lully's first fanfare. It is, however, German, made in Nuremberg in 1667 by Starck (Copenhagen, Claudius Colln., see Pl. VIII). It seems to be substantially in its original state except that the mouthpipe must once have been a little longer (the mouthpiece in the photograph may be disregarded). The single coil is 33 cm. across (just over a foot); bell, 10 cm., as in a trumpet; tube now *c.* 176 cm., tapered throughout to a present socket of 9 mm. The bell is brought right round close to the mouthpiece, but the hoop

---

[1] Readers of *GSJ* may have been intrigued by Thurston Dart's notice (XXI, pp. 73, 79) of 'Reversi' in Cotgrave's *Dictionary* (1611): 'A kind of Trumpe (played backward, and full of sport) which the Duke of Savoy brought some ten years ago into France'. *Reversi*, or *riversi*, was, however, a card game.

is too small to be placed over the head without disturbing one's cocked hat: slinging rings are still provided. The pitch, about modern F, an octave above the future F horn, matches the upper range of the spirals, and the instrument sounds easily up to h12 if one wishes it to. For whom it was made nobody knows. But in France shortly after the date of Lully's *Isis*, single-coil horns which, by their proportions, were certainly no bigger, were modelled in some of the sculptured trophies of Versailles executed from the end of the 1670s up to 1682. Marolles, who investigated these (*Monographe abrégée*), also noticed an engraving after a now lost painting by Van der Meulen dating from the same years, in which the king himself is shown out hunting while a piqueur gallops by sounding a horn of the same small size. In one of the trophies the horn appears to be two-coil, but very small and it would have been little deeper in pitch.

Such instruments would fit the motifs of Lully's fanfares. They would also fit the one in *Dido and Aeneas*, so that the 'French horns' recorded in England then may still have been of this small model. But a difficulty in this simple picture is that the time of the Versailles trophies coincides with the visit of Count von Sporck who, according to the well-known story, was so impressed by the French royal hunt and its music that he had two servants instructed in the latter, which he thus took back to his home in Bohemia, the land which became so renowned for its horn-players in the following century.

It seems hard to believe that the young count would have been so struck by the French sounds had these amounted merely to common-chord motifs across an octave—especially in the light of contemporary concert virtuosity close to his homeland on instruments named 'corno da caccia', probably of hooped rather than of spiral kinds; Sporck must have heard something of a different nature, and no doubt a clue to it is to be found in the opening phrase of Ex. 23c: a melodious phrase rising to h10, totally non-trumpet, non-orchestral, but pointing firmly in the direction of the future French *trompe* idiom (it is in fact the germ of 'Le Rapprocher', of which Ex. 23d is a short version.) No less striking in the manuscript are vagaries, as in the notation of rhythm in Ex. 23c, bar 2. It is as if Philidor were transcribing a musical vernacular which was quite strange to him. He may have noted down the call long before, soon after he became royal librarian in 1684, and Sporck may have heard it too. We may then imagine that it was about the time of the court's preparations for its final move to Versailles—when famous fanfare-writers of the future, like Morin and the Marquis of Dampierre, were still boys—that those royal and ducal huntsmen who were the most skilful with the small one-coil horn had begun to create the celebrated idiom, characteristically rising in lilting rhythm from G (h6) through C, D, E, so closely akin to the spirit of French folksong that the men may have had the songs of servants and others dwelling on the great estates in their minds. And so they tacked their tuneful fragments on to the existing formulae of triads on repeated notes, long reiterations of single notes, and pauses made with chin vibrato, the whole rendered the more stirring and energetic through a constant *tayauté*, or in English, 'jerked note' (Ex. 24.)[1]

Ex. 24 Notations and executions of *tayauté* (from Pompecki).

On a horn in high F, h10, sounding *a″*, is quite a high note. Paintings of Versailles by J.-B. Martin show that a pitch of about 7-foot D was in use by 1688 (Pl. VIII), but still no dated French instrument is known. Morley-Pegge cites an anonymous horn pitched nearly in modern 8-foot C, with hoop 44 cm., bell 14 cm., and ascribes it to the closing years of the seventeenth century. By that time, 12-foot F had been reached, and in England also.

This big lowering, which first gave to the horn its historic musical character, may have come about through adding to the horn in C a second coil. This would bring a pitch very close to F,

---

[1] The $\frac{6}{8}$ rhythm, later to predominate, may have been less prominent initially. Something of a far more free original delivery may be preserved in calls printed in mid eighteenth-century English 'Instructions for the French Horn'. These calls, while basically those of the French, are written without time signature and are peppered with long reiterations on one note. Some would have lasted a full minute in duration. Morley-Pegge (p. 79) gives an example. The French horn was used in the hunt less in England than on the Continent and little after the 1740s; the methods of 'winding' it may well have remained by Continental standards old-fashioned. The contemporary calls printed in Diderot (in the Plates, under 'Chasses'), confirm this impression.

and would be most simply carried out with cylindrical tubing, the separated parts of the original horn providing a long tapered mouthpipe and bell section. The earliest dated F horn, by Bull (1699, Carse Colln.), though built in three coils, has this cylindrical middle section (external diameter 11·7 mm.) as do the subsequent London horns and at least some of the German.[1]

In France, two-coil horns were soon in fashion, and by 1720 the pitch for the hunt had become stabilized at the rather gruff key— for the open air—of 14-foot D, which the *trompe* retains today (save when made in E flat for use with bands). With two coils the hoop is *c.* 54 cm. across. With three coils, the most frequent model from the mid-eighteenth century onwards, it is 40 cm. In most cases, even with the finest makers, these horns are built with a tapered mouthpipe of some 70 cm., after which a kind of overall conicity is obtained by joining lengths of cylindrical tube of slightly increasing diameters. The mouthpiece (Fig. 1, No. 9) helps to give a sound which quickly becomes brassy, and which players, as one hears them today, produce with great vigour. The *tayauté* is made on practically every crotchet, by a lip-movement 'ta-ee-o', sometimes indicated in written calls by a cross or other sign as shown in Ex. 24. The ornament starts *on* the beat and is executed at about semiquaver speed. The upper note may be omitted or fail to 'come out', the effect then being to turn the original crotchet into a pair of forceful quavers on the same note. The frequent importation of *tayauté* into concert music is illustrated in Ex. 25, in the demisemiquavers of bars 1 and 2.

Baroque horn music. In Germany a parallel development of the single-coil horn can be followed by a few dated examples. An unsigned horn dated 1689 (Leipzig No. 1661) and one by J. L. Ehe (I), 1698, said to be in the museum at Kaiserslautern, are in 8- or 9-foot C or B flat. Then, with the F horn, German orchestral writing for hunting instruments matured in the very characteristic style illustrated in Ex. 25, from a Concerto by Johann Baer (or Beer, *alias* Ursinus), who died at Weissenfels in 1700. Assuming that the piece, in which the soloist doubles on post-horn, is authentic (for the existing parts are written by a younger copyist, Fick), it is one of the earliest F-horn examples known, just antedating an Aria in Badia's *Diana rappacificata* (Vienna, 1700: extracts in K. Haller, 1970, p. 176) which refers to the hunt and

---

[1] *Note to the Dover Edition.* In this copper horn with Bull's name and the date on the bell-rim, the three-coil middle section and mouthpipe are crudely adapted from some later instrument, in which case we cannot

begins with low-note fanfares, then continuing in the same vein
as Baer. There was still nothing like it in France as far as is
known, except for some rather similar passages in Morin's *La
chasse du cerf* staged at Fontainebleau in 1708. Morin here supplied parts which oboe and violin could double, so that the horn,
in C, was presumably played in C alto up to h16—though the
Paris Collection has a gigantic single-coil horn in 16-foot C ascribed
to Crétien: 91 cm. across, its tube is in seven sections, the mouthpipe followed by stepped cylinders to a bell 29 cm. wide. To hold
it, the right hand must be stretched backwards to grasp the hoop
some 18 inches from the bell rim.

Ex. 25 J. Baer, *Concerto à 4* (Bibl. Schwerin MS), 1st movement, bars
16–37. Corne de chasse in F. Post-horn actual pitch.

The early F horn is represented splendidly by Viennese instruments of the Leichamschneider brothers, and Fitzpatrick (1970)
puts a strong case for seeing the enthusiasm of von Sporck behind
their design. A single-coil example of 1710 (at Vienna; hoop
68 cm.) is probably for the hunt, being very like the horns in
statues at Moritzburg in Saxony (Pl. VIII; this hunting castle was
built in 1670 but the figures are clearly later). However the
makers also produced two- and three-coil F horns, their smaller
hoops suiting orchestral and duetting use as well. A two-coil
Leichamschneider of 1718 (Bernoulli Colln., with its pair at
Basel, Pl. VIII) is 41 cm. across with 24 cm. bell. Meanwhile the
older and higher tonalities, matching trumpet pitch or just below
it, were orchestrally introduced by North German composers of

know the original form of the 1699 horn. (See *Galpin Society Journal*, 1982,
p. 157.)

Corne de chasse parts, as Keiser (*Octavia*, 1706, in high C). A number of specimens from the first half of the eighteenth century stand in such pitches, all of them two-coil, 23–25 cm. across inside and rather more widely flared (15–22 cm.) than the older spirals and single-coil horns. Most have slinging rings, and the bell darkened inside as was customary with horns that might be used by mounted players in order to prevent sun reflection frightening the horse behind. The earliest of these horns in date, 1713, was destroyed in the war (Berlin No. 478). Most were made in Nuremberg: M. Hainlein, Fr. Ehe. a pair by G. F. Steinmetz, and two by the youngest Haas (Bernoulli and Nuremberg Collns., see Pl. VIII). Two stand in Cammerton C alto but others are a tone higher. Their sockets are wide, of trumpet size, and with two examples there remains a tapered shank up to 85 mm. long, with the aid of which the horns could no doubt have been played in high tonalities next to those in which they stand. But the strong probability is that each of these instruments once had a set of crooks for playing in lower keys.

Horn crooks were introduced very early, first, as far as is known, by Michael Leichamschneider in Vienna; Fitzpatrick (1970, p. 33) found a bill sent by him to the Abbot of Kremsmünster in 1703 for 'a pair of great new *Jägerhorn*' with four new double crooks and four new tuning bits. Mattheson, in Hamburg, mentioned such accessories ten years later. Crookless horns in different keys continued, however, to be used in music. An inventory of the instruments of the Count of Sayn-Wittgenstein in Westphalia, 1741, includes both kinds: 'one pair of C *Waldhorn*, two pairs of D, two pairs of F, and two pairs of crooks'. In London, Handel's horn parts before 1740, in either D or F, were certainly first performed on crookless horns like those which were built in both these keys by Nicholas Winkings. These too have blackened bells. The horns in Fig. 27 (right) could be two of them. The coils are for the most part loose, held together by the leather binding. The sound, even with a *trompe* mouthpiece is sweet and musical.

It cannot be positively stated what the earliest crooks were like, no sets having yet been discovered. But one can appreciate that, as compared with the simple matter of making trumpet crooks, the horn's tapered bore presented the maker with a fresh problem. His procedure in theory would be to divide the horn at a point where the tube reached approximately trumpet width. The larger part with the bell would then be re-fashioned to form a hoop

smaller than before, or with three coils reduced to two, and with
a socket for the crooks placed at the top of the hoop. (In practice
the usual length for the horn, without the crooks, thenceforth
lay between 220 and 240 cm.)

Fig. 27. **Left** detail from the scene of a private orchestra, *c.* 1750, by
G. B. Propst, Augsburg. **Right** horn-players in band accompanying an
ambassadorial procession in London, 1763 (print, British Museum).

The other part, containing the precious taper back to the
narrow mouthpiece socket, would serve as the basis for a system
of crooks. The earliest known sets of crooks belong to horns made
in London about the middle of the eighteenth century shortly
after crooks were first introduced from Germany, and they may
well exhibit the original system. The tapered tube is formed into
a two-coil crook which puts the horn in G, the highest horn key
used by Handel (from *Samson*, 1741). This is the 'master crook'
(length about 120 cm.). For the lower keys, cylindrical crooks or
'couplers' are placed between the master crook and the horn.
There are four of these, their lengths found by simple ratios.
For F, the G horn is lengthened by 9:8 by inserting the medium-
sized single-coil coupler. Next, a lengthening of 4:3, for D, is
obtained by means of the two-coil coupler; this D horn is now
lengthened by 9:8 to reach C, by adding the largest of the single-
coil couplers. The latter also serves for E flat in conjunction with a
smaller coupler which may itself be combined with the F coupler
for E. All four together just reach low B flat. The main drawback
of this ingenious and economical outfit, apart from any awkward-

ness in holding a horn with a chain of crooks, lies in the heavy wear imposed upon the master crook.

The English master-crook outfits include when complete two or more small tuning bits, inserted next to the mouthpiece as required, and also (though not invariably) a small one-coil master crook and coupler for obtaining high tonalities above G.[1] The earlier of the two English instruments in Pl. IX shows this small master crook and some couplers. It is one of a fine pair of 'Concert French Horns' (as distinguished from a plain crookless 'French Horn') belonging to the Shaw-Hellier family, made before 1754 by Hofmaster and now on loan to the Warwickshire Museum in Warwick (hoop 23 cm., bell 23·5 cm.). The other horn, with G master crook, is one of a pair made by Rodenbostel (presumed successor to Hofmaster and likewise of evident German origin) which was purchased by the Frampton-on-Severn Volunteers in 1798 and is preserved in the City Museum, Gloucester. There are no signs that this pair was ever provided with the small master crook: B flat must always have been played *basso* in this band.

The instrument shown is in each case the 'left-handed' horn of the pair. Through much of the eighteenth century it was common though not universal practice to build one horn of a pair as the mirror image of the other. The instruments were grasped in one hand or held aloft by both hands (Fig. 27). A right-handed horn was held with the bell to the right, and was so constructed that the mouthpipe or crook socket lay below the bell tubing—as it normally lies in horns today, i.e. to the left of the main coil as the player sees it. The left-handed horn, its player standing on the right with the bell pointing to the left, should, to be perfectly correct, have the socket on the opposite side of the hoop in order to come likewise below the bell tubing—to the right of the main coil as a modern player would see it—and the crooks of the one horn do not fit the other. Even the advent of the hand-horn did not always change the custom. The Frampton pair were themselves played with the hand in the bell, though judging by the wearing of the bell paint, not in a true hand-horn manner—nor would the players' music have demanded it.

HAND HORN

It may have been largely through the unaccompanied duet, performed indoors or outdoors (Pl. IX), that players came to appre-

[1] For illustrations of complete sets, see Fitzpatrick, 1970, Pl. XIV.

ciate the vast potential compass of the horn, on which the tonic can be sounded in four octaves, and to exploit it in solo concertos as well. The collection of the latter at Lund University (described by Rasmussen, *BQ* V, 4) contains manuscript concertos from the 1740s, some possibly earlier, and in these the full range is employed with extreme virtuosity. It is significant that the apparent source of the collection is Dresden, adding to the evidence of technical advances made by the Bohemian players who held posts there, among them Hampel and Knechtel. Here 1st Horn players were able to take the high horn technique up to h24 and to reproduce virtually the idiom of the violin (e.g. Knechtel, Ex. 26).

Ex. 26 Knechtel, Concerto for Horn in D, excerpt from Adagio (Lund Univ. MS Wenster Litt. I). (Sounding a seventh lower.)

Meanwhile the 2nd Horn, of whom Hampel was one, found ways of accompanying his partner in a Duo concertante, or himself in a concerto, by imitating as far as possible the left-hand figurations of a harpsichordist. Though nature provided him with no subdominant in the bass, it was discovered that a low *f* (or as customarily written in bass clef, *F*) could be produced in falset from *g*— as indeed it can be very well (and remained an accepted way of producing this note among hand-horn players). Thus cadences could proceed through F, G, C in the bass, while by the same means h4 and h2 supplied B and h3 also *f* sharp and even *e*. These and other falset notes for 2nd Horn had become routine in works of Johann Stamitz, as exemplified in the pieces by him for clarinets and horns alone, quoted in the *Essai d'Instruction* by Valentin Roeser, one of Stamitz's many admirers in Paris (Ex. 27).

Roeser's work has, however, its main importance to horn history for containing the earliest first-hand description of *hand-stopping*, that weirdly beautiful technique with the horn held downwards and one hand in the bell which gave music the classic style of the horn, still every player's favourite music from the works of Mozart to those of Brahms and to its clear echoes in those of Richard Strauss. Though not dated, the likely year of Roeser's work has been shown by Cucuel to be 1764, while the sad terms in which he speaks of the death of Stamitz (1757) as a blow to the entire musical world suggests that it was compiled even earlier.

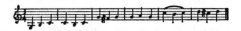

Ex. 27 Roeser, *Essai d'Instruction*. **Above**, from an Allegro in E♭ by J. Stamitz for 2 clarinets (top line) and 2 horns (*Cor 1er* and *Cor 2de*); **below**, notes to be made on the horn with the hand in the bell.

He gives the *f* and *f* sharp in the '2nd *Cor de chasse*' compass, adding that one can correct their intonation, and that of high *f″*, by placing the hand in the bell, especially on crotchets and minims. And, he goes on, there are four or five further notes to make with the hand, though to be employed with prudence (Ex. 27, below). His scale for 1st Horn, however, contains only the natural notes. As for *a″*, 'there is no way of making it correct, so that it must not be used in a chord and must be avoided in unison with other instruments as far as possible.' In London, Gehot's *Complete Instructions* (*c.* 1785) notices that the natural *a″* is 'either too sharp or too flat', from which it appears that some players were using h14 for this note.

A horn soloist who was employing stopped notes in Paris at this time was Rodolphe, from Strasbourg, who later became better known as a violinist and teacher and was an initial instigator of the future Conservatoire. Morley-Pegge reproduces (p. 206) the solo part played by him in an opera of 1770 by Trial. Ex. 28 shows part of this with the expression marks and stopping indications

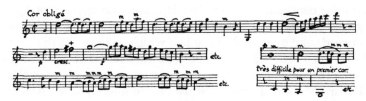

Ex. 28 Francoeur, extracts from solo part (in E) of Ariette from J. C. Trial, *La Fête de Flore*, 1770.

I 1. Mabu players (photo Beatrice Blackwood); 2. Didjeridu (photo Pitt Rivers Museum); 3. Thighbone trumpet, Bhutan 1907; 4. Rana sriṅga (*nagasinnam*), Ceylon, 1909; 5. Bucium, Rumania (after Alexandru).

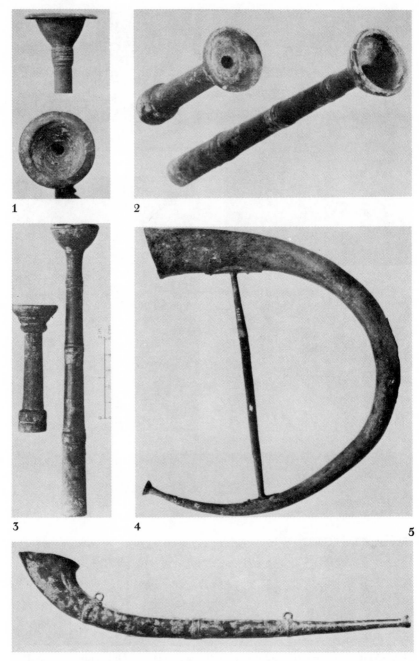

II *Mouthpieces*: 1. Lur (Lund, Hist. Museum); 2 and 3. Roman (Courtesy, Trustees of the British Museum); 4. Cornu (Rome, Villa Giulia); 5. *Signaltrompete* (Saalburg Museum, D 1090; courtesy Rheinisches Landesmuseum, Bonn).

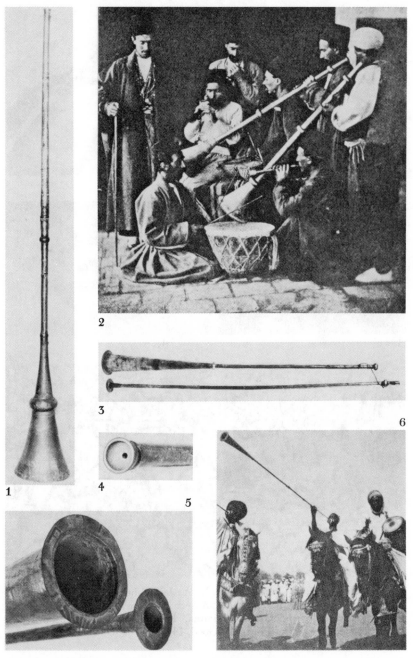

III 1 and 4. Karnaï, Usbek, 203 cm. (Brussels Conservatoire 746); 2. Nakkara khana, Meshed; 3 and 5. Kakaki, N. Nigeria, assembled 238 cm. (Pitt Rivers Museum); 6. Sultan's band with kakaki, Niger.

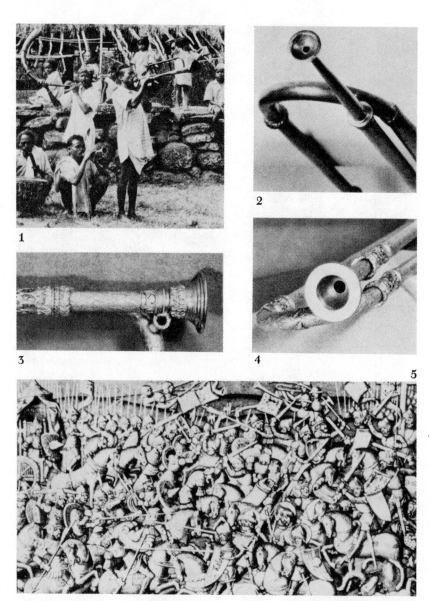

IV 1. Paidi tribe, C. India (photo N. A. Jairazbhoy 1963); 2. Trumpet, India (Crown Copyright, Victoria & Albert Museum); 3 and 4. Mouthpiece with Schnitzer trumpet 1581 (Vienna, Kunsthistorisches Museum); 5. Battle scene, Breviary of Philip the Good, 1460.

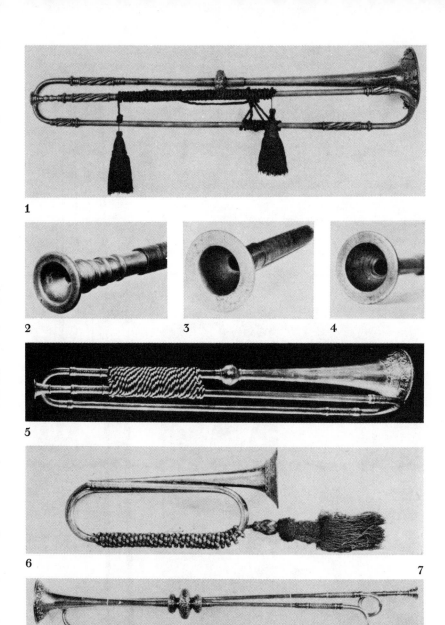

V 1. Trumpet, W. W. Haas (by permission of the Trustees of the Wallace Collection).
Mouthpieces: 2. trumpet, E. J. C. Haas (Nuremberg, Germanisches Nationalmuseum, MI 363); 3. trombone, Colbert 1593 (The Hague, Gemeentemuseum); 4. trombone, I. Ehe 1616 (Munich, Bayerisches Nationalmuseum).
5. Trumpet, Steiger 1578 (Basel, Historisches Museum); 6. John, Breslau 1735 (Leipzig, Musikinstrumentenmuseum, Karl-Marx University, 1820); 7. Bull (Ashmolean Museum, Oxford).

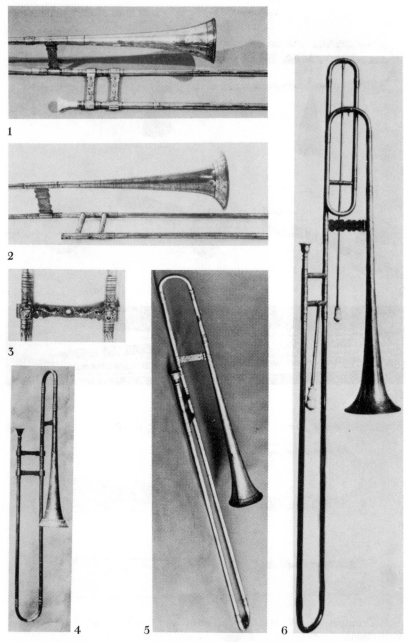

VI *Trombones*: **1.** Neuschel 1557; **2.** anon. German 1814 (Oxford, Bate Collection); **3.** slide stay of I. Ehe 1616 (as Pl. V 4); **4.** Alto, Goltbeck, Kottbus (formerly Berlin Colln.); **5.** Tenor, Drewelwecz 1595 (Nuremberg, Germanisches Nationalmuseum, MI 167); **6.** Bass, W. W. Haas (Berlin, Instit. für Musikforschung).

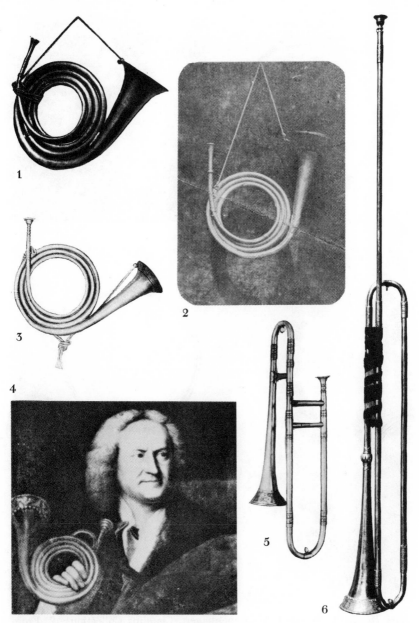

VII *Spiral instruments*: 1. Dresden, State Hist. Museum; 2. J. W. Haas 1688 (Sigmaringen, Hohenzollern Museum); 3. Pfeifer 1697 (formerly Heyer Collection); 4. J. G. Reiche in 1727 (Leipzig, Städtisches Museum).

5. Discant trombone *c.* 1770 (Stockholm, Musikhistoriska Museet); 6. *Zugtrompete*, Veit 1651 (Berlin, Instit. für Musikforschung).

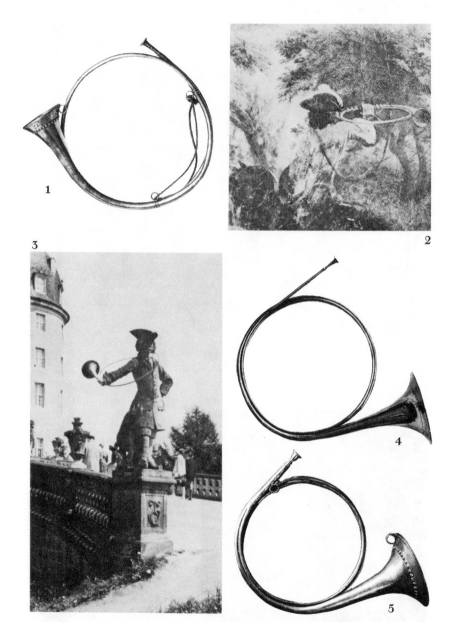

VIII *Horns*: **1.** Starck 1667 (Copenhagen, Claudius Collection); **2.** From painting by Martin *c.* 1688 (Musée de Versailles); **3.** Moritzburg, Saxony (photo by kindness of K. and H. Janetzky); **4.** M. Leichamschneider 1718 (Basel, Hist. Museum); **5.** E. J. C. Haas (Nuremberg, Germanisches Nationalmuseum, MI 178).

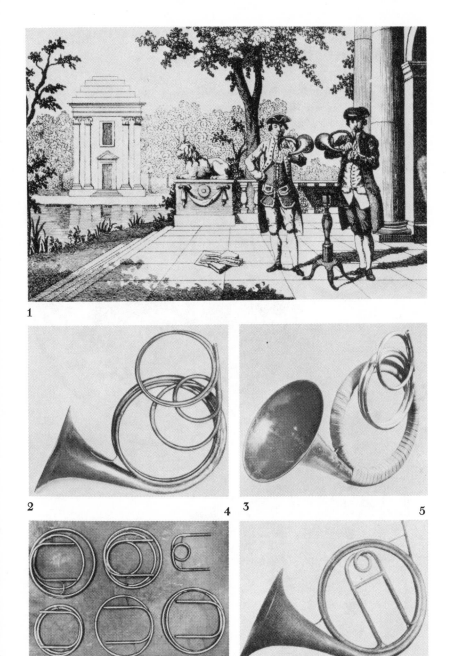

IX *Horns*: **1**. *New Instructions for the French Horn*, Longman & Lukey *c*. 1770; **2**. Rodenbostel, end 18th century (Gloucester City Museum); **3**. Hofmeister, pre-1754 (Warwickshire Museum, courtesy Miss Shaw-Hellier); **4**. slide crooks (some of set), Goodison *c*. 1830 (Bate Collection); **5**. Haltenhof 1776, as crooked in E flat (Paris Conservatoire).

X 1. Horn, Courtois *c.* 1820 (Bate Colln., Morley-Pegge Memorial Gift); 2. 'Caporal Cornet des Chasseurs', Dutch print, 1815; 3. *Jakthorn*, Petterson, Stockholm 1962 (21 cm.); 4. Post-horn, 19th century, with transposing hole (Munich, Bayerisches National-museum, 28/3245).

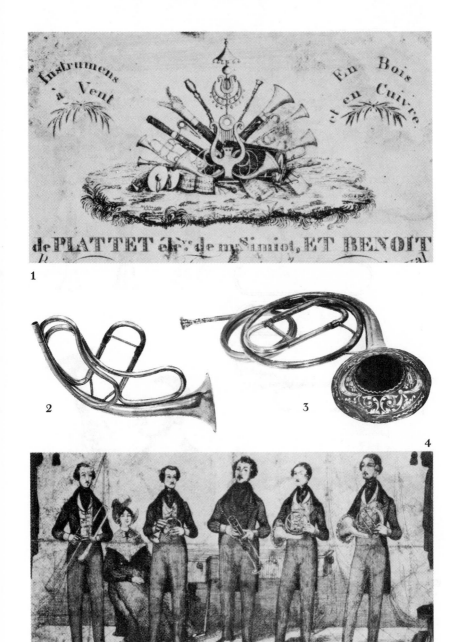

XI 1. Trade-card, Lyon *c.* 1836 (note dragon-bell *basson russe, trompette demilune,* and (right) trombone with bell to rear); 2. Demilune trumpet, Guichard post-1827, D crook (Bate Collection); 3. Circular trumpet, Jahn *c.* 1820 (do., Morley-Pegge Memorial Gift); 4. The Distin Family quintet *c.* 1834.

XII 1. Slide trumpet. Clementi *c.* 1820 (author's); **2.** *Mouthpieces*: *a* serpent, *b* the above trumpet, *c* ophicleide 1829, *d* keyed bugle, *e* cornet, early type; **3.** Trumpet, C. Missenharter, Ulm *c.* 1860, with D, C, B flat crooks (Nuremberg, Germanisches Nationalmuseum, MI 379); **4.** Keyed trumpet, J. Riedl, Vienna *c.* 1820 (Berlin, destroyed in the war); **5.** Keyed bugle, D'Almaine, in C with B flat crook; **6.** Bass keyed trumpet (as 3, MIR 127); **7.** An ophicleide player.

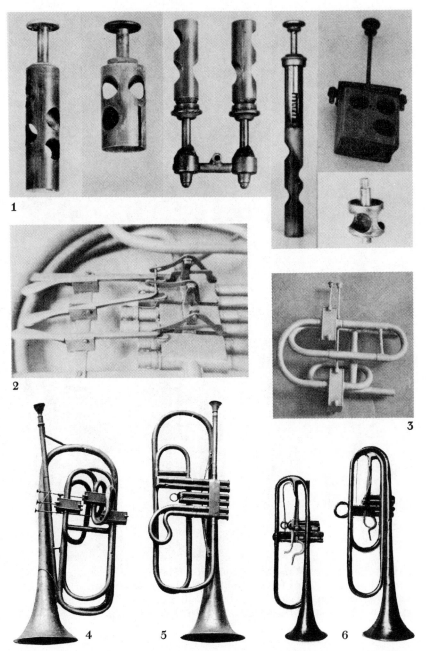

XIII 1. *Valves* (mostly cornet): Périnet, early type; Berlin; double-piston; Stoelzel; 'square'; (below) rotary; 2. Horn, Schott (Brussels Conservatoire 1314); 3. Schuster-type horn valves (do. 1310); 4. Bass trumpet, W. Schuster (Berlin, Instit. für Musikforschung 3104); 5. Bass trumpet *c.* 1825 (formerly Berlin 3105); 6. Trumpets in B flat (1837) and E flat, M. Saurle (Munich, Bayerisches Nationalmuseum).

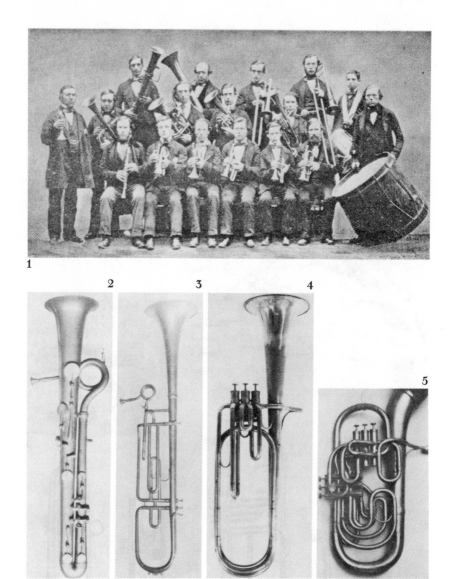

XIV 1. The Besses-o' th-Barn Band 1860 (Hampson); 2. Alto ophicleide, Printemps, Lille (Paris Conservatoire); 3. Clavicor, Guichard (Bate Collection); 4. Saxhorn baryton, Sax (Bate Collection); 5. Saxhorn basse, Sax, independent pistons (Brussels Conservatoire 2464).

XV 1. Tenor-bass trombone, J. Saurle (Munich, Bayerisches National-museum, 183 Mu); 2. *Tonwechsel* on tenor horn, probably Cervený (Bernoulli Collection); 3. Vienna horn (Brussels Conservatoire); 4. Tenor Wagner tuba, Alexander 1935; 5 and 6. Two celebrated London players of the past: John Solomon (b. 1856, Mahillon B flat trumpet) and Aubrey Brain (b. 1893, Labbaye horn, F crook).

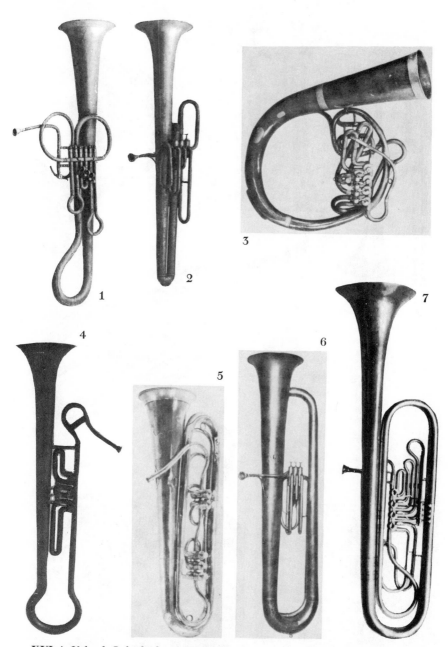

XVI 1. Valved Ophicleide in F, Beyde, Vienna; 2. Valved Ophicleide in F, Bachmann, Brussels; 3. BB flat Helicon, Stowasser *c.* 1850; 4. B flat Bombardon, Finke, Strasbourg; 5. F Bass tuba, J. H. Zetsche, Hanover *c.* 1840; 6. Saxhorn, BB flat contrebasse, Sax 1854; 7. BB flat Tuba, J. Saurle *c.* 1860. (1, 2, 4, 6, Brussels Conservatoire; 3, Nuremberg, Germanisches Nationalmuseum, MIR 71; 5, Oxford, Bate Collection; 7, Munich, Bayerisches Nationalmuseum, 182 Mu).

(m: *'main'*) as the part is quoted by Francoeur (1772, edited by
Choron, 1812). This work says that f'' and a'' were 'corrected' by
the hand, which suggests perhaps lowerings of h11 and 14, since
the other stoppings seem all to be lowerings. A trill, marked with
a cross, disguises the open f'' sharp. In Paris, also in 1770, a performance by Leutgeb, later Mozart's horn soloist, was applauded
in terms which also point to hand-stopping, which he would have
learnt in Austria about the time of Roeser's *Essai*. For one notes
that Roeser's evidence is not of invention, and the whole weight
of horn-players' tradition lies squarely behind the origin of the
practice among the Bohemian players of the Prague-Dresden axis,
of whom the first to teach it systematically, or the most successful
among the first, was said to be Hampel. We learn this mainly
from Domnich, a German who became a professor at the Paris
Conservatoire in 1795 and can be assumed to have got the information from Hampel's celebrated pupil Punto, another Czech,
real name Stich. Hampel was certainly an older man than either
Rodolphe or Leutgeb and died in 1771. There are in fact passages
among the concertos preserved at Lund which point to a dawn
zone of hand-stopping in Dresden as a concerto stunt of 2nd Horn
players and the raw material upon which Hampel built a method.

Ex. 29 Gehra, Concerto in D (Lund University MS): 1st movement,
bars 82–96. String parts reduced to short score.

In the excerpt quoted (Ex. 29, by Gehra) the initial quick descending figure in the lowest register would have been performed
simply in falset, but the words *con sordino*, which show that the

horn was held downwards, must refer to something rapidly inserted by the other hand, if not to the hand itself.[1]

Of Hampel's own works, *Lection pro cornui* (Dresden manuscript, lost in the war) includes the usual 2nd Horn leaps in the low register and some hand-horn passages essentially similar to those in Roeser. Morley-Pegge (pp. 204–5) quotes extracts and also from a manuscript set of Trios which, however, do not have the look of a man of the age Hampel must have been, but perhaps more the manner of Punto. An example from Punto's own *20 Duo Concertans* published in Paris, 1793 (Ex. 30), shows something of

Ex. 30 Andante from *Vingt Duo Concertans . . . composés par Punto*, 1793.

the mature virtuoso style with elegantly-wrought melody for the 1st Horn accompanied athletically by the 2nd.

Hampel, with the Dresden maker Werner, is also credited with the invention of slide crooks, by 1753 at the latest. With these, the integral mouthpipe of the crookless horn is preserved, while two-legged crooks are inserted further along the tube. No Werner example is known, though plain hooped horns by him exist, dated 1735 and 1740. Also in 1753 (according to Eichborn, 1883) the Munich maker Schöller supplied a pair of *neu-inventirte*

---

[1] The Shaw-Hellier Collection includes a curious mute of leather, the wider end perforated with a large hole and provided with a strap for the hand. It will lower the notes of the Hofmaster horns by up to a semitone.

Waldhorn to the Electoral orchestra for 'playing in six keys', but whether with slide crooks is not stated; Schöller's dated instruments, mostly trumpets, are from that year onwards. Slide crooks can be provided over the whole range from B flat alto to basso, and were so made in the next century; they can be very satisfactory in tone and tuning on all the principal crooks (Pl. IX). However, the earliest-known specimen of '*Inventions-horn*' with slide crooks, by Haltenhof of Hanau-am-Main near Frankfurt, and dated 1776 (Paris Collection, Pl. IX) is provided with independent mouthpipe crooks for F upwards, by-passing the fixed mouthpipe which serves the slide crooks of the lower tonalities. This system continued to be used in Germany by some makers into the 19th century, e.g. a horn by Korn, Mainz, in the Bernoulli Collection.

The more celebrated model with slide crooks is that used by the hand-horn soloists, Punto included, and known in France as *corsolo*, with crooks only from G (a plain bow) down to D (two-coiled), covering the tonalities in which fully-stopping can be used best to raise a harmonic by a semitone. The classic design produced by Raoux in Paris *c.* 1780 is two-coil, hoop *c.* 33 cm. The long, tapered mouthpipe of about 135 cm. occupies the whole of the first coil and crosses the bell leg to reach the slide. The construction could be very svelte, with tapered crooks, gauged thickness through the bell, and dissimilar metals in the slides to reduce wear by friction (as often today).

For orchestral use, in which all tonalities would be required, horns were mostly made in all Continental countries with independent mouthpipe crooks covering the whole range even up to C alto and handy for constant crook changes; the slide was retained as a tuning slide. The place and time of origin of this system is still in doubt, but complete sets of crooks survive with early nineteenth-century French, German and Austrian instruments. Table 6 lists the standard French crooks with a typical figure for the diameter of the coil of each. So often all but the F crook have failed to survive, instruments having been later converted to valve horns, and it is imperative today that every old crook is carefully preserved now that interest in the hand horn is returning. The crooks from F downwards are made in two or more lengths of tubing of which only the first, 60 to 80 cm. long, is carefully tapered, the rest being almost or entirely cylindrical.

The French horn alone, without crooks, has a tubing of some

Table 6

*French horn crooks, standard outfit of ten, with average mean
width across inside of coil in centimetres.*

Rare extra items included in *italics*. (Very rare—high B natural—
omitted.)

			Approx. length
B♮ alto (SB, SIB, = si bémol)	one-coil,	7	45
A (LA)	,,	13	65
A♭ (LA♭)	,,	17	83
G (SOL)	,,	24	102
F♯ (FA♯)	*two-coil*	*14*	*122*
F (FA)	two-coil	18	142
E (MD, = mi dièse)	,,	21	165
E♭ (MB, DIS)	,,	24	189
D (RE)	three-coil,	18	220
coupler to D crook for D♭, 8			*26*
D♭ (RE♭)	*three-coil,*	*21*	*240*
C (UT)	three-coil,	24	270
coupler (SB) to C crook for B♭ basso, 16			62
B♮ basso (SB)	*four-coil,*	*22*	*330*

225 cm. (a little greater than that of the D crook alone) and will
permit the rare crooking in C alto; for this, players are said to have
used a cornet A shank, lapped with paper to fit the socket of the
horn. Since a certain amount of the fixed tubing is consumed by
the tuning slide, the build of the French horn is in a single coil,
but many early nineteenth-century English and German instruments are made in two small coils—and may require a piece
of dummy tubing to complete one of the circles. The rather confusing makers' terminology of the classical period may be clarified
by extracts from two price-lists of the mid-1820s. First, of the
Malines firm of Tuerlinckx, reprinted in the *Bulletin du Cercle
archéologique de Malines*, 1914; second, of B. Schott, Mainz, printed in *Caecilia*, 1825, in French for their Antwerp branch. (Added
words in German are from contemporary Schott lists in that
language. *Coulisse* or *Pumpe* = slide; *ton* = crook.)

Tuerlinckx: *Walthörens*:

Cor à coulisse, tous les tons de B haut à B bas.

Cor à coulisse. B haut, F et C, un ton et un demiton, faisant tous
les tons.

Cor solo, Fa, mi dièze, et mi♭ doré [? = et ré]

Cor sans coulisse en Es.
Cor de Chasse à 3 tours
   „   à 2 tours
embouchures argent, ivoire ou cuivre.

Schott:
   Cors d'Invention:
      avec 9 tons à coulisse de Si haut jusqu'au Si bas
         (*Bogen auf die Pumpe*)
      avec 9 tons à l'embouchure de si haut à si bas
      avec 5 tons à l'embouchure de ut à ut bas
   Cors simples:
      avec 4 tons à l'embouchure
      en Fa, Mi ou Re
      de Chasseurs, grand (*Grosse Jagdhorn*).

Note.- *Cor à coulisse*: in Tuerlinckx, orchestral horn with mouth-pipe crooks and tuning slide, the second (cheaper) model having whole-tone and semitone couplers somewhat on the lines of the old master-crook system. Schott's list shows how *Inventions-horn* covers equally models with slide crooks (*tons à coulisse*) and those with mouthpipe crooks (*tons à l'embouchure*).

A few words on hand-horn technique are now due to those who are wholly unfamiliar with it. The normal position of the hand is with the fingers close together against the far side of the bell and with the thumb close against them. The hand is a little cupped (indicated below by *o*) and can then be straightened flat (indicated by *O*) to sharpen harmonics like h7, needed for B flat. This slightly-closed normal position also helps to equalize the quality of open and stopped notes. The fingers are never moved from this position in the bell. Some methods recommend resting the bell on the thigh, e.g. Gallay (Fig. 28). Increased cupping of the hand flattens harmonics by the various amounts required, e.g. h11 by half a semitone for *f″*, h8 by a semitone for *b′*, and (difficult, but in the curriculum) h5 by the smaller whole-tone for *d′*. Lastly, closing the bell completely, to raise a harmonic by a semitone (indicated below by +, in tutors by 1 or black spot).

The classic range is upwards from *e′* flat, where no whole-tone stopping is necessary. German instructions are very straightforward, with as far as possible a single instruction for each note, as Fröhlich and, later in the century, Richard Hofman and also early editions of Otto Langey's Tutor (London, Rivière & Hawkes):

b''	o or O	$a\flat'$	+ (O may be preferred in
$b\flat''$	O		slow passages after g')
a''	½	$f\sharp'$	½
$a\flat''$	+ (½)	f'	+
$f\sharp''$	½ (o is admissable in fast	$e\flat'$	½
	passages)	d'	+ (in later sources ½)
f''	¼	$c\sharp'$	+
$e\flat''$	½	b	½
$c\sharp''$	½	$b\flat, a, g\sharp$	+
b'	½	$f\sharp$	½
$b\flat'$	O	f, e	+ (or o, lipped down)
a'	½ [better expressed as ¼]	$e\flat, d, c\sharp$	+

Fig. 28. J. F. Gallay, *Méthode pour le Cor*, *c.* 1845. Cor-solo, F crook.

French instructions, of which Morley-Pegge gives a synoptic table (p. 101), on the whole make more of fully-stopping (+) on notes like a'', a'' flat, f'', e'' flat, d'' flat. Duvernoy (1803) gives these exclusively, but later methods stress them less. Morley-Pegge, who was himself trained at the Conservatoire in its hand-horn tradition, almost entirely used the partial stoppings on these notes. The methods, both French and German, allow certain fakes in fast passages, as in Ex. 31; in the third passage, the middle note of each triplet is to be made always in the same manner as the note before and after it (i.e. not as in Ex. 28).

Ex. 31 Domnich, *Méthode de Premier et de Second Cor*, 1808; some expedients for fast passages.

A special instruction in most tutors is to make the low A flat between Gs, and D flat between Cs, in slow tempi, as wide-open sounds, while cupping the hand more than normally for the G or C. The small resulting semitone fitted a concept of leading notes (*notes sensibles*) with which the Conservatoire professors, woodwind also, were much occupied, i.e. sharpened leading-notes, and flattened minor sixths (*sensibles descendantes*). With this, a flat comes lower than its enharmonic sharp, the opposite to Meantone. The cause of this reversal of earlier principles remains to be properly investigated, but the two concepts are not mutually exclusive, the one being concerned with horizontal (melodic) intonation and the other mainly with vertical (chords, keeping the natural major third), and a good musician's ears are alert to both.

In many Conservatoire horn methods sharps and flats are given distinct instructions, like:

g'' sharp, O (h13) but a'' flat, + (h12), a lower sound. But in instances like d'' sharp, ¾ (h10) as against e'' flat,+ (h9) the difference seems to be sought also in colour, the brighter sound for an ascending interval with the sharp and the muter with the flat. Dauprat's directions (1824), given in the form of scales in different keys, are evidently a corollary of this, examples being as follows (ascending, as written for horn):

C major from c'': o o o + o + O o
E♭ major from $e♭'$: ¼ + o + O o o +
from $e♭''$: + + o + O o o +

D major from *d′*:	¾	o	¼	o	¼	¼	¼	o				
from *d″*:	o	o	¾	o	¾	O	O	o				
F♯ harmonic minor from *f*♯′:	¼	½	¼	¼	¼	O	O	¾	O	¾	O	O
E major from *e′*:	O	¼	½	¼	¼	¼	¼	O	¾	O	¾	O

The A flat major scale has of course become famous through Beethoven's Ninth Symphony, with which Dauprat's *Méthode* is contemporary. Whether the original players of the 4th Horn part (i.e. second horn of the E flat pair) observed a French succession of fully-stoppings, or preferred calmer-toned partial stoppings, one cannot say. Either way it must have had a magical effect. Thus the critic after the second performance, in Aachen, 1825: 'the wind instruments breathe out a heavy sorrow, and the horn in particular sounds a deeply melancholy appeal, so that everything appears to combine in uttering a silently-weeping lament'. Much later, a correspondent in *Musical Opinion* in 1892 remembered how the passage was so much more effective when he had heard it performed with the hand than when played with valves. (The question whether the elder Lewy may have used his valved horn in Vienna to transpose the scale into hand-stopped G major, by changing valve, is discussed in Blandford, 1925.)

The differences in quality between open and stopped sounds were minimized almost to vanishing point by skill in blowing, moderating the strength of the former where necessary and particularly, stressed in both French and German sources, not forcing the stopped notes (except in the occasional *sf*). Thus the hand-horn was played at a moderate dynamic level when passages contained stopped notes. The dynamic contrast in the first two phrases of Beethoven's Sonata (written for Punto) is observed by the hornist today because it is in the music, but by the hand-hornist because it is in the instrument also. The slow movement of this work, incidentally, provides a very suitable moment for re-acclimatising audiences to the sounds which classical composers heard as they wrote, for which the modern horn can be used without the valves effectively if not ideally.

A problem arose with the hand-horn over stopped passages marked *con sordino*. At the end of the Beethoven *Rondino*, for example, a non-transposing mute is needed, and with any ordinary form of this (precluding use of the hand) the 2nd Horn can sound the low *b* in falset. But the 1st Horn needs a special mute introduced by Türrschmidt and described by Fröhlich and by

Fitzpatrick, with a stopping ball inside the mute on the end of a rod.

POST-HORN AND BUGLE

From the time when state mail services began to operate in the fifteenth century (among the earliest were those in France and Venice), the postal courier would announce his arrival and impending departure by a distinctive call on a small horn, curved or looped. In the seventeenth-century Nuremberg trumpet-makers' apprentices were allowed to try their hand first in making such things (Fig. 29, above). For the signal, at any rate in Germany, the *Postillons* had appropriated to themselves the interval of the octave, as in Ex. 25 and imitated on other instruments by Bach and Telemann (copied by Handel in *Belshazzar*) on the same two

Fig. 29 Above Austrian Post-courier, 1648. **Below** from *City Scenes, or a Peep at London*, anon., c. 1814.

notes, *b'* flat and *b"* flat, representing h1 and 2 of a one-coil horn measuring as little as 3 inches across the outside (7·5 cm.). A copper example at Munich (Bayer. Nat. Museum) is engraved with a mail coach-and-four and the scene of a hare-hunt on the brass garland and the two notes sound modern-pitch *a'* and *a"*. After this period the post-horn became longer-tubed, pitched in or below 4-foot C and built in several tapered coils, still no wider than the palm of the hand; S. Halle wrote that one often saw it carried on the whip handle. The octave now came to be sounded in a more leisurely manner, but carrying farther, on h2–4, or h3–6, and perhaps with a cheerful tune joined to it (Ex. 32b). This is the instrument to be visualized where Mozart requires the horn-players of an orchestra to change to post-horns, as in the Serenade K.320 (here in A) and in the *Deutsche Tanz* K.605 No. 3 with the 'Sleigh Journey', where the F post-horn may well have been a deeper-pitched instrument, not merely the B flat post-horn with an F crook.

Ex. 32 a. Post-horn call, Germany, 19th century; b. *Marcia* for post-horn and orchestra, c. 1778 (British Museum, Add. MS 32173).

In Germany and Austria after 1800 the common keys were F and E flat (Fig. 30). The octave call now vanished from the tunes, as in Ex. 32a, said to have been a great favourite with the public during the last century[1]. Meanwhile in France, Gevaert recalled: 'How many of us over fifty do not nostalgically remember from childhood the little *cornet de poste* with its cheerful sound which enlivened the tedium of a stay in a country town, bringing the bored townsfolk to their doors as the postboy tore by, hoofs shaking the paving of the street'. The instrument was given solos in band

[1] A page of Prussian calls reproduced by Heinitz (p. 69) from F. Gumbert's *Posthorn-Schule* includes this call and others all written between *g* and *c"*, some very much as quoted by Beethoven (*Deutsche Tanz*, Woo.8 No.12: 'Cornetto' in C) and Schubert ('Die Post', *Winter-reise*, in the key of E flat).

and *Harmonie* music, as in Spohr's Notturno Op. 34 (1815) with post-horn in F in the *Polacca*, range h3–6. Schott advertised band and dance arrangements with solos for one and two post-horns, and these might require crooks. Also, to entertain passengers on the coaches, post-horns were obtainable with the mechanisms then coming into use on other brass instruments. To quote Schott's list:

Cors de postillon:
    Cornet en Ut (*also* en Fa, en Re)
    Cornet à coulisse, avec 4 tons
        ,,   ,,   en forme de trompette
    Cornet avec 5 clefs.

Examples of all these exist in collections; also, from the mid century, post-horns with valves—virtually circular cornets—and such is Mahler's *Posthorn in B* in the Third Symphony, in a neat piece of brass painting as its tune retreats into the distance and the F trumpet breaks in *forte* and 'schmetternd wie eine Fanfare'.

Some nineteenth-century German post-horns have a 'transposing hole', a small fingerhole placed where it will, when uncovered, transpose the harmonic series upwards by a fourth, to sound perfectly clearly though with some loss of amplitude. The Bavarian instrument illustrated (Pl. X) is in 6-foot F, four-coil (14 cm. across outside), with 13 cm. bell and total tube 175 cm. including mouthpiece. The bore is lightly tapered and the hole is oval, 9 × 8 mm., the perforation slightly raised by a brass surround and centered 119·5 cm. from the mouthpiece—a shorter distance then might be expected for subdominant transposition, but it works. By alternately opening and closing the hole a useful scale for tune-making is obtained from (sounding) *a'* upwards, e.g. using the hole-open *b'* flat as keynote and closed h7 for *e''* flat. Sometimes the hole is covered by a key, or it can be shut off by turning a sleeve. On instruments which can be lowered by a crook a second hole may be provided to suit the increased tube-length.

In England the post-horn was developed differently, changed from the small coil (shown in Bull's trade card which is reproduced in Langwill's *Index* p. 20) to the straight form of the English hunting horn and at first of about the same length (Fig. 29, below). From around the 1840s it was made longer, 70–75 cm., kept in a wicker basket by the guard's seat (Fig. 30). The pitch was largely settled at A flat to suit cornet-players' use in band concerts, the

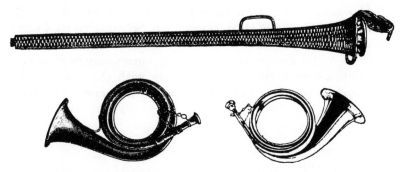

Fig. 30 Left to right German post-horn in E flat, 19th cent.; Prince-Pless hunting horn, B flat (see p. 175). **Above** English post-horn in basket.

post-horn key matching, in the octave above, the then favourite cornet crook. Koenig's famous Galop ('Post Boy's Return', 1844) reflects the common currency of post-horn and the contemporary bugle calls, though the former were not regularly taken above h4. The calls in Ex. 33a are from the 1890s. The 'coach horn' (Ex. 33b,

Ex. 33 a. English post-horn signals: *i* 'The Start', *ii* 'Clear the Road', *iii* 'Change Horses', *iv* 'The Post Horn Call'. **b.** Two 'Original Coach Horn Flourishes'. (From Turner's *Complete Tutor*.)

with a strong flavour of regimental bugle calls) of copper or brass, usually with a bugle-profile bell, varied in length from 3 feet (also called 'tandem' horn, as used from the same period with gigs drawn by a pair of horses in tandem) up to 4 feet (or 'drag' horn, used with some of the heavy mails even up to the first world war, and even more by coaching clubs). Today these instruments must be firmly distinguished from the various copper objects manu-factured for the hotel and antique trades. For a similar market in Germany and Switzerland the coiled post-horn is now manufactured, usually from stock cylindrical tube and the bell engraved with the name of some fictitious postal route of the past.

Infantry cornets. To the virtually new military arm born in the eighteenth century, namely the Sharp-shooter or *Jäger-corps*, recruited in Germany from forest communities, marksmen to a man, fell the function of harassing the enemy from the woods, clad in a uniform of dull camouflage green, armed with their hunting weapon the rifle, and equipped for communication with the horn of the forester which in one shape or another has been the emblem of Light Infantry ever since. Small horns, seldom carried in warfare since the fifteenth century (Pl. IV), thus come on the scene as regulation military instruments, first mentioned in Hanoverian sources of the time of the Seven Years' War. One is the U-shaped *Halbmond* described below. The other (likewise to be seen among old German sets of tin soldiers) is a coiled horn, a little larger than a post-horn and similarly held forwards, bell upwards. Specimens are difficult to identify among the various small horns, hunting and other, which were made in Germany but they are generally two-coil, about 24 cm. across inside, with 15 to 17 cm. bell and pitch of 8-foot C or D. The sockets are wide as if for a bugle-like mouthpiece. In England too, the Light Cavalry, who fought largely on foot, are said to have adopted in 1761 'horns like those of postboys' (Grose, *Military Antiquities*, 1788). During the Napoleonic wars these small military instruments, in French called *cornet*, were much in evidence right across Europe from the Netherlands to Italy, usually with *Chasseur* or *Jäger* regiments (Pl. X) though also with artillery. Tuerlinckx lists under 'Trumpets' a *cornet sans coulisse* in E flat, probably this type of instrument. It went out of use everywhere by about 1850 following a swing in favour of the bugle.

Bugle. The Hanoverian *Halbmond* ('half-moon') is normally of copper shaped in a rather ungainly 'U', with leather cross-straps by which it was raised for blowing, very much in the manner of a Roman small *cornu*. The pitch is D, an octave above the D trumpet. The prototype is the old *Flügelhorn* of the princely hunt (Fig. 24), of which an example by Werner, 1733, is in the Brussels Collection (illustrated in *Grove*, 5th edn., 'Bugle'). The military version appears in Hanoverian records of 1758 in association with a mixed corps of Light Troops organized by Capt. von Scheiter and supplied with a handsome variety of military music: H.Q. with six *Hautboisten* (band) and the Drum-major; squadron of horse with 2 trumpets; Grenadier company with 5 *Tambours* and fifer; and the Jäger company with 2 *Halbmondbläser* (von Sichart, III, p. 16ff.).

The *Halbmond* arrived in England before the end of the war under the name 'bugle horn'. Robert Hinde, when a retired officer in 1778, set down the drill for Light Troop's evolutions with almost a Byzantine emphasis on obedience to the sound of different instruments, for example (p. 290): 'At signal of Trumpet, centre divisions front and halt.... Signal of Bugle horn, skirmishers join their divisions, and the centre moves briskly up, and the whole charges in line and halts; signal of French horn, centre divisions retire, and the rear rank of the flank divisions should skirmish in front immediately, and remain in front till the Bugle Horn sounds'.

The English bugle calls themselves were first taken over from Hanover, where the code (given by Kastner, 1848, as it was in 1821) shows signs of affiliation to hunting calls. The code of the German hunting *Flügelhorn* is not itself recorded, but it must be at least partly preserved in Germany where the *Halbmond* is still the traditional instrument for the hunt. The chief region for this is Sauerland, to the east of the Ruhr, where game is hunted on foot with a pack of *Bracke* hounds. Old half-moons are prized above the new ones that can be sought in shops. Among the calls used by the Deutscher Bracken-Club, communicated by the late Dr. Joseph Zimmermann, the 'Set forth' (Ex. 34a) is the same as our bugle call 'Rouse'—an archetypal kind of call further imitated

Ex. 34 a. *Brackenjagd*, 'Aufbruch zur Jagd'; b. ditto, 'Wild tot' (Deutscher Bracken-Club, Olpe i.W./Sauerlandt). c. *Trompe de chasse* fanfare 'L'Hallali sur pied'; d. Hanoverian bugle Reveille (after Kastner; also a greeting call for Prince-Pless Horn).

in the post-horn 'Start' (Ex. 33a). The Brackenjagd 'Game killed' (34b) does not appear among the bugle calls but is interesting for its strong flavour of the herdsman and its resemblance to tunes made on the shorter alphorns (Ex. 6f). Yet other *Halbmond* and bugle calls are founded on existing diatonic tunes by substituting an e'' for an unobtainable d'' and so on, much in the manner of some of the early trumpet sonatas (Ex. 14). On the Sauerland *Halbmond* the continuation of Ex. 34a seems to parody a celebrated French air in this way. Earlier than this, the 'Halali sur pied' of the *trompe de chasse* code was borrowed by the Hanoverian bugler for a Reveille (Ex. 34,c,d); traces of this adaptation endure among our Rifle Brigade calls still.

Over most of Germany the hunting *Halbmond* or equivalent instrument became widely replaced during the later nineteenth century by the circular brass horn in two or three coils of bugle-like bore wound with green cloth, known as 'Prince Pless horn' after a Silesian nobleman who was Master of the Prussian hunt and a close friend of Kaiser William I. He is said to have preferred a smoother sound than the somewhat barking tone of the *Halbmond*. The Pless horn (Fig. 30) is in B flat and sounded bell-upwards. The repertory, published in many booklets, preserves the custom of a call for every quarry and includes composed tunes for pauses in the hunt. For the latter it may be supplied with valves. Some hunting people disapprove of this, but the Grand Duke of the Palatinate before the 1914 war had a band of circular 'hunting cornets' which played waltzes in the woods during the luncheon interval.

About 1800 the English military bugle-horn in *Halbmond* form was remodelled in bell-front trumpet form, perhaps by William Shaw of London by whom examples in both half-moon and folded form exist. Pitched in C (with a B flat crook for playing with bands) this became official in 1812 and was soon afterwards adopted on the Continent where it remains a standard type of bugle in, for example, France (*clairon*). The compact twice-looped British bugle in B flat became official after the Crimean War and has also been used abroad, while some German hunting bugles are made in the same format, or even smaller, in three loops like the horn for the elk hunt in Sweden (Pl. X). The British military calls are published in *Trumpet and Bugle Calls for the Army* (Ministry of Defence). Many remain much as they were in the late eighteenth century, but there was a certain amount of reciprocity between bugle and trumpet calls in most European states during the nineteenth century. For instance Suppé's overture *Light Cavalry* begins with the bugle adaptation of the older Austrian trumpet 'Retreat'.

Bugle bands date from the Napoleonic wars. Hyde's *Preceptor*, written for the War Office, includes some examples of the music, observing the usual bugle harmony. Detachable valves, offered by Distin in 1855, enjoyed a temporary success in 'Chromatic bugle bands'. More lasting use was found for models with a single valve (possibly an idea of Pelitti, Milan). This usually lowers by a fourth, giving a diatonic octave after a fashion; or it may lower by a whole tone, to give a scale which again lacks the written *a'* (a third below the keynote). The valve is often fitted to the American trumpet-like bugle in G; also sometimes to German E flat fanfare-trumpets, here apparently to raise the pitch to the B flat above.

Russian Horns. In order that huntsmen should sound concordant whilst signalling to each other, Prince Narishkin, Master of the Hunt to the Empress of Russia, in 1751 caused to be made sixteen metal horns tuned to a chord of D. At that time in service with the court at St. Petersburg was the Bohemian horn-player Maresch (who is said to have later experimented with a bitonic compound horn; see Fitzpatrick, 1970, p. 101). To Maresch the count entrusted the task of developing the harmonious new hunting horns

Ex. 35 A. F. Anacker, *Bergmannsgruss*, Funeral march for Russian horns.

into a musical band. After an abortive initial scheme (described by Seaman, p. 93) Maresch decided upon a set of one-note horns, which together provided a scale of C over several octaves, each of thirty-two men sounding his note as his turn came. No doubt for economy, the horns were made as straight conical tubes, sharply bent round at the narrow end close to the cup-shaped mouthpiece. The band performed at a Grand Hunt concert in 1757. Ricks (1969) reproduces the full score of a march from a work published in 1796; semiquaver runs are but one feature of what these men were forced into achieving.

The Russian horn band created a fashion which spread to other countries and lasted up to the 1830s, when the idea was continued among workmen's bands in the East of Germany. Here, whether as a further economy or whether to give the players something more interesting to do, each horn was used both for the note and its octave, and also, except with the largest sizes, hand-stopped for one or both semitones below. Ex. 35 is an example from an opera of pre-1834 by A. F. Anacker, 'the miners' friend'.

SEVEN

Transitional Methods

——

SLIDE TRUMPETS OF THE BAROQUE

Identification of the eighteenth-century German *Zugtrompete* hinges on two things: the reasonable certainty that a trumpet with sliding mouthpipe had existed in earlier times (Chap. 4); and one actual baroque specimen which acts on the same principle. This last is not from Nuremberg, whence there is not a whisper of a slide trumpet after the sixteenth century, but from the Wenzelskirche in Naumburg, Saxony, from which the Berlin Collection obtained the instrument in 1890 along with a plain trumpet and numerous other wind instruments. Both trumpets are by Veit of Naumburg and that with the sliding mouthpipe is dated 1651 (Pl. VII). Its main tube is wide, 12·7 mm. in outside diameter; the mouthpipe, now a replacement of the much-corroded original, is 11·5 mm. with bore 10·6 mm. (matching average Nuremberg dimensions for a normal trumpet). The extension allows two tones in comfort but not more, and the pitch is Chorton D. The church's inventory of 1658 (A. Werner, p. 415) mentions 2 *Zugtrompete, ganz neu*. Seven years from 1651 may not match 'quite new' though there could be several explanations for this, and the entry can reasonably be taken to confirm that the Veit instrument represents what a *Zugtrompete* was then and later; the two instruments are in fact listed again, in 1728, as still serviceable (ibid).

The italianate expression *tromba da tirarsi* (cf. modern Italian *trombone a tiro*, slide trombone) occurs only in cantatas written in Leipzig by Kuhnau and Bach before about 1723. During the period of these, *Zugtrompete* is mentioned in Leipzig documents as an instrument of the town players. Otherwise there is peculiarly little mention of the instrument, though Altenburg (p. 12) says that town musicians customarily used it. Identification of *tromba da tirarsi* with *Zugtrompete* thus seems reasonable.

Ex. 36 shows some passages from Kuhnau's cantata (listed No. 26 in *DDT*, LVIII–LIX, p. xlvi); the part is headed *Obboe overo tromba da tirarsi* and seems very good *Zugtrompete* music, combining normal clarino passages in the high register with the diatonic chorale in the lower. Possibly it was played by Reiche, who left a *Zugtrompete* among his effects on his death in 1734.

Ex. 36 Kuhnau, Cantata No. 26. Two passages for 'Oboe or Tromba da tirarsi'. (D trumpet written at sounding pitch.)

Some of Bach's non-natural trumpet parts, whether or not '*da tirarsi*' is written on them, are very difficult, and it has often been suggested that the intended instrument was the smallest trombone, *Discant-posaune*, known by several eighteenth-century specimens of which the earliest was actually made in Leipzig in 1733 by J. G. Eichentopf, the town's leading maker of both woodwind and brass instruments. A later example, *c.* 1770, from the Swedish Royal Chapel (Stockholm Collection, Pl. VII) stands in about modern B flat, probably a choir-pitch A. The bell diameter, 83 mm., is less than in a contemporary trumpet or alto trombone; slide bore is 10 mm. and the length of inner slide, 21 cm., allows a two-tone extension, sufficient for the ordinary compass of a chorale. But in Leipzig, as Terry has pointed out (p. 36), it seems that this is all that the discant trombone was required for. Bach's successor Doles, auditioning candidates for a *Stadtpfeifer* vacancy, refers to ability on *Zugtrompete* for the *concertirende Choral* (the difficult part) and also on the four trombones including *Discant* for the *simpel Choral*; one example of the latter may be in Cantata 21. Since a discant trombone in A has a semitone shift of 4 cm. against the 13 cm. of a *Zugtrompete* in D, this seems at first paradoxical. But the shorter tube allows no clarino register. Also very small movements of the wrist are difficult to control at speed and have in subsequent history proved an obstacle to wide adoption of the smallest trombone, whether described as 'soprano' or 'canto', or nowadays as 'slide trumpet' by jazzmen who have occasionally experimented with it.

Probably the new research on Bach's scores and parts now being undertaken by Alfred Dürr and the *Neue Bach Ausgabe* will disclose the extent to which Bach's non-natural, non-'tirarsi', trumpet parts were meant for *Zugtrompete*. Meanwhile it would be rash to say too much, or equally about the still outstanding mystery of the *corno da tirarsi* parts in early cantatas: Nos. 46 (*tromba o corno*), 67 and 162. It has to be proved which copyist penned the words *da tirarsi* and when. In No. 162 the part is added to an older version and runs mostly with the viola. But in Nos. 46 and 67 the parts appear to be written very purposefully for a diatonic instrument which on the face of it was played in Cammerton C with a Chorton orchestra playing in A in one case and in B flat in the other; or else was itself pitched in Chorton A or B flat, which would indeed suggest a horn. Many diatonic parts written by Bach himself and headed *Corno* are scarcely less perplexing. The period seems too early for hand-stopping and anyway the parts are not in character with the early exhibitions of this technique so far as they are known; nor is abbreviation of 'Cornetto' a fully convincing solution. A slide horn is not, of course, an impossibility. An easy-moving slide arranged like a tuning slide would have to be moved only 9 cm. for a semitone on a horn in A. In Leipzig, Eichentopf was certainly an enterprising maker, but the two extant horns by him, dated 1735 and 1738, are of the usual crookless kind of the period. Yet no slide horn is actually described until 1812, when the *Allgemeine musikalische Zeitung* (col. 761–2) reports a hand-horn with a playing slide by Dickhuth, Mannheim. His slide could be pulled back 'half a span' by the left thumb against a clock spring. The writer of the report quotes the *ff* theme in the Finale of the Eroica Symphony as an instance where the device might be used advantageously and also observes that bad hand-notes like *d'* would become semitone stops with the help of the slide.

Flat trumpet. From France two neat drawings by Cellier, *c.* 1585, of the instruments of cornett and shawm bands show above '*Sacqueboutte, basse-contre*' not a trombone but an instrument of trumpet shape which differs from a normal trumpet through the presence of a stay at a little distance from the rear bow (*GSJ* X, Pl. VII and p. 88; also Jeans and Oldham, *GSJ* XIII, p. 26). Basse-contre parts in the music of those bands occupy a diatonic compass upwards from *c*, so that this trumpet must have had a slide, while the stay possibly suggests that this may not have been of the 'Renaissance' type but a backwards-drawing rear bow. Fifty years later Mersenne alludes rather sarcastically to experiments in applying the form of the sackbut to the trumpet, but he discloses no details. Then, more than fifty years later again, comes the English 'Flat Trumpet', of which Talbot's description (*GSJ* I, pp. 21–2) may be paraphrased thus. 'The mouthpiece stands obliquely towards the right. The rear bow is by the left ear and by it [there is no mention of a stay] you draw out the slide, of which one leg reaches inside the bell branch as far as the boss; the other reaches outside the lower branch as far as the front bow and measures 58 cm. from the end of the rear bow ferrule. When closed the size is the same as that of the ordinary trumpet.' The accompanying chart shows a chromatic compass from c to c''' for a trumpet in C.

Musically this flat trumpet, so-called from its capacity for minor keys, is known by two short pieces by Purcell, printed and discussed by Squire (1903, p. 225). One occurs in music for *The Libertine*, probably for the revival of this play in 1692: Don Juan's arrival in the infernal regions is heralded by a solemn piece in four-part homophony headed 'Flatt Trumpets' (British Museum, Add. 5333). The other is in music for the funeral of Queen Mary in 1695 (Oriel College MS). This includes the same piece as in the play and also a *Canzona* on the same theme, headed simply 'Tremulo' and descending to B flat in the fourth part (Ex. 37).

Ex. 37 Purcell, 'Canzona. As it was sounded in the Abbey after the Anthem' (Oriel College MS, after Barclay Squire).

Both of these contexts, descent to hell and funeral lament, were then properly for trombones, for which there had been no regular players in the King's Music since Charles II, and Talbot evidently did not find a complete set among the profession in London. However, it has been suggested by Halfpenny (1951, p. 110) that two former sackbuttists of the royal music, Fittz and Flower, are shown playing flat trumpets along with a cornettist in the coronation procession of James II (1685) among the engravings in Sandford's *History* of the event. The instrument here does not quite match Talbot's description, but the design could have been altered in the interim.

Nothing further is heard of the flat trumpet as such. Yet the appearance of a modified version late in the eighteenth century shows that the profession had not wholly forgotten it. John Hyde and a maker Woodham claimed to have invented this 'Chromatic Trumpet' which became under the name 'Slide Trumpet' a celebrated orchestral and solo instrument in England through much of the nineteenth century. Many fine examples are by Köhler, London, who (as the younger Harper told Blandford) took early eighteenth-century trumpets by Harris as his model— or possibly Harris trumpets which had already been converted to slide trumpet, as with specimens which still exist; one is now on loan to the Bate Collection, Oxford. The slide is drawn back with the second and third fingers by a finger-piece fixed to a telescopic rod, and returns by means of a length of gut, such as violin D or A string, wound three or four times round the drum of a clockspring enclosed in a brass spring box, a duplicate box containing a spare spring. From the 1840s the clock-spring began to be replaced, at first by a rather unsatisfactory spiral spring and then by an elastic rubber cord, evidently an idea of Harper junior. The travel is about 9 cm. in early specimens, increasing to 11 or 12 cm. in later models, theoretically just short of a whole-tone on the D crook, though players were certainly able to play f' (sounding g') with this crook. The main intention was to correct intonation: Hyde refers in his *Preceptor* to Burney's criticism of the fourth and sixth in the natural scale. However, Cudworth's examination of Vauxhall Gardens musical programmes (*GSJ* XX, pp. 31ff.) indicates that the slide trumpet may have already been used by Sarjant in 1790 and not only to correct intonation, for though he performed the 'March in Scipio', in which he might have left non-natural phrases to the accompanying orchestra, he also played the Aria 'Se l'arco' from *Admeto*, which would be musically futile without playing the vocal line, and this has a plagal compass requiring a' and b' (regarding the trumpet as in C).

The *Preceptor* includes various diatonic arrangements like 'Drink to me only' as a duet in the key of A (for the D crook) and some Irish melodies in the same key. Epoch-making though these are in the general history of brass playing, a more interesting arrangement is that of 'God save the Queen' in the elder Harper's Tutor (*c.* 1836, see Ex. 38). Here, besides the two slide trumpets,

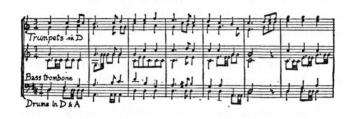

Ex. 38 'God Save the King', in Harper's *Instructions for the Trumpet, c.* 1836.

are two natural parts, the lower with a very Teutonic *schmetternd*, while the trombone disputes with the kettledrums on the bass line. The next example, 39, illustrates what could be done on the slide

Ex. 39 Harper's *Instructions for the Trumpet*, part of a study by Norton for slide trumpet.

trumpet technically, at least with the crooks down to D (their normal range was down to C; for lower tonalities required by classical works crooks were coupled as they were on the plain trumpet, though some instruments have with them separate crooks down to low A). Among the great soloists, Hyde junior, Norton, the two Harpers, were succeeded by McGrath and in later Victorian times by Morrow and by John Solomon, a great artist whom many still remember though not on slide trumpet. Through the Handelian favourites repeatedly performed by these men, solo and in oratorio, England may claim to be the country in which obbligato clarino playing continued longest in the concert room without interruption—that is until Morrow and Solomon changed to valve trumpets for such parts about 1890. Of Harper senior, his 'smooth, silvery, unforced sound' may be fittingly added beside earlier comments on clarinists, as those quoted in chapter 5.

The slide trumpet was one of the English instruments to be noticed and copied in Paris after the peace of 1815. The French, however, reversed the position of the slide, bringing it to the front, drawing forwards. There were two patents in 1821, the first, by Legram of the Guards, allowing a 16 cm. extension (tone and a half on the G crook). Later on the slide was much reduced in width to clear the bell (Fig. 31, b), with 25 cm. travel, and a tuning slide placed in the rear bow. Dauverné recommended this in preference to the valve trumpet on account of its potentially superior intonation. Courtois was still offering this instrument after the mid century, but with little success, probably for the reasons mentioned earlier in connection with the soprano trombone.

HAND-STOPPING ON TRUMPETS

During the last third of the eighteenth-century endeavours to complete the scale of natural instruments were prosecuted with a new and steady determination from London to St. Petersburg by musicians, professional and amateur, some of them skilled mechanics like clock-makers, and all, particularly in Germany, encouraged by local musical circles and the appreciative interest of an increasing number of widely-read musical journals. Among them were trumpet-players experimenting with side-holes and keys, and also exploring the possibilities of hand-stopping the bell. Not surprisingly the old clarino music itself was wearing thin as composers and players alike felt a growing boredom with its stereotyped, out-of-date, thematic scope; it was in a fresh idiom based mainly upon the perpetually evocative *principale* that natural trumpets kept a place in the Classical orchestra. But even an old and devoted member of the Guild like Altenburg hoped for extension of the instrument's musical powers in new directions. His criticism of makers for failing to discover how the defective intonation might be corrected, and his favourable expectancy of a

complete low register in the future (pp. 111–12) show tha
the aim of his great book was to set down the history
ancient art he was no enemy of innovation.

Hand-stopping he does not mention. Yet there had been positive news of it in a *Reformierte Trompete* invented by Michael
Woeggel of Carlsruhe and performed on by him in 1774 when he
was twenty-six. Junker's Musical Almanach of 1782–3 describes

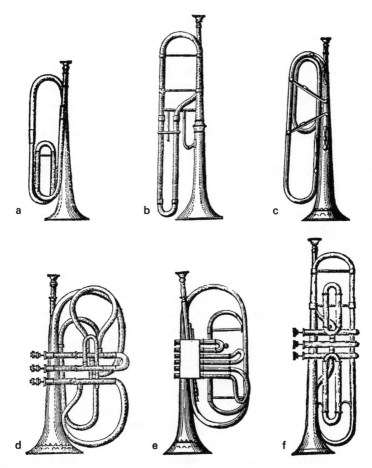

Fig. 31 From Dauverné, *Méthode pour la Trompette* (not in original
order). **a.** Trompette d'harmonie, for crooks from G downwards; **b.** slide
trumpet, French system, in B flat; **c.** 'Italian keyed trumpet', German
system; **d.** trumpet with 3 valves, Stoelzel system, model sent to France
by Spontini in 1826; **e.** valve trumpet, German system; **f;** valve trumpet,
French system (Périnet).

in the affable style of this journal how Woeggel curved the trumpet somewhat downwards and brought the crooks to the side so that he could more comfortably and securely, like the hornist with his hand in the bell, 'apply the shades of his painting . . . these happy alterations have brought the trumpet very close to the human voice without taking away its heroic war-cry; in short, it has won grace without losing its vigour' (remarks which indicate that the *principale* register was mainly concerned). In a Stabat Mater by Schmittbauer, the Carlsruhe Kapellmeister, Woeggel played a vocal part, 'altering it only a little, handling his trumpet with knowledge and taste, and with special sweetness in the Adagio, in which he can better use his middle tints' (etc.). This all refers to the trumpet re-styled partially on hand-horn lines which became well known in the early nineteenth century, called in French *trompette courbée* or *trompette demilune* (Pl. XI). Of this, makers over the period 1800–40 are known in much of Europe but not apparently in England, Prussia or Austria. A dated example of 1802 is by Eschenbach, Markneukirchen (Berlin, 3027).

In 1787 Tuerlinckx supplied to a regiment a *trompet invention* with three crooks, along with eight clarinets (ranging from 'amour in F' to 'F octav'). This trumpet was perhaps not the *cromme trompet* (demilune) which appears in the firm's books for 1803 but a short-model trumpet with tuning slide (Fig. 31, a) of which an example by Haltenhof is known (Berlin 3034). Gerber mentions *Inventions* trumpets made around 1796 by Krause, instrument-maker to the Berlin court and a noted clarinist. They had slide crooks from A to F on which 'all semitones can be made with the hand as on a horn'. He does not describe the shape, but a trumpet by Krause dated 1793, picked up on the battlefield of Jena, is of this short model with slide crooks (Leipzig No. 1829). Evidently when the question of hand-stopping arose the two builds of the instrument might be regarded as alternatives, the demilune preferred in some regions and the short model in others.

Further extracts from Tuerlinckx and Schott give a shop-window view of trumpet models and terminology just after those times:

Tuerlinckx: *Trompetten*:
    Trompette d'ordonnance (*duty trumpet*)
    Trompette d'harmonie à coulisse, F ou Es
           ,,   F, Es, D, C, et B
           ,,   F, à clefs

Trompette d'harmonie courbée, de F à B
Trompette d'harmonie, B haut à B bas.
Schott:
  Trompettes d' Invention
    Avec 9 ou 10 tons à coulisse de si haut jusqu'au si bas
    Avec 6 ou 7 tons à l'embouchure, de sol jusqu'au si.
  Trompettes simple
    En Fa avec les tons de Mi♭, Re, Ut, et Si♭
    En Mi♭ avec les tons de Ut et Si♭
    En Fa ou Mi♭
  Trompette à 6 clefs et tons Fa, Mi♭, Re, Ut
  Trompette de Basse à coulisse en Fa avec les tons Mi♭, Ut, Si♭
              (*Basstrompete*)
    ,,   ,, ,, simple, en Fa ou Mi♭.

Of major importance both in connection with trumpet stopping
and in the post-eighteenth century advancement of brass instruments, was cavalry music, which in previous epochs had been
bound so rigidly to the splendid but primitive harmony of natural
trumpets all in one key with kettledrums below them. It then
found fresh directions: in France through the Revolution, and in
Germany through emancipation from the dying clutch of the
Imperial Guild, finally dissolved in 1815. In Prussia and parts of
Eastern Europe especially, the trumpet corps now became a
Trumpet Music, capable of some of the harmony and modulation
of other music by addition of trombone or serpent to the bass and
by combining natural trumpets of different sizes and pitches, discreetly employing hand-stopping on some of them. The little work
on military-band instrumentation by the Berlin clarinettist Sundelin (1828) does not specifically mention stopping but states that the

Ex. 40 Illustrations of hand-stopping on trumpet: **a.** Sundelin, 1828;
b. Bargans, *The Harmonicon*, 1830.

notes b, f', f' sharp, a', b' flat, b' and e'' flat may be written for the
1st Trumpet of a cavalry music in solos only, and that any good
player should manage phrases like those in Ex. 40a. This was
certainly by hand-stopping, which indeed can be quite effective.

The article by his fellow Berliner of the same period, the trumpeter Bargans (translated in the *Harmonicon*, 1830, pp. 23ff.), goes further, noticing how a short-model trumpet allows comfortable stopping with the hand and how one must try to equalize the strength of the notes. His scale includes three whole-tone stoppings *d'*, *f'*, and *g'* sharp marked 'very difficult', but a good Berlin player, he adds, would have no fear of a passage like Ex. 40b, played in the Royal Prussian Artillery without aid of either keys or valves. The passage itself may, from its smack of Spontini, come from the band's opera transcriptions, a field in which these cavalry bands won some renown later on.

Sundelin's trumpet in high C, or as more usually built in B flat (*B haut* in the first list above), is an earlier nineteenth-century innovation which enabled arpeggio figures played in the tonic key on the standard E flat cavalry trumpets to be answered in the dominant. Among early specimens are those with an all-silver trumpet-music outfit in the Army Museum, Brussels, made for a Cossack regiment in 1812–13. The trumpets range from high B flat (with crook for A flat) down to the thrice-looped bass trumpet in 13-foot E flat, while a double-slide bass trombone, the only chromatic instrument, completes the set. Ex. 41, from a set of trumpet *Aufzüge or Fanfares* by J. Küffner, *c*. 1815, shows how such instruments were used. All the trumpets are written in the old notation (*c'* = h4) so that the 'Alt Tromp. in B' (high B flat) sounds a seventh higher, or a sixth higher with the A flat crook (in *As*), while the ways in which the melody is thrown from one natural instrument to another may have been inspired by the methods of Russian horn bands of the time as much as by other uses of differently-pitched instruments as in Mozart's Divertimenti with five trumpets, K.187–8. The two bass trumpets in 9-foot B flat come early in the sequence of cavalry-band instruments of that pitch, later also made with valves. The 13-foot bass trumpet in E flat, at the bottom of the score with very little to do, corresponds to the last item in Schott's list above and has continued to be made up to the present, now known in Germany as a *Bassfanfare* for large fanfare teams. A thrice-looped example from Sax's factory is in the Paris Collection.

The sharps written for the smaller trumpets, *ff* in the *tutti*, might just conceivably have been produced in falset by some players, but Fröhlich for one is very dubious about the effectiveness of this above low *b*, while these pieces also include *b'* and *a'*

Ex. 41 J. Küffner, 10 *Trompeten-Aufzüge (Fanfares) für Militär Musik*, Offenbach a/Main, *c.* 1815. Quick March. (**Beneath** the melody at sounding pitch, indicating the trumpets concerned: 1st E flat, B flat alto, and A flat.)

for the leading E flat trumpets; use of the hand must therefore have been the composer's intention. Küffner's works were quite popular in France and the Netherlands as well as in Germany, and bandmasters must have been reasonably satisfied with the results of scores such as this, probably helped in the former countries by demilunes for the medium trumpets. In the parallel context of *Jäger* 'horn music', Neefe (1896) cites the Saxon use around 1809 of *Inventions* trumpets with their stopped notes and two bass trumpets, filling in the harmony between the horns and *Halb-mond* and the trombone or serpent on the bass.

In France, Dauverné briefly notices the demilune and also a

circular orchestral model which he says was used in the Opéra for hand-stopping up to 1826 when the first valved trumpets arrived in Paris. This is in fact practically a natural cornet, with tuning slide and tapered crooks, made possibly from as early as 1816 by Jahn (Pl. XI). An example in the Paris Collection by Raoux, 1820, is said to have been made for Dauverné himself, then a young man of twenty. That such instruments were employed as trumpets is proved by the almost certainly original mouthpiece with the Jahn instrument: the cup is wide and shallow (19 mm. wide and 8 mm. deep) and the long stem is narrow enough to fit the 9 mm. sockets in the crooks. Hand-stopping is confirmed by places where the fingers and ball of the hand have worn away the red and gold painting inside the bell. The crooks resemble those of Haltenhof's horn: the higher (of which only A flat survives) communicate directly with the bell-leg of the slide; the lower (F to low B flat) fit into the main socket, a tuning bow then being inserted into the slide as shown in the Plate.

In orchestral use this type of instrument was evidently found to give better results with the hand than the short-model trumpets which Berlioz presumably refers to when pronouncing unfavourably on this procedure—save in the sole matter of h11: this perhaps allows us to believe that the climactic high Fs in the first movement of Beethoven's Ninth Symphony were assisted in this way.

KEYS

Over the first experiments with side-holes on brass instruments information is very fragmentary. In England William Shaw's fine E flat trumpet bearing the royal arms and the date 1787 is described by Halfpenny in *GSJ* XIII pp. 7ff.: it has transposing holes to the dominant, one hole for each crooking down to B flat, shut off by a rotating collar when not required, except for the B flat hole which is covered by a key. Here we have a case of a well-preserved instrument the purpose of which is not disclosed by contemporary sources. The Continent on the other hand offers a number of sketchy descriptions which, without being able to see the instrument, one can only explain theoretically and not always then. Thus Altenburg, musing over the possibility of completing the lower octave by means of a small key-covered opening low down on the side of the trumpet (p. 112), recalls how of old he saw an instrument of the Weimar court-trumpeter Schwanitz on which, by a small leather slide over such an opening, one could produce a perfectly pure a' and b', leaving only f' and d' wanting from the scale in this octave. This could have been as far back as 1760, but how a single opening served for both of these upper notes yet for neither of the lower is inexplicable without further details. Equally mysterious is Kölbel's *Amor-schall*. All histories relate how this Bohemian horn-player produced in 1766 or thereabouts a horn with keys like those of an oboe (their number was unspecified) and a bell like a bowl onto which fitted another bowl which had small holes in it and could somehow be moved to lower the pitch. Kölbel, then employed at St. Petersburg along with the no less inventive Maresch, won much admiration, playing fluently on the *Amor-schall* in F minor and E major (as written for the horn, thus implying a chromatic compass over a considerable range). Something similar or the same received appreciative notice in Paris a few years later (*Avant-coureur*, 1771), named *Taille d'amour*, 'a kind of *cor de chasse* played by some musicians from Bohemia, furnished with keys (*touches*) and folded *en quarté* (whatever this may signify; the full quotation is in Marcuse, 1964, under 'Amorschall'). No instrument answering to either description has been found. Possibly some music exists, however, for instance the part for 'Dalie' in Rosetti's Quintet in E flat for wind, a work patently adapted to five parts from a composition written basically in four. The part, for an instrument in F, is in one place very deliberately taken down to a sounding *e* flat, a tone lower than could have been managed on the contemporary cor anglais (which a 'taille' in F could mean) while its solo in the Rondo pointedly quotes the famous 'Saint Hubert' of the *trompe de chasse* repertoire. If intended for a horn, this must have been built in E flat with an open-standing key for the F series and at least one semitone key unless the hand were used when the keys were closed. Possibly some visiting player was still using the *Taille d'amour* now and then around 1780.

Returning to the trumpet, Schubart, in his undated *Ideen* (he died in 1791) tells that a Dresden trumpeter had experimented with trumpets 'with keys' but that their sound was so uneven that they were discarded. In 1793 Nessmann, a young Hamburg silversmith and amateur player, made a chromatic trumpet (which Gerber, reporting it in 1814, calls *Inventionstrompete*) with keys concealed under the cordage to give all semitones in the lower octave purely and freely even in fast passages. Sachs (1930, p. 266) states that a 'secret hole' under the cords was still familiar to postillions and buglers and that it raised the natural series by a semitone. Some instruments with this device should therefore still be in existence somewhere.

Haydn's celebrated *Clarino* concerto in E flat (1796) is unquestionably for a keyed trumpet of the four-keyed type which is well known (Fig. 31, c), and it is plausibly held that it was written for Weidinger, the ex-dragoon trumpeter who was the foremost Viennese performer on it. Two years later Weidinger was reported as playing his *organisierte* trumpet in a concerto by the Bohemian composer Kozeluch for piano, mandolin, trumpet and bass, with a rather dull keyed-trumpet part in E flat, all below sounding d''. In 1803 *AMZ* noticed a performance in Leipzig by 'Weidenmeyer' (whom Gerber concluded to be Weidinger) of among other things a 'truly excellent' Trio for piano, violin and trumpet by Hummel (whose difficult concerto in E for keyed trumpet is now well-known). The report commends the player's sound as full and penetrating, yet also as soft and sweet as a clarinet can sound. The player was perhaps helped in achieving this by a deep funnel-like mouthpiece like the apparently original one preserved with a fine five-key trumpet by Doke, Linz, in the Bernoulli Collection (cup width and depth both 16 mm., total length 65 mm.). Years later in 1817 Weidinger was playing concertos on keyed trumpet with his son on 'Klappen-Waldhorn', whatever that was.

Robert Minter has recently come across other Central European composers for *Klappentromba*, etc. including Neukomm (Ex. 42), Fiala and Jan Ryba. All wrote for the instrument in D, E flat or E, and for playing in so close a group of tonalities four keys suffice, raising the low g, h3, by semitones to b. The short-model was used. An exceptional specimen in long format without tuning slide is by Bauer, Prague, 1817 (Berlin 1063); the four keys, situated on the bell branch, require both hands. The normal form is fingered with one hand, and in many Austrian and Czech instruments this is the left hand. The keys themselves resemble woodwind keys of the period, mounted on brass saddles, two of them usually on cross-struts, and are heavily sprung to close with flat springs riveted to the levers. The tone holes are raised by brass inserts to present a level edge for the leather pads. Naturally, notes issuing from a hole close to the bell-mouth match the bell

Trombe in Es

Corno 1ᵐᵉ in Es

Corno 2ᵈᵉ in Es

Corno 1ᵐᵉ in As

Corno 2ᵈᵉ in B basso

Ex. 42 S. Neukomm, Vocal Requiem for M. and J. Haydn, 1815. First part of *Zwischenspiele* for 'Weidingersche Inventions-Trompete', 4 horns and 3 trombones (the latter here *tacent*). **Below** reduction of first 8 bars at sounding pitch.

notes best—a point well taken by Haydn in his semibreves on low *g, a* flat, *g* in the 1st movement of the concerto.

A complication arises with a keyed brass instrument if it is to be played with many different crooks since keys, unlike valves, are not tunable. If placed correctly for E flat crook (adequate also for E and D crooks) the keys are much too far apart to serve a crook a fourth higher, giving instead of semitones practically a series of whole-tones. Yet it was found practicable to use numerous crooks on a keyed trumpet by laying out the holes on the basis of a high crook like G. With a lower crook their positions are then too close,

bunched towards the bell; but by adding a fifth key farther from
the bell, and then missing out one of the four existing keys when
fingering by semitones up to b, satisfactory results were obtained.
Thus on a five-key trumpet built primarily for G or A flat crook
the semitones with the E crook might be made with keys (numbered from the bell) 1, 3, 4, 5. The fingering became largely
empirical and did not necessarily correspond from one harmonic
to another. An often-reproduced fingering chart for crooks from
G down to C in Roy and Muller's Tutor presents a weird scheme
which, allowing for misprints, might yet make sense to a pains-
taking student of the instrument.

Keyed trumpets were made well into the 1840s in Italy, whence
the brothers Gambati number among the prominent soloists after
Weidinger, appearing in every country during the 1820s though
without earning quite the praise accorded to the Austrian. Playing
for a time in the orchestra of the King's Theatre, London, they
were 'a perpetual source of destruction and head-ache... their
execution is wonderful but their tone is rough and raw in comparison with that of Harper', the latter of course on the slide
trumpet. In England the keyed trumpet never took root, nor in
France. The parts for *trompettes à clef* in the Paris score of
William Tell, and in Meyerbeer's *Robert the Devil*, were in
Dauverné's recollection performed on valve trumpets and not on
the actual *'trompette à clef dite italienne'* which he had heard the
Gambati play and not thought much of. In France, plain *'trompette à clef'* denoted the keyed bugle (equally *'bugle à clef'*), as
descriptions by Kastner, both in his *Cours* and his *Traité générale*,
make clear.

A few examples of bass keyed trumpet exist, for instance an
early left-handed four-key specimen in the Nuremberg Collection
in low G, with a wide flat-rimmed mouthpiece and a quite good
tenor trombone-like sound (Pl. XII).

Keyed Bugle. The patent of 1810 granted to Joseph Halliday,[1]
bandmaster of the Cavan Militia, is for 'Certain Improvements in
the Musical Instrument called the Bugle Horn' (Fig. 32). This
was the Keyed bugle or, in honour of the Commander-in-Chief,
'Royal Kent Bugle'. Halliday could scarcely have got the idea from
the Austrian keyed trumpet since Irish regiments were confined

---

[1] *Note to the Dover Edition.* Or 'Haliday', born in Yorkshire and brought
up in Ireland: see Ralph T. Dudgeon, *Journal of the American Musical Instrument Society* IX (1983).

to the island; but his band no doubt used the Bass horn (mentioned later) and this had a few keys of the pattern he employed on his bugle. This has the form of the recently-introduced bell-front bugle in a single loop. It is held in a vertical plane and the keys are placed to suit this position, occupying both hands, thumbs included. Theoretically their number should have been six, since

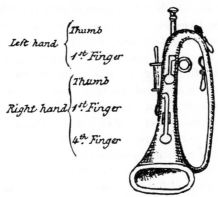

Fig. 32 Keyed bugle, Halliday's patent specification of 1810 re-drawn for the Patent Office records in 1856.

on a bugle h2 requires to be raised in chromatic steps to f' sharp (on the bugle in C). Halliday's patent, however, provides five (Fig. 32), this last note being made by opening the two higher keys together. The right middle finger is anchored over a brass bridge and operates no key. This original fingering is given in the left column below, showing only h2 and h3, the higher notes following logically. A rare example with these five keys by Turton, Dublin, was in the Shaw-Hellier Collection and is described in Day, 1891, p. 355.

	five-key	*six-key*	
Bugle as it stands	C, G	C, G	
Right little finger	1. C♯, G♯	O. (open key)	low B, F♯
,, 3rd finger	not used	1.	C♯, G♯
,, 1st finger	2. D, A	2.	D, A
,, thumb	3. D♯, B♭	3.	D♯, B♭
Left thumb	4. E, B	4.	E
,, 1st finger	5. F	5.	F
both these	F♯		(improves F)

Very soon, evidently by 1815 when the instrument was first copied in Paris by Halary, it was improved by lengthening the bell to jut out well beyond the front bend to give the series of B. The C series is then emitted through a large hole under an articulated key sprung to rest normally open. When this open key is closed by the right little finger, the player gains a proper F sharp and also a good b', which as h3 to low E with the left thumb comes too sharp on the five-key bugle and anyhow blends poorly with c'' as a leading note. The C sharp /G sharp key is accordingly taken from the little finger and given to the third finger (right column above). The best fingering chart is in the anonymous tutor published by Purday; it also contains tunes and duets much as popular tutors have chosen them since: 'The Portuguese Hymn' ('O Come all ye Faithful'), 'Carnival of Venice', etc. etc.

A seventh key very frequently added is for the right-hand first finger or ball of the thumb, opening on the left side of the root of the bell to give a good low E flat; the original thumb key was tuned to give a good b' flat (h3) but the e' flat as h2 then came too flat. Purday's tutor gives this note as D sharp, stating that before addition of the seventh key, low E flat was unobtainable. Less often provided are 8th and 9th keys on the lower branch for the trill F/G, respectively for the C bugle uncrooked and crooked in B flat (a crook in one small coil, used 'when playing with B flat clarionets'). Purday's statement that these two keys were for the trill on middle D cannot be correct. A 10th key, opening near the rear bow, will give b flat and a in fundamentals, which can be continued downwards by the other keys; but although Halary in one of his specifications provided systematically for a fundamental octave, this was going further than the nature of the instrument called for. Mouthpieces are deeper than field bugle mouthpieces and also have narrower rims (Pl. XII).

Bishop was writing for the keyed bugle a few years after its invention in his operettas for Covent Garden, where one of the trumpet-players played it for an extra fee. Ex. 43 looks simple compared with the music which had already been written in Vienna for keyed trumpet. But collections of variations by McFarlane and others, from about fifteen years later, include fast chromatic scales and virtuoso passages similar to those written for the cornet, and intended for the bandstand where the keyed bugle played its important role in the growth of the amateur band movement in England. John Clegg, of the cotton manufacturers

Ex. 43 Bishop, *The Miller and his Men*, 1813. Part of an Arietta (accompaniment condensed).

in the village of Besses-o' th'-Barn just north of Manchester, had himself played keyed bugle in 1818 in his 'Reed Band' which later became so famous; with him were C and F clarinets, piccolo, trumpet (probably slide), two horns, trombone, two bass horns and bass drum. The bugle and the woodwind were replaced in 1849 by cornets when the band adopted the valved instruments then flooding in from France. Yet keyed bugles continued to be made by Köhler, the London maker who most staunchly kept to native traditions. It reached America in 1816 from Dublin and remained long popular, the E flat soprano having been a particular favourite (Eliason, 1972). On the Continent, regimental bands used the bugle extensively from 1815 or soon after, in Germany up to as late as 1866. Many instruments (in Germany *Klappenhorn*, *Kent-horn*) are of brass or nickel alloy, and mostly in B flat. In Tuerlinckx and Schott they are listed below the field bugles:

Tuerlinckx: *Buglehorns en Klappenhorns*:
   Cor de Signal ou Buglehorn. F sans clefs
       ,,   ,,   Es ou D
       ,,   ,,   C ou B
       ,,   ,,   demilune. B (*i.e. Halbmond*)
       ,,   ,,   demilune basse. C
   Bugle, cor à clefs. F, Es, C ou B
    ,,   basse

Schott:
   Cors de Signal
    à 7 clefs
    en forme d'une demilune (*in the German*: Halbmond-form)
       ,, de trompette
    Cor de signal de Basse à 9 clefs avec tête de Dragon

As for 'Basse', there exist a few specimens which might answer to this. Kastner gives a sketch of an 11-keyed *bugle-basse* designed for playing in upright position but distinct from the ophicleide; of this, no specimen remains.

Some English keyed bugles after 1850 include a whole-tone valve (usually rotary) for the left hand, whereby the normally left-hand notes E and F may be made as h3 with the bell key, open and closed, plus the valve. The keys are then reduced to those for the right hand (an example is illustrated in Baines, 1966, Fig. 762).

Ophicleide. This tenor-bass development of the keyed bugle and longest-lived of the keyed brass instruments was invented in Paris by Halary (real name Jean-Hilaire Asté) in 1817 after he had seen the British keyed bugle in a military review following Waterloo. He patented it in 1821 and it was still in Couesnon's catalogue in 1916. Historically it is only by a few years an older instrument than Stoelzel's earliest deep-pitched valved instruments; but to Halary's credit the original ophicleide required no significant alteration for the rest of its existence whereas valved basses remain in some state of flux even today.

For over a quarter-century prior to the ophicleide, bandmasters seeking to strengthen their resources in the bass had depended largely upon the serpent tribe, either the old serpentine instrument itself or a large variety of wooden 'upright serpents' (*serpent-basson, basson-russe*, etc.) made roughly in bassoon shape, 90 to 100 cm. tall, with smaller initial bore than in the old serpent and better-focused notes of brighter quality. These often carried the *tête de dragon*—the brightly painted metal dragon bell (Pl. XI) as made also for the *buccin* model of trombone and inspired no doubt by the fantastic drawings in La Borde's *Essai* (I, p. 233) of the 'tuba curva' from Roman monuments in Italy; these give the *cornu* the zoomorphic bell of the *carnyx*. The six fingerholes of these serpents provide a scale a fifth lower than the bassoon's, descending to *C* (written *D* in many French instructions) below which *B'* flat could be made in falset. There are generally three keys: C sharp, F sharp, and B (the last because the all-uncovered note is *B* flat, corresponding to *f* on the bassoon). The sound—'the deepest and fullest bass tone of all wind instruments'—was felt to confer a contrabass effect—'what the double bass is to the orchestra the serpent is to wind music' (Fröhlich,

'Zum Serpent'). Some were made of brass or copper: firstly the species invented by the French serpentist Frichot while in refuge in London in the 1790s, built in a tall 'V' and the first model to have the name 'Bass horn'. This was copied by some makers on the Continent, as Sattler in Leipzig, but in Germany as a whole this name came into wider use than the actual instrument and nomenclature became very muddled. Thus Schott: '*Russisches Basshorn*, dragon or plain bell' (wooden *basson russe*); cf. '*Metall Serpent* or *basson russe* of brass' (variety of Bass horn). Perhaps the best of all these instruments for sound is the part-wood, part-brass upright serpent made in Paris from *c.* 1820 by Forveille, a better instrument, really, than the more scientifically-designed *Chromatisches Basshorn* by Streitwolf in Germany with 10 to 12 keys covering holes laid out in 'correct' positions instead of in two clumps of three in the old serpent fashion.

These various three-keyed instruments were still sold on the Continent in the 1840s, as were ordinary serpents and Frichot-pattern Bass horns in England. When *Rienzi* was produced in Dresden in 1842 the Serpent part may have been played on anything of these kinds. Berlioz recalls among adventures over his ophicleide parts at that time how in Brunswick he had to assent to a *basson russe* called by the performer *Kontrafagott* which replaced the ophicleide after a fashion, and was obliged to since though the orchestra (he continues) possessed a magnificent *basstuba*, the young man in charge did not seem to understand how to play it (1844, p. 120).

The ophicleide's first appearance is said to have been in the stage band of Spontini's *Olimpie* (Paris, 1819) in a coronation march which was much admired by Berlioz and helped to inspire the march in *The Trojans*. Spontini's band is on the French cavalry pattern of the time, with natural trumpets and horns, and a diatonic bass for trombone plus the new instrument discreetly on trial with the simplest possible part, but nonetheless the send-off for four generations of players up to Bandsman Lydyard of the 1st Battalion, Connaught Rangers, marching with his band across India down to Bombay in 1914 to embark for Europe, playing the BB flat Bass part on the ophicleide.

The instrument is a wide, almost exactly conical tube of brass, slung across the body with the left little finger resting against the tube (Pl. XII). The mouthpiece at first resembled the ivory serpent mouthpiece, hemispherical with wide sharp throat but broader rim than in most serpent mouthpieces (Pl. XII); specimen dimensions are: max. width 37, cup 27, throat 8, depth 34, length 72 and end-bore 10 mm. Later mouthpieces are more euphonium-like. The crook into which the mouthpiece is inserted is either coiled, or U-shaped with a tuning slide which has one leg wider than the other to interrupt the cone as little as possible. The original patent provides for two crooks for playing in either C or B flat like the keyed bugle. But unlike the latter, the ophicleide requires keys to fill the fundamental octave, whence lowering the C instrument to B flat by an alternative crook introduces more severe intonation difficulties than on the bugle. In fact, ophicleides are built either in 8-foot C or in 9-foot B flat. The B flat ophicleide

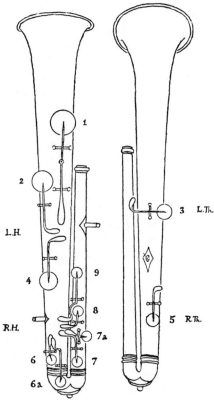

Fig. 33 F. Berr & Caussinus, *Méthode complète d'Ophicléïde*, Paris, c. 1837. Diagram of 9-key system, here amended to show the 10th and 11th keys (6a, 7a). Crook and mouthpiece not shown.

is some 108 cm. tall and a C ophicleide is 10 to 12 cm. less. For purposes of description it may be best to follow the French tutors and refer to the C instrument, which comes to the same thing as treating the Bb ophicleide as a transposing instrument, as some composers did.

The number of keys was at first fewer than were necessary to fill the fundamental octave in a strict sense. Caussinus, co-author of the best tutor (*Méthode complète* by Berr & Caussinus) and himself according to Berlioz the only decent player in Paris, tells how one could still see in the Halary shop the first ophicleide made, with only seven keys. The patent shows nine keys, and this number continued to be provided on some instruments though it still left two notes in the fundamental octave, F sharp and A flat, which had to be faked. This system forms the basis of Caussinus's fingering instructions, which can be summed up as follows (N.B. for C ophicleide):

Left hand, first finger: closes key 1 for B series.
     second finger: opens key 2 for C sharp series.
Left hand, thumb: opens key 3 for D series, while keeping key 2 open also.
Left hand, third finger: opens key 4 for E flat series, keeping keys 2 and 3 open also.
Right hand, thumb: opens key 5 for *E* and *e*.
Right hand, little finger: opens key 6 for *F* and *f*, while keeping key 5 open also.

The left-hand keys are employed from the fundamentals up to h5 or above and offer alternatives on the high notes from *f'* sharp upwards. The above right-hand fingerings are normally used only on the fundamentals and h2. (A minor point of interest is that in the patent, key 5 is for the little finger and key 6 for the thumb, the opposite to the normal arrangement).

The next fingerings are required only in the fundamental octave:

Right hand: F sharp: thumb and little finger as for *F* and close key 1.
    G: third finger opens key 7.
    A flat: third and second fingers (keys 7 and 8) and close key 1.
    A: second finger opens key 8.
    B flat: first finger opens key 9.

In order to make low *F* sharp and *A* flat correctly Halary had added in 1822 the two keys **6a** and **7a** with their finger-touches overlapping keys **6** and **7**. Thus key **7a**, for A flat, automatically also opens key **7** to vent the note. Caussinus advises students to be provided with this key. Both of them are present on the standard eleven-keyed ophicleide but they cannot be used in many legato passages (e.g. from G to A flat) so that the old fingerings of the nine-key ophicleide still have to be mastered, which is no doubt why Caussinus grounds his pupils on them. It should be mentioned that some individual ophicleides show unconventional layouts of the right-hand keys where someone has added to a nine- or ten-keyed ophicleide after his own fashion.

Ex. 44 Berr & Caussinus, *Méthode complète*. Part of a study (for C ophicleide; to test the key numbers on B flat ophicleide, take the piece a tone down, into A flat).

The fingering may have to be modified on a particular instrument and in quick passages (Ex. 44), also (in the days of Caussinus) in the tuning of leading notes and other *sensibles*, like raising C sharp between Ds and lowering D flat between Cs. An important practising point was that descending passages are the hardest (as with other deep brass instruments) and should be studied most strenuously and with a crescendo. Caussinus's notes on performance follow customary brass precepts (detaching notes etc.) while his warning to bandsmen not to render the crotchet-quaver in $\frac{6}{8}$ time as a dotted $\frac{2}{4}$ has interest as being the opposite to a common tendency today. An excerpt from a published brass band arrangement (Ex. 45) gives an idea of what an average player was expected to manage in the days before the euphonium. Favourite concert solos later played by Samuel Hughes and others included Bottesini's selection of 'Airs from *La Sonnambula*' and 'O ruddier than the cherry' from *Acis and Galatea*, with its bold arpeggio figures.

To make pads, Caussinus continues, cut out two circular pieces of *molleton* (swanskin) and wash leather a fraction wider than the key to allow for shrinkage on gluing. Sew them together and cover with a disc of goldbeater's skin wide enough to fold over and be sewn on the underside. Warm to candle heat and glue to the key with sealing-wax. Use wash-leather for key buffers to minimize noise. Clean the crook with shot and boiling water.

Ex. 45 Rossini, *La Gazza Ladra*, last part of Septet (più andante) arranged by W. Childe in Book 12 of *Wessel & Co.'s Journal for Brass Band* (after 1839). (Score from the original parts, retaining inconsistencies in markings etc.)

With a wide bore uninterrupted by cylindrical tubing the ophicleide offers little resistance, and the bright, free sound can today be most refreshing. In its day it could sound in the orchestra, as Prout put it, very powerful but somewhat savage and obtrusive (*The Orchestra*, I, p. 240). Prout heard it often enough and the comment must have been fair at the time, but it also goes to show how the weight and volume of orchestral wind has increased since: Berlioz judged the tuba the more powerful, alluding to the old Moritz tuba which itself would be completely drowned in the orchestra today. The ophicleide was not, however, finally replaced by the tuba in English orchestras until near the end of the century, and it is an unconfirmed suspicion that the gentleman in Pl. XII is Guilmartin, a leading young player of that time who doubled on both instruments.

On the Continent outside France and especially in Germany and Austria, Halary's invention sparked off a profusion of bass instruments with 8 to 12 keys, some copying the ophicleide in wood, with or without dragon bell; or in brass with a narrow bore and a flared bell, suggesting a kind of keyed bass trombone and no doubt the 'thin copper instrument with scarcely any tone' which Berlioz was offered in Leipzig. German makers rarely used the name 'ophicleide' but instead *Bombardone*, a word which seems to have been remembered from the past in connection with the old one-piece fagotto (precursor of the bassoon), described by Eisel and in the 1795 treatise of Reynvaan as *Bombardo*. Thus Schott again: '*Bombardone* or *Basshorn* of brass with 10 keys'; '*Bass Flügelhorn* (i.e. bass bugle) called *Bombardone* with 8 keys'; and a 12-keyed *Bombardone* with dragon bell. Museums can produce instruments which appear to match such descriptions, though by 1830 Austria and Germany were already in the lead in constructing equivalent instruments with valves, also called bombardons. Nevertheless Mendelssohn's Ophicleide part in the Overture to 'A Midsummer Night's Dream' (1826), though the work followed a visit to Paris, was probably first performed in the North German cities on a quite primitive wooden instrument, named in London parts printed by Cramer and also in an autograph score of the later 'Wedding March' as *Corno Inglese di Basso*, italianising the German 'Englisches Basshorn'.

An *Alto Ophicleide* appears in Halary's patent as *quinticlave* with eight keys (later eleven) and 'in sound intermediate between horn and bassoon, and stronger than the latter'; pitched in E flat with alternative crook for F, the compass is B to c''. In fact, as with the ophicleide, the two pitches were made separately, the E flat instrument standing around 90 cm. tall. The French instruments were built with proportionately narrower bore than the bass ophicleide; examples with bore of full proportions exist, but are comparatively few and of late date; it appears that whereas the ophicleide was invented, as the patent states, to replace the serpent, the alto version was deliberately designed to replace or reinforce the less sonorous instruments named above.

The alto ophicleide found considerable use in French and Belgian military bands of pre-Sax days, for instance a pair of them playing parts (treble clef, transposed for E flat) just as one might now write for two E flat Tenor Horns. Kastner prints in *Cours* (1st edn., 1837) a part of what must be a fairly early march score, with one cornet in A, the only valved instrument and still written in the old notation. Besides this and the two *Ophicléides alto* are *Bugles* (keyed) in B flat and high E flat, horns (hand), E flat trumpets (natural), three trombones (all bass clef), two bass ophicleides in B flat, plus piccolo, clarinets and bassoons. But Kastner says that the sound of the alto was 'criard et perçant'; the instrument was also said to be hard to play in tune. It was replaced at the first possible moment by valved instruments. Even so, Adolphe Sax made at least two examples of a smaller *ophicléide contralto* in A flat (Paris and Berlin Collections); they must have been played by someone, if only for a day.

The *Contrabass ophicléide* was never a regular species either, though it is mentioned in the report of the 1821 patent as *ophicléide contrebasse en fa*, with $11\frac{1}{2}$ feet of tube, 9-inch bell, and descending a semitone lower than the orchestral double bass. An unsigned example in E flat is in the Brussels Collection. There is also a Bavarian type of the narrower German kind by Barth, Munich, and this must be the 'Kontrast (kontra-est?) Bombardon' which Barth patented in 1840. An eleven-key specimen in the Deutsches Museum, Munich is in tuba F, about 140 cm. tall, with the bottom end curved out in a loop. Since on ophicleides the notes just above those of the basic series are closest to the latter in strength, whereas on valved instruments they are the weakest, this instrument probably gives a better-balanced low F' sharp and G' than any brass bass made since.

EIGHT

Valve Era

In 1815 the *Allgemeine musikalische Zeitung* printed the historic communication from Breslau (col. 309), signed by the director of the theatre there:

NEW INVENTION

Kammermusikus Heinrich Stölzel of Pless in Upper Silesia has, for the perfection of the *Waldhorn*, devised a simple mechanism by which a chromatic scale of nearly three octaves, with all non-natural notes clear and strong, and similar in sound to the natural notes, is obtained by means of two levers for the right hand.... He has laid his invention before the King of Prussia and now awaits a favourable outcome.[1]

[1]   NOTIZEN

1 *Neue Erfindung*

Der Kammermusicus, *Heinrich Stölzel,* aus Pless in Oberschlesien, hat, zur Vervollkommnung des Waldhorns, einen einfachen Mechanismus an demselben anzubringen gewusst, nach welchem er alle Töne der chromatischen Scala, in einem Umfange von beynahe drey Octaven, wohlklingend, rein und stark erhalten hat. Alle unnatürlichen Töne— welche bekanntlich bisher durch Stopfen des Schallstücks mit der rechten Hand hervorgebracht wurden, und jetzt blos durch zwey Hebel, mit zwey Fingern der rechten Hand dirigirt, hervorgebracht werden— sind den natürlichen Tönen vollkommen ähnlich, und behalten den Charakter des Waldhorns. Ein jeder Waldhornist wird bey einiger Uebung im Stande seyn, darauf zu blasen. Hr. Stölzel hat zu weiterer Anwendung und Verbreitung seine Erfindung Sr. königl. Majestät von Preussen zu Füssen gelegt, und erwartet nun ein gnädiges Resultat.

Ich habe mich von diesem Mechanismus und seiner Brauchbarkeit überzeugt, und bekenne, nach meiner Einsicht und der Wahrheit gemäss, dass die Anwendung desselben dem Waldhorn eine bis jetzt noch nicht erreichte Vollkommenheit giebt, und dadurch bey vollstimmiger Musik eine noch nicht gekannte Wirkung hervorgeht.

Ob ich gleich diese Erfindung bis jetzt nur an dem Waldhorn angebracht gehört habe: so glaube ich doch überzeugt seyn zu dürfen, dass sie, in ihrer Einfachheit, auch an Trompeten und Signalhörnern, und mit ähnlichem Erfolg, anzubringen sey. Welch ein neues Reich an schönen Effecten eröffnete sich hierdurch den Componisten!—

Breslau   *G. B. Bierey*

Heinrich Stoelzel (as he was sometimes more conveniently spelt) was then a thirty-eight year old horn-player in the orchestra of Prince von Pless. At once[1] he began to advertise the new horn, performing on it at Leipzig in 1817, upon which a further report appeared in the *AMZ* (col. 814ff.) to much the same effect as the previous but mentioning two 'airtight valves (*Ventile*) for the right hand, pressed down like piano keys and returned by springs'. Next year he found himself a place in the royal orchestra at Berlin. He had, however, left out of the reckoning his younger collaborator, Friedrich Blühmel, a member of a miners' band (*Berg-Hoboist*) and for all we know a horn-player too. Blühmel chased to Berlin, to claim that the horn had been his and sold by him to Stoelzel. A ten-year Prussian patent was then issued in 1818 jointly to the two men (according to *AMZ* 1818, col. 531, where both are described as coming from Waldenburg, today Walbrzych, southwest of Breslau, where Pless had a castle). The patent has long been inaccessible and a copy which Mahillon saw was largely incomprehensible because of the absence of the drawings; it was apparently signed by Blühmel only, which has never been explained. Stoelzel finally bought off Blühmel on the expiry of the patent. Both were evidently mechanics as well as musicians. But the only writer who knew them both personally, the great Berlin bandmaster Wilhelm Wieprecht, said that though the two men had worked together in Silesia for many years, their subsequent quarrels made it quite impossible to find out which of them had conceived the idea first.

Wieprecht, in 1845 when he was still only forty-three, described in the *Berliner Musikalische Zeitung* (see Kalkbrenner, pp. 88ff.) the early development of the valve so far as he knew it from times when he was daily in and out of the workshops of Griessling & Schlott, with whom Stoelzel had been associated in Berlin, 'directing improvements in the external construction of the instruments'. The essence of his remarks is paraphrased below in *italics*, the rest being free commentary. *Kasten* is taken to mean a square 'box', and *Büchse* a round 'canister' like a pill-box.

---

[1] *Note to the Dover Edition.* Valves are actually first announced (not described) by Stoelzel in a letter of December 1814 to the King: see Herbert Heyde, *Das Ventilblasinstrument* (Wiesbaden, 1987).

(i) *Stoelzel had made various attempts to improve the valve, e.g. through Schiebekastenventile* ('push-box valves') *in which the windways follow a circular path.* These would be a form of square-section valve, and Fétis, writing in 1828, also said that Stoelzel made such a valve. 'Circular path' must, if internal, signify semicircular, perhaps as conjectured in Fig. 34, c.

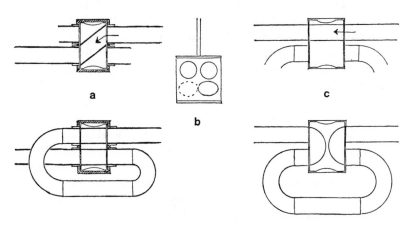

Fig. 34 a & b. Square valve, Schuster pattern. **a.** plan (**above,** valve up, **below** valve down); **b.** face of valve; **c.** conjectural plan of Stoelzel square valve with windways 'following a circular path'.

Three examples of square valve are known, two sets being on instruments signed by W. Schuster of Carlsruhe, a maker who had got to know of them through a horn-player of that city who had seen the valve in Berlin in 1816. Schuster was still making this valve in 1828. The three examples are: (1) a two-valve Schuster E flat trumpet in the Nuremberg Collection (illustrated in Baines, 1966, No. 768); (2) a Schuster B flat bass trumpet with three valves which passed from the Snoeck Collection in Ghent (Pl. XIII) to the Berlin Collection (No. 3104); (3) a two-valve set for F horn (Fig. 34, a, and Pl. XIII)—exactly corresponding to (1) and to the Schuster horn valves illustrated by Fétis in 1828— preserved in the Brussels Collection attached to some nonsensical pieces of later tubing to give an appearance of a trumpet (No. 1310). The valve bore in (1) and (3) is 11·3 mm. and the travel is 13·6 and 15 mm. respectively. The valves have spiral springs below, and straight windways throughout, thus having no 180 degree change in direction as there is in Fig. 34, c. As often in two-valve instruments, the 1st valve of the Schuster trumpet is for the semitone and the 2nd for the whole-tone. This became changed after the addition of the 3rd valve for a tone-and-a-half, for with this it became convenient with some types of valve for the maker to place the shortest valve loop in the middle, and this arrangement remains standard.

(ii) *Stoelzel found that the preceding valves proved impracticable, so he finally returned to Röhrenschiebeventile* ('tubular push-valves', or as Wieprecht also terms them *Schieberröhrenventile*, 'push tube-valves'). He adds: *all Berlin players were against the invention, but it was received abroad, especially in Russia, France, and parts of Austria.* He later notes that this valve brought right-angle bends into the windways. The likely interpretation is that this was the open-ended piston valve which in fact became known in France as the Stoelzel valve (Fig. 35, left and Pl. XIII). The windway leads down through the piston, out of the bottom of the casing to the bell (or to another valve by a short bow). The sharp bends in the windway are usually softened by inclined brass partitions, though in many French instruments up to the

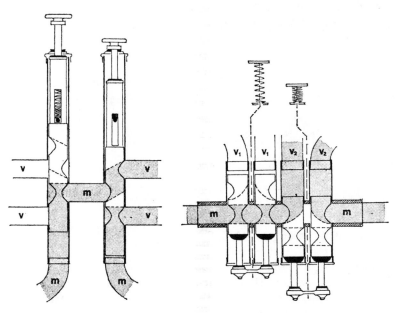

Fig. 35 left Stoelzel valves; **right** double-piston or 'Vienna valves. *m*, main windway, *v* valve loops.

mid-century, even by Raoux and Courtois, the partitions are simply of wax. Some trumpets and horns sent from Berlin to Paris by Spontini in late 1826 had this valve (Fig. 31,d). Labbaye worked on it and patented an improvement next year: *a trompette à ventilateur* (i.e. *Ventil-trompete*) 'to supply with the brilliant quality of the natural trumpet all those semitones which otherwise can only be obtained by means of the hand or keys, which alter the sound'. Up to the 1840s the Stoelzel valve was the most-used system in France, England, and Italy, and some cheap French cornets were still provided with it well into the present century.

There is also to be noticed at this point the other early type of valve with tubular open-ended pistons, namely the double-piston valve, often called 'Vienna valve'. This employs, for each valve, a pair of short pistons linked by an external bar and drawn out together in order to direct the windway down through one casing, through the loop, and up through the twin casing and so out through the twin piston (Fig. 35, right; Pl. XIII). The valve has to be lifted, not depressed as with other pistons, and therefore may be placed upside-down, or the instrument (if a trumpet) may be held upside down. A valve of this nature was made in 1821 by Sattler (*AMZ* for this year col. 397; see Fig. 36) with two valves

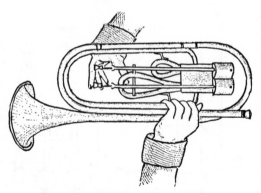

Fig. 36 Sattler's trumpet, *AMZ*, June, 1821.

placed longitudinally on a trumpet, and with three on a horn. This valve must have then been developed very rapidly by makers in several centres, for it soon became the commonest pattern over all Germany except Prussia, where it seems not to have been made. The earliest dated instrument with double-piston valves is a two-valve trumpet by M. Saurle, Munich 1829 (New York, Metropolitan Museum, No. 1098). It shows a neat form of the valve with the tops of the pistons emerging partially protected from dust by short caps as in the later example shown in Pl. XIII. In Mainz, C. A. Müller may have been making this type for Schott already in 1826, when they advertised a *Ventil-trompete* in *Caecilia*. An improved Viennese pattern with pistons enclosed under screw caps and the levers sprung with clock springs was patented in 1830 by Uhlmann, and is the model still used on the Vienna horn.

(iii) *Blühmel returned to Berlin from Silesia in 1828 and produced (but failed to secure a patent for) the first conischen Drehbüchsen-ventile* ('conical turning-canister valves'). *These were only outwardly different from (i), having a similar interior construction, and both these formed the fundamental basis of the invention.* These would be rotary valves. Their windways follow a quarter-circle and the rotors are normally tapered enough for grinding in; Blühmel's may have been more visibly so, but Wieprecht's terse description does not allow certainty on this point.

Wieprecht now compares (ii) with (iii), observing in the latter a superiority in that the circular passages offer the air-column no serious interruption of direction, and that the strength and quality of the notes is therefore better than with the tubular design (ii) where the air-column includes sharp right-angle bends, though the tubular type has the advantage of ease of manipulation (i.e. direct push on the piston as against the cranks and links of a rotary valve). However (continues Wieprecht) Blühmel's *'Dreh'* valve (iii) was at once improved in Prague—according to another writer (Rode, 1860, p. 242) by the hornist Kail in 1829—in two respects: reduction in size, and use of spiral springs. This suggests that Blühmel had employed the flat strip-metal springs that one sees on early rotary-valve instruments made in Mainz but that Kail's *Maschine* was more like the rotary valve as now known, often said to date from a patent of Riedl, Vienna *c.* 1832.

(iv) Wieprecht now took a hand himself in conjunction with the Berlin maker Moritz. *With the object of combining the light feel of Stoelzel's piston* (ii) *with the better tonal results of Blühmel's rotaries* (iii), *the latter were changed to produce* (Wieprecht's) *Steckerbüchsenventile* ('pin capsule-valves', these patented 1833) *which were then used in my chromatic brass instruments for army bands, especially cavalry bands.* These are the Berlin pistons (Fig. 37, Pl. XIII), in principle little different from the square valve and kept in alignment by a stationary guide pin fixed to the inside of the casing. *They are simple and strong. The improved Prague*

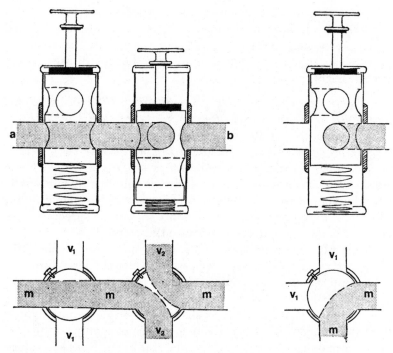

Fig. 37 Berlin valves (*Berliner Pumpen*); **left** main windway arranged diametrically; **right** in a right angle.

rotaries proved rather delicate for cavalry musicians, though infantry bandsmen are able to take better care of their instruments and can be trusted with the rotaries, with which, especially on the smaller instruments such as cornets and high trumpets, the tone is freer and less 'grell' than with the 'stickers'; but these last are much the best for the deeper instruments like trumpets, horns, tenor horns, tubas, etc. Such has proved the case inasmuch as the last three of these continued to be made with Berlin pistons by Moritz and makers in Sweden (brass-wise mainly within the Berlin orbit) in the present century and were familiar objects among North German troops in the first world war. The Swedish Royal Guards only abandoned their last Berlin-valve tubas some twenty-five years ago and some are still doing fine service in amateur bands in that country. In Paris, Adolphe Sax, much to Wieprecht's displeasure, pirated this valve for his early saxhorns, on which he also tried rotary valves before finally settling on the Périnet type. The foregoing summarizes the story of the early development of the valve as told by an eminent and fair-minded man who was on the spot for much of the time. Other accounts do not differ substantially. Next, in 1839, the Paris maker Périnet, noted for his horns and cornets, patented his 'gros piston' which is virtually the modern piston valve and is still known under his name in Germany and Austria where it has long been manufactured for export instruments and dance-band trumpets. Like the Berlin valve it has three inserted passages (coquilles) across each piston, this being wider than the Stoelzel piston but narrower than Wieprecht's. Instead of passages placed side by side as in the latter, one is horizontal or nearly so, while the others slope in opposite directions, all with their long axes at 120 degrees to one another or thereabouts. Countless subsequent modifications have aimed to minimize or abolish humps where one passage passes closely over another and to provide a full bore throughout in the confined space available.

To mention a few other valve systems known by extant examples, the earliest are the remarkable inventions of N. Adams of Lowell, Massachusetts, 1824–5, described by Eliason in *GSJ* XXIII (pp. 86ff.). In his 'Permutation Trumpet' in F, inside each of the two junctions of the valve loop with the main tube is a turning leather vane faced with brass on both sides; the two vanes for a given valve are simultaneously turned by external flexible wires connected to the finger lever. His other valve, of the same date, is a small-diameter rotary valve, apparently invented quite independently from the European rotary valve and in fact the first rotary valve of which details are accurately known.

The 'Patent Lever' valves of J. Shaw of Glossop, Derbyshire, 1838, commonly referred to as 'disc valves', were made by Köhler around the mid century for every kind of brass instrument (Fig. 38). Each valve has a rotating brass disc which is held airtight against a fixed disc by a spring. The rotating disc has four apertures at which are attached, in the earlier designs, the valve loop and the small straight-through bow, the windway passing through the one or the other as the disc is turned through 90

Fig. 38 Instruments by Köhler, London, with Shaw's disc valves, 1851:
Patent Lever Cornopean (**below**). Patent Lever Trombone (**above**).

degrees by a rod with finger-button. Later the valve loop was
transferred to the fixed disc so that only two small bows were required on the rotating disc. A rather similar system had been proposed earlier in France by Halary (*plaques mobiles*, 1835). Another
French invention, by Coeffet in 1843, is a valve called *emboliclave*
(Fig. 39, b). Somewhat as in Adam's Permutation trumpet but
with plunger action instead of pivot, each valve comprises two
three-way tube junctions within each of which a leather disc
supported by brass washers is moved up and down on the end of a
fine rod. This passes to the exterior through a hole in the upper-
most tube; the two rods for a given valve are connected to a finger-
button. At the time the idea was rated as very promising. A B flat
bass by Raoux with these valves is in the Brussels Collection, No.
1275.

Further American rotary systems of 1848–50 are described in Eliason's article. In a design by T. D. Paine, Smithfield, Rhode Island, the rotor has three passages through it, one being a central straight-through passage, so that the rotor is wide but requires to be turned only 45 degrees. As with Adams and Coeffet, use is made of flattened entry tubes—narrowed in one sectional direction but widened in the other—to save sideways space at the approaches to the valve. Finally we may notice the type of valve in which a sleeve, open at both ends but with a partition in the middle and two apertures in one side, is moved up and down by a lug which issues through a slot in the casing and is connected to an external push rod with spiral spring. An early form is seen on an

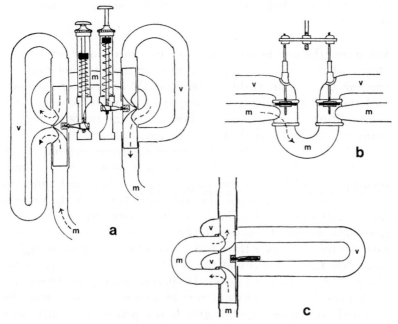

Fig. 39 a. Samson's Finger Slides, London, 1862. **b.** Coeffet's *Emboli-clave*, Paris, 1843, showing valve raised (*m*, main windway, *v*, valve loop). **c.** An antecedent to **a** by Charles Pace, London.

instrument by Charles Pace, 49 King's Street, Westminster (so pre-1849): a long-model trumpet with two horizontal valves (Shaw-Hellier Collection, see Day, 1891, No. 386) now on loan to the Warwickshire Museum. The partition deflects the windway either through a short by-pass loop, or, when the valve is moved, through the valve loop (Fig. 39, c). The sleeve can be extracted when desired by removing the bow situated beyond the valves. Extremely simple, but involving a series of right-angle bends in the main windway. This is avoided in Samson's 'finger slides' (London, 1862, Fig. 39, a) which Rudall, Rose & Carte fitted to many of their brass instruments until it was abandoned owing to the expense of making it.

The rest of the inventions of the second half of the nineteenth century were almost wholly concerned with compensating arrangements or extra valves in order to overcome the intonation defects of valve combinations. Two will be referred to later and others are described in the works of Constant Pierre, Morley-Pegge and Bate, but a word must now be said on the problems themselves.

Valve lengths and intonation. With two valves only, an instrument had a chromatic compass from *e* (in the later notation, *e'*) upwards save for the G sharps (which could be made on the horn with the hand). To calculate the lengths of the valve loops the early and traditional method is to observe the natural ratios of the B-C semitone and C-D whole tone, the loops, measured along the centre line, being one fifteenth and one eighth respectively of the open tube-length of the instrument as it stands—i.e. without mouthpiece, without considering end-correction, and ignoring the length of extra passages through the valve when the valve is lowered. By mutual cancellation of such factors the results come close to prediction. However, the two valves together do not quite give the natural minor third 6:5 (since a fifteenth plus an eighth make less than a fifth) and the result is in theory 12 cents too sharp. This, with the missing G sharps, made good reason for adding the 3rd valve which lowers by a correct minor third. The 2nd and 3rd valves together give G sharp at a fair compromise between Mean-tone G sharp and A flat. The other combinations are very sharp but are needed only in the low register where they are most easily tuned by the lip. Though the 3rd valve can be tuned to give the minor third correctly, by itself, the 1st & 2nd are normally employed for this interval instead, since A, for example, mostly comes in music next to B or B flat, and it is smoother to move one finger alone than to move two fingers in opposite directions. This leaves the 3rd valve free to be built on the long side, or tuned down by its slide, to help counteract the sharpness of other combinations.

These natural fractions for the valve loops are large ones, theoretically lowering an open harmonic by 204, 112, and 316 cents respectively. The 112 cents for the 2nd valve in particular makes an alarmingly wide semitone to be committed to, for instance inhibiting the niceties of the leading-note. In practice this valve is usually shortened to an empirical length of about one seventeenth of the open tube-length. Another basis for measuring valve loops is by Equal Temperament, the valves then adding by ratios of 1:1·05946 (an increase by the twelfth root of two); 1:1·12246 (its square); and 1:1·1892. These, corresponding to 100, 200 and 300 cents, are smaller proportions than the natural ones, giving the player greater range for tuning. But the combinations come sharper, and so the 1st valve is often lengthened somewhat to help the minor third.[1]

A fourth valve lowering by a perfect fourth and adding one third to the total is frequently fitted, chiefly to the deeper instruments, to extend the compass of h2 downwards to meet the open fundamental. Then, the combination of 1st & 4th ($\frac{1}{8} + \frac{1}{4}$) adds up to $\frac{11}{24}$; but the amount required is $\frac{1}{2}$ (perfect fifth), leaving $\frac{1}{24}$ short, or six inches on an F tuba. With all four valves lowered the sharpness is 145 cents or nearly three-quarters of a tone, or with unadjusted E.T. valves 178 cents, obliging the player to lip down with consequent loss of power and attack. This is where Blaikley's Compensating Pistons (1874 etc.), long manufactured by Boosey (from 1930, Boosey & Hawkes), have proved so valuable in British tubas, euphoniums, etc. They employ a simple principle which had long been known to the makers in Paris but not effectively proceeded with there. It can be applied with either three valves or four. With three (Fig. 48), a small bow is soldered

---

[1] The following are theoretical figures in cents for the lowering-intervals given by valves according to the two main bases for determining their dimensions:

Valves lowered	Natural	Equal-tempered
2nd	112	100
1st	204	200
1st & 2nd	303	290
3rd	316	300
2nd & 3rd	409	384
1st & 3rd	487	467
All three	572	546

to each of the cases of the 1st and 2nd valves just above their normal loops. The 3rd valve loop is led to enter the 1st valve on this
higher level and, if the other valves are 'up', continues straight
through their pistons by special passages and thence back to the
3rd valve. All this amounts to a normal 3rd valve loop. But when

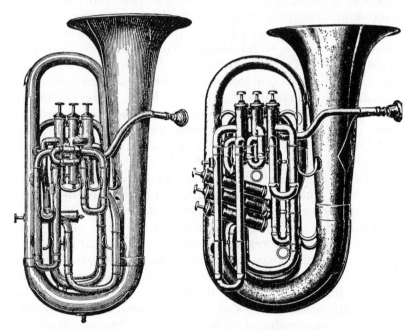

Fig. 40 Two remedies for valve-combination problems. **Left** Euphonium,
Boosey & Co., with the compensating 4th valve on Blaikley's system.
Right French orchestral tuba in 8ft. C, Besson's six-valve system (p. 258).

one or both of the other valves are lowered as well, further passages in their pistons divert the windway through the small increment bows, bringing combinations with the 3rd valve correctly
in tune (or with all three, very nearly). With four valves, the
4th valve loop similarly passes through the other pistons, the 3rd
valve being provided with an increment bow like the other two
(Fig. 40), whereby an E flat Bass will come naturally in tune from
B' flat (4th valve) down to G' and below that be considerably
better than a plain four-valve instrument.

But in sum, and when the natural intonations of the harmonic
series are taken into account as well, it is clear that whatever

fractions are chosen for valve loops and however these may be modified, or tuned by the player—and even with a good compensating system—a pre-set system of valves can never give all notes in tune without help from the embouchure. Certainly the enormous majority of brass-players since valves came into use have not felt unduly put out by this, overcoming the deficiencies barely consciously by ear and lip. Still, this state of things is not, perhaps, ideal. On trumpets a simple mechanical help is the mobile valve slide, first thought of in Paris a century ago and frequently fitted to French cornets from the 1880s. The 1st or 3rd valve slide, or both, can be moved while playing by means of a lever ('trigger', Fig. 43) for the 1st and a ring (usually) for the 3rd. Combinations can thus be flattened if there is time, also extra low notes supplied (e.g. *f* on C trumpet) and even quarter-tone music becomes to some extent feasible. (Another simple idea for the trumpet, though not capable of adjustment, has been by Shediva, Odessa: a fourth valve with a very small loop which adds about a third of a semitone, and this of course can be used in fast passages.) By far the most radical solution has been put forward by Vogel (1961) and worked out mechanically by Alexander in Mainz. This is to tune the valves to one, two and four eighteenths of the open length, and to provide slides which can be simultaneously drawn out by a system of levers to larger fractions like sixteenths and fifteenths. Vogel's ingenious argument is, however, too complex to try to condense here.

BRASS INSTRUMENTS THROUGH THE VALVE ERA

HORN

No doubt there were German bandsmen who used the valves on the horn from the start much as they are used today. But for a player of serious pretensions the only thinkable path lay in sympathetically integrating their use with the prevailing and very successful practice of the hand-horn. This established the valved instrument's tonality from the first as in F, one of the good hand-horn keys and allowing, on the two-valve horn, normal hand playing in keys down to D, using the valves both to save crook-changes and to substitute for a weak hand note a better one; or even in certain circumstances to play an open note as a stopped one, e.g. a C leading to D flat, as Meifred's *Méthode* (1840), the first French tutor for the valve horn, goes into in great detail. J. Rudolf Lewy's studies, published in Leipzig, expressly forbid wholesale sacrifice of the hand to the valves. Morley-Pegge (p. 211) quotes some of his examples and Ex. 46 is another, illustrating the kind of passage where the valves may take over. The studies are primarily pedagogic, but the precepts were certainly observed in general by the first generation of artists on the valve horn.

Ex. 46 J. R. Lewy, *12 Etudes pour le Cor chromatique et le Cor simple*, Leipzig, n.d. Part of a study. The valves may be employed save where marked *la main*. . . . (All sounds a fifth lower.)

Yet inevitably the bias among orchestral players changed in favour of the valves, despite protests like that of Gleich (1853) that to use these in Beethoven or Weber was a 'Vandalismus'. Many had begun to speak like Fahrbach, the professor in Vienna, against the uneven sound of 'the old stifling of harmonics with the hand'. Fahrbach is one who advises the use of crooks from G or F down to D, but evidently for the sake of the clarity of the open notes, which is a matter not necessarily bearing on hand-stopping, for the valves were of course re-tuned for the crook. Kling (p. 127) strongly recommends, for example, the G crook in Mozart's G minor Symphony for the Trio of the Minuet, which becomes ruined, he says, when played on the F crook. Consequently these crooks continued to be supplied, being totally ignored only by theatre players and so on. The crooks for low C and B flat, dull in sound and apt to be wild in intonation, were continued only in France, where the Conservatoire training was on hand-horn for most of the century. (By 'Horn in A flat basso' in *Otello*, Verdi subtly conveys to the F-horn player the intended musical effect; valve slides able to be matched to this key being as mythical as the crook itself.)

Among leading types of the old valve horn, the *German F horn* has become the rarest in use today, though it was played in its home country, in Eastern Europe, and in American orchestras well into the 1920s (Fig. 41).[1] The valves are rotary, in many older models sprung with clock springs (*Trommelwerk*). The crooks are usually slide crooks, e.g. for E, or for the military, E flat. Models were also made with mouthpipe crooks, for instance in G with crooks to D, or covering a wider range of tonalities down from high B flat. Bores reach 11·5 mm., wider than elsewhere. Bell proportions are variable but tend to be wide. Mouthpieces are conical with wider rim than in France and with a distinct throat. In all, good, safe instruments with a good safe sound, and under the name 'single F horn' still manufactured for schools where it is felt wise to start pupils on the 12-foot tube-length only.

The *French horn*—to use the expression in the restricted sense of the traditional French type of horn—keeps the form of the French orchestral hand-horn, having the same narrow bell-throat and mouthpipe crooks. The valves are placed on the slide, and formerly could be removed and replaced by a plain slide for hand-horn playing. Since their position is low on the instrument, the valves need long stems up to the finger-buttons, protected by screw-on 'chimneys'. In another model, but less strong, the tuning slide immediately follows the crook socket, pointing downwards, and the valves are placed high up (Fig. 49; apparently an idea of Sax). The French bore varies from 10·8 to 11 mm. (though some larger bores were made for military bands) and the mouthpiece remains a deep funnel (Fig. 1, 1). The musical quality is light and poised but rather harsh in the low register around h3.

The French horn was the normal professional instrument in England up to 1930 and has amateur devotees still, while many will remember it from school days, often an instrument adapted from the old sharp pitch by a lengthened tuning slide. Though normally played in F, a high crook—B flat alto or more usually A—was kept handy in case a work like Beethoven's Seventh Symphony appeared in a programme. It could prove a tricky instrument under concert conditions, usually having one or more valved notes just below or above written g'' which tend to break, whence the horn's old reputation among concert-goers as the most difficult instrument in the orchestra—i.e. that from which one heard the most wrong notes. The f'' was so apt to be troublesome

[1] Acknowledgement is due here to Mr. Jeremy Montagu for kindly lending the Moritz illustrated catalogue, dating from the first decade of this century, from which a number of figures in this chapter are taken.

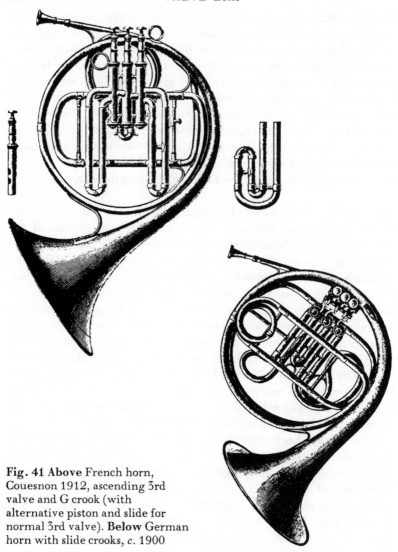

Fig. 41 Above French horn,
Couesnon 1912, ascending 3rd
valve and G crook (with
alternative piston and slide for
normal 3rd valve). **Below** German
horn with slide crooks, *c.* 1900

that the opening of Brahms's second Piano Concerto was a night-
mare to many players: London students of the 1920s shared a belief that the infallible Aubrey Brain had cured this bogey (on his
Raoux model by Labbaye) by placing a splinter of wood somewhere in the 1st valve—not necessarily true but it shows the
phobia.

In France this horn has generally been made with an ascending

3rd valve (Halary, 1849; Fig. 41). This is a whole-tone valve in which the passages are so arranged that with the valve 'up' the windway leads through the loop. To play as one did normally in F, a G crook must therefore be used (usually of a less fragile two-coil type). The G series obtained on lowering the valve offers many excellent notes to replace uncertain notes on the F horn, as a'', played with the ascending valve alone (h12), and f'', adding the 2nd valve (h10). The extraordinary confidence of French playing must be largely due to this modification (which leaves low e flat to be made with the hand). In Ravel's *Pavane pour une infante défunte* (orchestral version, 1908) 'Cor simple en sol' signifies the horn played with the ascending valve down, thus in G, and otherwise '*simple*', i.e. hand-horn.

The *Vienna horn* corresponds with the French horn in that it is a pre-valve orchestral horn with valves added to it with minimal change in the format. The basic format is in this case that of Leopold Uhlmann, in which the mouthpipe crosses back over the main circle before reaching the tuning slide: Fitzpatrick (1970, Pl. XIIa) illustrates a fine example in his own collection. Uhlmann then placed his double-piston valves on this cross-tube, where they remain today in the famous model used by the Vienna Philharmonic Orchestra but otherwise superseded in Austria by the safer German-style double horn, said to add ten years to a player's life. In some respects the Vienna horn is the extreme opposite to the French horn, with a much wider mouthpiece (socket 8·7 mm.), main bore only 10·7 mm., but with the wider, more full-throated bell section which Austria, like most of Germany, had adopted while hand-horn playing came in in the eighteenth century but the Paris makers to a certain degree resisted. The Viennese F crook is tapered throughout, and since the fixed tubing of the horn is long, the high B flat crook is reduced to a short shank. When this or the A crook is required for a dangerously high part and the valves are also to be used, a set of short valve slides is inserted in place of the normal set, since double-piston valves leave insufficient spare external length for B flat slides which will pull out for F. Musically, while an indifferent orchestral player can sound appallingly tenor-horn-like, the darkly romantic quality in the hands of artists like the late von Freiburg can give, especially in legato, an unsurpassable effect, while the full, velvet lower register elevates those interminable sustained octaves of classical horn parts to a contribution of rich beauty to the whole.

Double horn. While in France Debussy's totally original and non-Teutonic horn writing made no severe new demands upon the players, in Germany, with Richard Strauss's writing advancing inexorably towards *Ein Heldenleben* and presenting every difficulty including very high notes constantly sustained loudly in the tuttis, players had begun to fly to the high B flat crook. This had long been employed among military players, like the '*B-Hornists*' of the Prussian Jäger Guards from 1837. But great orchestral conductors of the old school like von Bülow objected to the change of quality when the shorter tube was used in place of the F tube-length; neither could one change in a hurry from the one to the other since valve slides had to be re-tuned or even replaced. Out of this situation Kruspe of Erfurt, in conjunction with the nephew of the great Leipzig hornist Gumbert, devised the compensating double horn—no doubt without the knowledge that the idea had been thought of in Paris forty years earlier. The instrument was exhibited in Markneukirchen in 1897: *Waldhorn in B mit F-maschine*. A critical observer could now no longer *see* whether the horn was being played in F or B flat and it remained up to the player to conceal any difference in sound. Strauss commented favourably on the invention with the proviso that the tone on the B flat should be mollified as far as possible.

The double rotors allow two sets of valve loops to be controlled by one set of finger-levers.[1] A thumb valve switches the horn from one valve circuit to the other. There are two main types. *Compensating horn* or B flat/F horn, Kruspe's first model, intended for playing mainly in B flat. The B flat loops are permanently in the circuit. Behind them are the shorter increments which become added to the circuit when the horn is in F (which it normally is with the thumb valve at rest). A tuning slide is provided for the main circuit and an auxilliary one for the F-increment circuit.

---

[1] Note for beginners: (1) the top cap on a rotary valve (on the same side as the 'horse-shoe' and levers) has a milled edge like that of the bottom cap but it is brazed to the casing; only the bottom cap can be unscrewed. (2) For lubrication, most players rely upon water condensed from the breath, though some makers recommend an occasional touch of a special light oil on the spindle under the bottom cap. Horn-players seem to be resigned to the problem of the *gloux-gloux désagréable* (as the *Encyclopédie* terms it) caused by accumulated water in the instrument: water keys as used on other brass instruments have been tried, but a horn has so many potential sumps that no one or even two such keys can be very useful.

The *Full double horn* or F/B flat horn first appeared about five years after the other. Beyond sharing mouthpiece and bell-section the F and B flat sides are independent circuits, each with its complete valve loops, the longer ones for the F being placed in front. Each circuit has its own tuning slide.

As to bore, it was found early on that an enlargement improved the tonal match between the two sides of the horn, minimizing the buglish tint which can be very marked in B flat alto with small bores. The celebrated double horn of Alexander has had a bore of 12·1 mm. for upwards of fifty years. As to sound, in England, where the instrument arrived late— its powerful advocate in 1930 was Alan Hyde—the old bright sound has generally been sought, the horn being held well up as of old. In America, where it was introduced by Anton Horner nearly thirty years earlier, many players support the bell on the thigh and allow the sound to be partly blanketed by the clothing, producing a thick, dark quality which can have a very beautiful effect especially in the late Romantics. This has also been an Italian tradition, but dispensing with hand-control in the bell. For example the first player in the Rome Opera a few years ago grasped the horn at the farthest side of the circle over a green baize cloth which hid the horn entirely except for the valves, protecting it from tarnish. Yet Italian playing can be as fine as any.

A French double horn was introduced in the 1930s, using the compensating principle with double-length piston valves and the 3rd valve ascending on both sides. With Selmer's enlarged bore it still preserves much of the old French timbre, but it has failed to hold its own against the German models which a few players in Paris were already using before 1940.

Single B flat horn. This is integrally designed as a wide-bore B flat horn without crooks. It requires an extra valve for hand muting. This effect requires the fully-stopping which hand-hornists employed to raise the pitch by a semitone. On a B flat horn the rise comes nearer a three-quarter tone and the muting valve compensates by this amount. It is also often incorporated in professional models of the double horn to enable the players to mute on the B flat side. On the single B flat horn it can be adjusted to lower by a semitone in order to give more fluent fingering in sharp keys, and it can further be provided with an alternative slide which lowers the pitch to F ('open F'), useful in fast natural arppegio passages in this key and, by re-tuned combination with the 1st valve, in E flat also. At one time it looked as though the B flat horn might supersede the double horn: some orchestral sections have used it entirely, as in Berlin. Latterly this trend has weakened, many having returned to the view that the properties of the traditional F pitch are too valuable to be wholly thrown away.

The elder Gumbert was one among others who envisaged the *F alto horn* or *Diskant-horn* in 6-foot F. This was in 1883 for high parts like the off-stage call in *Siegfried*. The pitch had already been known in substitute horns (tenor cor, etc., see note, p. 260) made for military bands, in which a man might serve for only three years during which to learn to play horn parts from scratch. In 1906 Alexander built a Diskant horn in high G (with F crook) for Handel's *Judas Maccabeus* and Bach's B minor Mass at the Mainz Festival in that year. Then the F alto horn lay dormant until recent years, being now best known in the form of a double horn in B flat/F alto or F/F alto or even a triple horn in all three. Paxman, London, have done much to improve it and its future will be watched with interest.

CORNET

Forestier's *Méthode pour le Cornet à pistons* contains a historical introduction contributed by Dauprat above the date 1834 saying that 'it occurred to Halary to apply the valve system as perfected by Meifred to the *Post-horn des Allemands*, known in our military bands by the name *petit cornet*'. By the last term he evidently means a natural post-horn with tuning slide and crooks. The statement refers to some seven years previously and must be true as far as it goes. There is no patent, but we have seen that in Germany, 1825, Schott was offering a natural post-horn in trumpet form (as opposed to circular) with four crooks and tuning slide, and this form the cornet had from the start. Moreover the Germans would seem on all counts to be the most likely people to have first valved a post-horn. Yet there is no positive evidence to this effect (a Griessling & Schlott cornet in the Paris Collection is of the early pattern, with Stoelzel valves as used by Halary, but is undated). Also they took over the French word to name their own versions of the instrument.

Occasional doubling on post-horn by horn-players in Germany was noticed in Chapter 6. Now in France, or rather in Paris, which was at this time both a leading centre of horn-playing and the seat of a comparatively new type of mass audience, a number of the younger horn-players, some still barely out of the Conservatoire and no doubt, like students always, habitués of the premises of their favourite makers, were drawn by the new little valved instrument on which there were no traditions to inhibit them from exploring to the full the totally novel scope and facility of execution which it offered and to exploit it profitably at popular concerts. The oldest among them was Dufrène, for whom Musard wrote solos and variations for his Promenade Concerts from 1833 onwards. In one bound advanced cornet technique became virtually what it is today, and this was a remarkable achievement.

The early cornets are cylindrical from the Stoelzel valves back to the crook socket (with a main bore of c. 11·6 mm. as since), though some show a slight taper through this section. Like horns and trumpets of the period they were supplied with a wide range of crooks as a matter of course. These ran from B flat (tapered shank) down to F (oblong loop, fully or partly tapered), and below that down to D with either individual crooks (looking like the F crook with an extra twist in it) or else the F crook with cylindrical couplers. Valve slides can be pulled out to match the low crooks except, in most cases, that of the 2nd valve, which students were anyhow advised to keep sharp-tuned for the sake of leading notes. Early tutors like that of Carnaud (Paris, undated) require all these crooks, often in duets wherein one student or amateur player with a high crook is accompanied by his fellow with a low crook, e.g. A (a long shank) and D (sounding a seventh lower than written), apparently for pleasure in the tonal contrast as much as for gaining proficiency on every crook. For each operatic tune these tutors prescribe a suitable crook, e.g. for 'Voi che sapete' the G crook, the air sounding in this key. (The 'cornets in E flat' in the *Symphonie fantastique*, incidentally, are in the score only; Berlioz includes a note to the effect that the parts are written in B flat.)

Crooking below F was soon given up; (where 'Cornet in D' appears in mid-century sets of band parts it is likely to signify the soprano cornet in E flat with D shank, sounding a tone *higher* than written). The set down to F (Fig. 42) was still supplied in 1916 by Couesnon, but in fact players through most of the second half of the last century were using the B flat, A and A flat crooks almost exclusively. Old photographs confirm the special popularity of the

last of these in brass bands (Pl. XIV); it finally disappeared from
them through the exclusive use of the B flat cornet in military
bands and of B flat and A in theatre arrangements and in orchestral editions with the trumpet parts set out for cornets. The B flat
cornet with rotary change-valve for A then became popular, still
provided with the separate B flat shank.

With the Périnet valve, fitted to the best French cornets from
the mid 1840s, the instrument acquired the classic format with
three reversals of the tube before this enters the 3rd valve. The
cornet became heavier to hold but more solid in sound thanks to
the improved valves. The last bow, just before the valves, may
contain a short extra tuning slide formerly known in England as
the 'piano slide', used for tuning a sharp-pitch cornet to a low-
pitch piano (Fig. 42, a). The valves are located at a considerable distance from the mouthpiece, so that the bell section is some 15 cm.
shorter than in any B flat trumpet, though the profiles otherwise
are similar or different depending entirely upon the model of
each instrument which is chosen for the comparison. In fact it was
not unknown in Paris for the patterns for cornet bells to be used
for trumpets also. The increasingly superfluous B flat shank was
first integrated with the mouthpipe in France and America early
in the present century. The mouthpipe could then be made with a
planned taper up to 35 cm. long if desired. From the same period
and in the same two countries cornets have also been made in
various more streamlined formats known as *cornet-trompette* or in
America 'trumpet cornet' (one of them is seen in the hands of
La Rocca in an old photograph of the Original Dixieland Jazz
Band).

The vital difference between a cornet and a small valved trumpet lies in the cornet mouthpiece, which is much the deeper in the
cup. It is this which above all gives the cornet that flexibility of
execution and relatively unfatiguing nature when played for
hours on end, to which the Brass Band has so largely owed its
success from the days of the instrument's first manufacture in
London by Pace and Köhler under the name Cornopean, 'horn of
triumphal song'. The tone-quality has however undergone a
change, for the early mouthpiece, in England as well as in France,
was somewhat horn-like (Fig. 1 and Pl. XII), narrow-rimmed,
thin-walled, with a conical interior up to 17 mm. in depth merg-
ing gradually into the backbore. These mouthpieces were said to
produce a 'rounder and more velvet sound' than the rather harder,

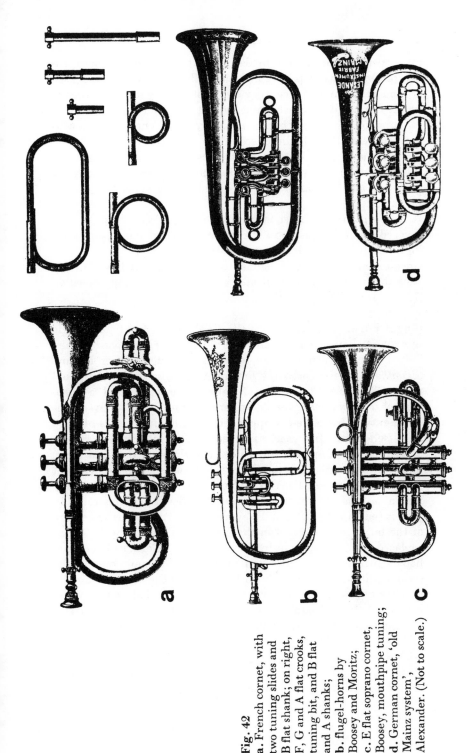

Fig. 42
a. French cornet, with
two tuning slides and
B flat shank; on right,
F, G and A flat crooks,
tuning bit, and B flat
and A shanks;
b. flugel-horns by
Boosey and Moritz;
c. E flat soprano cornet,
Boosey, mouthpipe tuning;
d. German cornet, 'old
Mainz system',
Alexander. (Not to scale.)

more penetrating sound made with the cup mouthpiece advocated by the trumpet-trained and influential Arban, and used
around the turn of the century by artists of staggering virtuosity
like I. Levy and H. Clarke, and by all today. Not that the instrument suffered much change in its musical character in consequence, for though the effect of an early cornet with the old
form of mouthpiece can be sweetly nostalgic, it must be granted
that Arban was not yet twenty when the instrument had already
gained a label among classically-minded musicians for 'snappy
vulgarity'.

In Germany and Austria the name 'cornet' (*Kornett* etc.) has
covered many designs, most of them with a short mouthpipe leading directly to the valves as on the German trumpet (Fig. 42, d).
Once extensively used in bands, these instruments have latterly
been disappearing from the catalogues, the parts being played on
trumpets, now taught so much in schools.

Flugel horn. (Fig. 42, b.) As the English bell-front field bugle
was adopted in Germany and the old name *Halbmond* thereby
ceased to be descriptive, the name of the bugle either became
Signalhorn or else (probably first in Austria) reverted to the old
term *Flügelhorn*. In Berlin, Stoelzel then advertised a *chromatisches Signalhorn* among other chromatic (i.e. valved) instruments in his price-list appended to Sundelin's works of 1828
and itself dated that year. Five years after this early news of a
valved bugle, Wieprecht introduced the virtually flare-less form,
known in Prussia as *Sopran-Cornett*, to replace the B flat trumpet
in his cavalry music. For this purpose it was built with the strong
Berlin pistons: an example by Zetsche, Berlin, is illustrated in
Baines (ed., 1961, Pl. 29g). Elsewhere in Germany the wide flare
of the bugle was retained in the *Flügelhorn*, which by 1840 had
replaced the keyed bugle in the majority of German bands and
had begun to attract attention in France. Kastner notes in the
second edition of *Cours* how with the valves the *bugle* acquired a
nobility of sound which it was far from having before (i.e. when
keyed). In his *Manuel générale*, written in 1847, he illustrates
various *bugles à pistons* including *Flugelhorn de Vienne* and *alle-
mand et belge*, all with double-piston valves, and an *autrichien*
with rotary.

Sax then produced a bugle of *ancienne forme, proportions
nouvelles*, with Berlin pistons and the modern French and English

format: short cylindrical mouthpipe, telescopic for tuning, leading straight to the 1st valve, then following a wide loop expanding throughout to a wide bell (Fig. 42); the mouthpiece has cornet width but greater depth, *c.* 18 mm. This was imported into England by Distin and by Jullien and by 1860 was allotted the regular place in brass-band editions which it has held since: one flugel-horn, reading from the same part as the Repiano Cornet, *à due* or solo as marked. Continental bands have used it a great deal more, valuing the blend of its full, buglish sound with the tenor horns etc. beneath it; French editions may contain three parts for *grand bugle* (B flat flugel-horn) as against two for cornet.

Sopranos in high E flat (sometimes F) include: in England the Soprano cornet (Fig. 42, c) which preserves the form of the bell-front soprano saxhorn; and the Continental small flugel-horn (*petit bugle*, in Germany usually simply called *Pikkolo*). Both are built in flugel-horn format with mouthpipe tuning-slide leading straight to the valves.

Symphonic orchestration has, apart from stage bands, not been generous to the cornet and other such post-classical novelties. Berlioz used the former largely for parts which could not safely be entrusted to the trumpets of his time, and some later composers for purposes of caricature. When thrown in sharp contrast with French C trumpets the effect of the cornet in its own right can however be memorable, notably in the start of the third part of *La Damnation de Faust*, where it is used as a quasi-natural instrument. But otherwise, orchestral managements know well enough that with things as they are, audiences hardly recognize a difference between the sounds of cornet and trumpet, and the parts are usually left to trumpets. The flugel-horn, on the other hand, has suffered at least as badly by the opposite treatment. There is no question of mistaking the individuality of its sound when mixed with others—a sound which to many in Germany has stood for lofty nobility. Why, says Kuhlo's *Posaunenbuch* of 1910, use sparrows and chaffinches (cornets and trumpets) when you can have a nightingale (flugel) for the same money? But British brass-band arrangers know that it can quickly grow monotonous, and it was not fair when two works composed in 1957–8, Stravinsky's *Threni* and Vaughan Williams's Ninth Symphony, each contained a solo cantilena, longer than had been written for any brass instrument since Tchaikovsky's Fifth, for of all things the orchestrally-unknown nightingale. Small wonder that a critic described its effect in the second of these works, very well played though it was on the occasion, as a nasty noise. Much fairer was Respighi, whose *flicorni* (flugel-horns) in the *Pines of Rome* serve merely to suggest the sounds of a Roman army.

TRUMPETS

In Prussia, Wieprecht, who detested hand-stopping on this instrument, had valve trumpets in his cavalry music from 1824— apparently before he scored for valve horns—and these were in high B flat as well as in E flat (Ex. 47). No very early specimens from Berlin are known, but there are the double-piston C and B flat trumpets from Munich by Saurle (Pl. XIII), and from Adorf (near Markneukirchen) by J. G. Roth; those of the latter are not dated, but his dated hand-horns and Inventions-trumpets run only up to 1826. The B flat trumpets have bores from 10·3 to 10·7 mm. and the format which has been kept in Germany since (Fig. 43). The 1829 Saurle trumpet is inscribed with the name of a Bavarian Jäger Regiment. Bandsmen often, however, served in the local orchestra and though an orchestral valve trumpet was held to be properly in F with crooks, it seems fairly certain that by the 1850s the higher instrument had largely found its way in and become (with crooks down to G) as Mandel wrote in his Kneller Hall treatise, the 'ordinary trumpet' in Germany.

Tonalities specified in orchestral scores are small evidence of what instruments players actually used or use. Behind the glorious scoring in *Parsifal* where Wagner writes F trumpet *sehr zart* up to h12 there is the belief in Germany that the instrument used was the B flat (or C), said at the time to give a better sound than the F (Eichborn, 1881, p. 104). In fact, from those years round 1880, it was the military band which continued to find a place for the deeper pitch, allotting the F or E flat trumpets rather dull inner parts plus an occasional fanfare passage while the orchestras adopted the smaller instrument which stood further from classical tradition. In a report of the trade exhibition in Markneukirchen in 1897 (where Kruspe showed the new double horn) the B flat and C trumpets are termed *Orchestertrompeten* and only one F was shown. In England the use of Mahillon's long-model F trumpet, even as late as 1910, really amounted only to a forlorn gesture of protection for the classic pitch. Since crooks might still be used, a shank was provided for the normal key, and with this maker's B flat trumpet also.

Fig. 43 French C trumpet, mobile 1st and 3rd valves, Cousenon, 1912; Below German B flat trumpet, c. 1900

In Paris, following Labbaye's Stoelzel-valve instruments, trumpets in G or F with crooks were in regular use (Fig. 31, f). But trumpet-playing in France ran into a weak phase, due partly to the popularity of the cornet as a substitute and partly, according to Pierre, to the suppression of cavalry bands under the Empire. The lull however gave makers and players the opportunity to reconsider the instrument without classical prejudice. Millereau, successor to Labbaye and Raoux, advertised their new B flat trumpet in 1874. Then Besson's B flat and C trumpets of the 1880s placed the valves on the return branch following the tuning slide in the front bow, to create the modern Franco-American format (Fig. 43) which has now become so widely familiar. This model introduced the long straight mouthpipe instead of a short tube leading directly down to the valves, and though there was no mention of an integral mouthpipe taper at this period, it made this development possible in America later. The taper, from 15 to 25 cm. in length, increases flexibility and is said also to improve intonation, though the tuning of old cylindrical models could be extremely good. A shallow mouthpiece, 9–10 mm. deep, ensures a ringing trumpet sound. Bores earlier this century were as small as 10 mm., conducive—especially with C trumpet—to the incisive silvery tone characteristic in France. But elsewhere, following the later view that symphonic brass must be able comfortably to overwhelm the orchestra in the popular Romantics, the choice in dimensions has been progressively widened even to near 12 mm. for the instrument to be capable of the required maximum volume without the tone breaking up, yet with minimal harm to the trumpet's traditional bright clarity at every degree of loudness.

A classic model of *German B flat trumpet* up to early this century was that of Heckel, Dresden (related to the famous woodwind firm). The short mouthpipe contains a taper. Otherwise, the instrument retained up to some forty years ago the old and well-tried narrow bore dimensions noticed already. The intrinsic tone quality has a golden clarity unmatched by any other B flat trumpet, with notes extraordinarily well centred in the instrument, whereby detached playing can be superlatively crisp while the legato is effortless and singing. The mouthpiece is rather deep, with rounded throat and usually of nickel-silver. This most beautiful of orchestral trumpets lacks, however, weight and power beside the massiveness of the other German brass; older musicians recall how a great opera conductor would be satisfied with the balance at the rehearsal knowing that the singers and others were reserving their full strength for the evening and assuming that the trumpets were doing likewise, though in fact they were giving their best and at the show no one could hear them. Bores therefore often became enlarged, in some models to around 11·3 mm., yet without much alteration to the instrument's character, and to not a few ears it may seem a loss that the German trumpet has recently been replaced so widely in Eastern and Central Europe by American-style instruments. It has of course some minor disadvantages, being awkward to play with one hand when turning pages or inserting a mute, while rotary valves are useless for half-valving in jazz and the like. For international-style dance music German and neighbouring players have always used trumpets of American types, listed in one Hungarian catalogue as '*B Jazz Piston*' (i.e. with Périnet pistons).

The weakest register of the old narrow-bore German trumpet is decidedly the low one, which probably explains why in Russia

Rimsky-Korsakov conceived the use of an F trumpet, *tromba contralta*, to provide a fuller sound as the lowest of three trumpets in his scores from *Mlada*, 1889; but, he added, avoiding the four lowest available notes since the part would often have to be played on B flat trumpet. Some of his pupils and grand-pupils have also included this instrument, e.g. Stravinsky in his recently-published sketches for the *Rite of Spring*. The parts are written in modern notation ($c' = $ h2).

Bass trumpets. An interesting aspect of the rapid developments in cavalry music during the early nineteenth century is the quick attention given by Stoelzel and his associates in Berlin to the recent deep natural trumpets mentioned in the last chapter (Ex. 41). The first news of his valved versions is in *AMZ* of 1821 (col. 122), reporting a performance in Leipzig by Belcke, the Berlin trombonist, of a pot-pourri of his own on the *Chromatische Tenor-trompetenbass* invented by Stoelzel. The instrument went 'from tenor B natural down to bass G or perhaps lower, and stands a third above Stoelzel's new *Chromatische Trompetenbass* made by Griessling & Schlott, and is provided with the same mechanism'. Its natural tonality was said to be G and it excelled the tenor trombone in fullness of tone, being more horn-like, smooth and pleasant in the tenor and stronger in the bass, so the report continues.

The open tonality was probably in fact B flat, as with the Stoelzel-valve *trompette basse* which Labbaye copied in Paris in his specifications of 1827. At least two early specimens are known of this large instrument: the Schuster square-valve instrument already mentioned; and, also from the Snoeck Collection and later acquired by Berlin (No. 3105) but unfortunately destroyed in the war, an anonymous instrument with double-piston valves and stamped 'Tenor H' (Pl. XIII, no. 6). If not in B natural, 'H' could mean 'Horn': it seems that in Germany the designations 'trumpet' and 'horn' were used synonymously in these early days for such instruments. Thus in 1828:

	Sundelin (*instruments for cavalry bands*)	Stoelzel (*price-list printed in Sundelin*)
tenor	Chromatic Tenor Horn in B flat	Chromatic Tenorhorn or Tenor-trompete in B flat
bass	Chromatic Bass Horn, compass $C — g'$	Chromatic Basshorn or Basstrompete in F or E flat

Stoelzel's double nomenclature may be explained by his appended
note that he supplied all instruments needed by *Horn- und
Trompeten-Musik*, i.e. Jäger bands based on horns as well as
cavalry bands based on trumpets, these two new species being
suited to either. No early example of this bass is known, but it was
probably bell-front like the tenor and like the low E flat natural
trumpet of the previous cavalry music. It may have been what
Kastner's *Traité générale*, written in 1836, shows as a bell-front
ophicléide monstre in F with three Stoelzel valves and 'which
seems to be known in Germany as Bombardon or as some say,
Corno basso chromatico'. In Distin's advertisement (Fig. 49) the
same instrument is drawn more carefully, showing fairly wide
proportions and the valves placed horizontally at the front of the
wide main loop, the rear part of which would be tucked under the
player's right arm. An extant baritone in C by E. J. Bauer, *c.* 1850,
has exactly this form (Prague, Museum of Musical Instruments,
No. 244).

Ex. 47 W. Wieprecht, start of 'Lob der Cavallerie', from *6 Lieder für
Preussens Soldaten*, Op. 18 (*c.* 1829). 'Trompeten-Musik' (vocal parts
omitted).

Wieprecht used some of these instruments in his cavalry music
from 1824. Ex. 47 is the accompaniment to a soldier's song, to be
performed at the tempo of a slow march. The four chief trumpets
are richly *schmetternd* (with, in defiance of Fröhlich, some double-
tonguings on main beats) and include, by the look of it, hand-

stopped f' sharp and a', which seems surprising for Wieprecht. They are accompanied by two valved trumpets (that in high B flat written in the old notation), two keyed bugles ('*Kenth*'), two tenor horns written in tenor clef at sounding pitch, and two trombones. The *Tenorbasshorn* which Wieprecht also had at this time is absent and so is the Basshorn, unless this reinforced or replaced the trombones, as Sundelin says that it might.

By the 1840s the German bell-front '*Tenorhorn*' in B flat was a well-known instrument in bands, made with various proportions following regional traditions. The illustrations in Welcker (1855) show a trumpet-like pattern, perhaps from Mainz, beside another of clearly Prussian design with wide bell-section but small flare, and a sound that was 'thicker and more woolly'. From the same period and still up to quite recently Austrian and Bavarian military bands used a wide-bell version known as *Basstrompete*, while a narrow-bell true bass trumpet survives as the *tromba bassa* of large military bands in Italy, likewise in 9-foot B flat and chained to the duty of padding out the harmony.

Wagner's bass trumpet. Deep trumpets of the above kinds would not have escaped Wagner's keen eye in course of his not infrequent dealings with military bands. His first intention for *The Ring* was said to have been a *Basstrompete* at the old 13-foot E flat pitch mentioned in the last chapter, and from the first entrance in *Rheingold* one might suppose that this was indeed what he had in mind. But the part soon rises to a sounding g'' flat. This would represent h19, which no composer of the period who understood wind instruments as well as Wagner could possibly have demanded. True, the bass trumpet is here partly covered by other brass, but not so in the great moment in the 1st Act of *Valkyrie* where Siegmund prepares to draw the sword from the tree, and as he does so the *Basstrompete* forces the famous theme, solo amidst the orchestral *tutti*, up to a sounding e'' which would be h18 on the 13-foot instrument, here crooked in D.

Either Wagner had changed his notion of the bass trumpet, or he had always imagined it an octave higher, which is what Oscar Franz, the eminent horn-player, implies in an article in the *Zeitschrift für Instrumentenbau*, 1884: 'originally the bass trumpet was to stand in low E flat, but since the low notes were very uncertain on this the instrument has been built in low C, sounding an octave lower than written as against a sixth lower with the

E flat instrument'. Thus the E flat in question was higher than
the C, which certainly could not mean 16-foot C. Franz continues:
'in shape it resembles the ordinary trumpet but has a wider
tubing and a correspondingly bigger mouthpiece, whereby the
trumpet quality becomes somewhat veiled, and melancholy rather
than bold'.

Fig. 44 Bass trumpets in C, pre-1910, by Alexander (**left**) and Moritz
(**right**).

A bass trumpet in 8-foot C with crooks for B flat and A was
supplied to the Munich theatre on Wagner's personal order by
Moritz—or so says a later article in the same periodical (1908).
Unfortunately the firm's records are not preserved, but a C bass
with these crooks appears in their post-1900 catalogue and has
something of the wide proportions of a military *Basstrompete*
(Fig. 44, right). Meanwhile, Alexander offered an instrument of

true trumpet proportions (Fig. 44, left), built in either E flat or C, opera houses preferring the one or the other, and today a four-valved model of this type is the most used, in C and normally played by a trombonist since it requires a wider mouthpiece than most trumpeters are prepared to work with. Yet there were said to be theatres which held that the correct sound for *The Ring* was dark and mellow (rather as Franz described) and therefore used an 'Althorn-like' instrument—perhaps the Moritz type in Fig. 44.

Bach trumpets. Prior to the great Bach revival at the bicentenary of the composer's birth, various high-pitched brass instruments had already been made, mostly for military purposes. A German cavalry-band trumpet in high D was advertised in *Caecilia*, 1845, and a few years later in Paris the piccolo B flat pitch was reached in the smallest saxhorn. Again in Paris, a sopranino cornet in this latter pitch was offered by Millereau ten years later as a curiosity. Physically-speaking, therefore, it was not new when, as Pierre relates, the player Teste of the Paris Opéra, engaged in the bicentenary year (1885) by an amateur choral society for Bach's *Magnificat*, feeling that a high D trumpet which Besson had offered him would not be adequate, had the firm make something higher. The result was a straight G trumpet, in an outfit with F and E flat crooks (Fig. 45). While executing

Fig. 45 Besson's trumpet in high G, 1885.

this order Besson also made some high F trumpets, and E flat trumpets with D crook. D trumpets were next made in Germany and Belgium,[1] and in 1894 Alexander supplied an F trumpet for the Second Brandenburg Concerto, stressing that no smaller mouthpiece than the ordinary need be used with it. For the same work Mahillon made a piccolo B flat trumpet for the Brussels Conservatoire concerts in about 1905. The curious story of Kosleck, the Berlin player to whom some, during the 1870s, gave credit for rediscovering the secret of sounding extremely high notes, is told in full by Bate (p. 176), to which it may be added

---

[1] Where D trumpets for Bach and Handel are already mentioned by Mahillon in 1874 (*Eléments d'acoustique*, p. 144).

only that Kosleck was a genuine advocate of the old *Clarin* and took much trouble rehearsing old-style *Aufzüge* on the natural trumpets of the Hussars in Berlin.

The small trumpets made today are in ascending order of pitch: D trumpet; E flat trumpet (tunable to D); F trumpet (3-foot); G trumpet (coming in again with alternative slides for F); piccolo A trumpet; piccolo B flat trumpet (some tunable to A). Most are built in folded format though the straight D, once known to British makers as the 'Handel model' and to audiences as 'Bach trumpet' has been returning to favour. Traditional British oratorio showmanship rightly expects the obbligato trumpeter to stride to the front of the platform opposite his singer, to aim the straight instrument at one section of the audience after another like the trumpet angels atop a baroque organ case.[1] With a piccolo trumpet, a 4th valve is needed to produce the sounding *d'* of the old D trumpet parts; if this can also be tuned to a fifth, the low *a* written for instance in 'Let the Bright Seraphim', need not be taken as a fundamental (or, as some former players of the D trumpet did, played an octave higher to avoid having to strike a low note in an otherwise high part).

Very high notes are of course obtainable on the ordinary trumpet: jazz players often sound the highest note of the Second Brandenburg Concerto. But of course in baroque works the notes have to be produced in a very accurate and articulated manner, and moreover the audience knows what they should be. The comparative safety which a small trumpet brings, through wider spacing of the harmonics in the high-sounding register, may be illustrated by Ex. 48, a laborious stream of notes from the B minor Mass ending on sounding *e'''*, shown as it would be written out in modern notation for piccolo trumpet in A.

These small trumpets are all intended to produce much the same quality of sound as an ordinary trumpet of similar bore, and

[1] In London the first 'Bach trumpet' was a straight two-valved A, inspired by Kosleck's performance and made in 1886 by Silvani, Paris; Solomon's instrument (length 140 cm.) is now in the Bate Collection, Oxford. Boosey was advertising this model still in 1905, as 'Bach trumpet'. Among other straight valved trumpets are those supplied to opera houses for the *Trombe egiziane* parts which announce from the stage the entrance of Egyptian soldiers in Act II of *Aïda*: six instruments are specified, in A flat and in B, in each case requiring a whole-tone valve only for the famous tune. For visual effect a sort of 'oriental' bell has long been the custom on the Continent for these.

their bores have likewise been increased in recent years. Modern composers have scored for D trumpet mainly to be able to write high notes, but the small instruments have also been tried, in England at any rate, on other counts: for a lighter weight of sound in classical works when played by chamber orchestras or

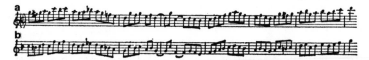

Ex. 48 J. S. Bach, *B minor Mass*, 'Credo' (miniature score p. 185): **a.** as written (sounding a tone higher); **b.** transposed for modern piccolo trumpet in A.

small touring orchestras; and for the advantage of open notes in favourite classical tonalities like E flat and D. Haydn's Concerto is often now played on the small E flat trumpet.

Clarino. As a modern instrument the name denotes a natural trumpet in 7-foot D, invented by Otto Steinkopf and produced by him and Helmut Finke of Herford in 1959 as a version of the baroque trumpet suited to modern requirements through use of nodal vents and transposing hole. Built in three-coil spiral format, 22 cm. across, it initially incorporated a 4 mm. vent situated halfway along the tube; when open, the odd-numbered harmonics, which have a node here, become silenced, so that by opening and closing the hole, fast diatonic passages in the range h8–13 can be executed with greater security—an idea first thought of by Anton Leichner in Vienna seven years earlier. Experiments were also made with a hole which silenced the even-numbered harmonics; but the major addition was a larger hole, 6 mm. in diameter (later up to 9 mm.) placed somewhere approaching three-quarters of the way from the mouthpiece—the position has to be found experimentally—to raise the pitch to the fourth above (as on the old German post-horns, which the designers knew about). Thus h11 and h13 of the C series can be replaced by h8 and h10 of an F series, circumventing the main problem of intonation. A further hole was for some time provided to give a correct f'' sharp, rather weakly, from a b series. The three-hole design was professionally introduced in the Bach works with success by Walter Holy of the Capella Coloniensis. Usually all but the important subdominant hole are now omitted, the instrument itself being designed as far as possible for h11 (hole closed) to favour the sharp. The clarino allows baroque parts to be performed with a commendable approach to authentic effect, with intonation acceptable to the record companies and a welcome relief from the rather monotonous articulation of valved instruments. It is now also made in normal trumpet format.

TROMBONE

A major change with the trombone in the early nineteenth century was the erosion of the old A-T-B trio, not in number, which of course has been preserved in orchestral tradition, but in differentiation of size and pitch of the instruments. In France, in the time of Gossec, trombonists followed other wind players over from Germany and the instruments were scored for, alto, tenor and bass, in their funereal role in this composer's *Messe des Morts* of 1762. They would have been sharp to the French pitch, but the parts were simple and they managed. Then, before the end of the century, '*8va*' appears above low E flat in Gossec's scores: the newer players and the first native makers for over a century—Cormery and Courtois must have been among them— had refused the bass trombone, which has rarely been seen in France since. The alto for a time continued to be used along with two tenors, but by Berlioz's time all parts were normally played on the tenor. In settling on one single species players had merely bowed to a new professional logic. The instruments were no longer a set of three owned by a municipality. Players provided their own as they have done since, and the tenor, on which any part, whether a single part or one of three, could be dealt with somehow was the obvious choice, particularly when serpent or ophicleide became subjoined as a bass voice below the trio.

Similar considerations led to a change in the German-speaking countries, the former guardians of the traditional trio. It is described by Fröhlich ('Von der Posaune', p. 29), by Gottfried Weber (*AMZ*, 1816 col. 51ff.), in Vienna by the bandmaster Nemetz, and called for instruments all of B flat pitch but with different-sized mouthpieces: for alto, a trumpet mouthpiece (Nemetz adds with the cup deepened); for tenor and bass Fröhlich and Nemetz practically agree on cup diameter 23·5, depth 15 for tenor; 28 and 21 mm. for bass; also that the instrument used for bass should also have a larger bore and bell. Thus the low Cs and Ds of Haydn and Mozart were lost for a time, and, which particularly disappointed German critics, the low E flat-D in the *Freischütz* Overture. But the lowest note in Beethoven and Schubert is usually *F*: Beethoven's *Equali* of 1812 may literally be named for the four equal trombones—and the Trombone basso who fires the start for the Trio in the Ninth Symphony, might be the widest of them: the best-sounding instrument and, from his important position in military bands, the firmest player.

The *French trombone* at first retained the old narrow bore. Dieppo, whose performance of the solo part in the *Symphonie funèbre et triomphale* was greatly admired by Berlioz, described in his *Méthode* his instrument as having 10 mm. bore, i.e. in the old Nuremberg range, though his bell was a little wider, 12 cm., and of course he used the French conical mouthpiece (Fig. 1, 10). Then, before 1860, the classic French narrow-bore trombone was perfected by Courtois, with bore *c.* 11·4 mm. continued up to the commencement of the tuning slide, then expanding through the bow to a 15 cm. bell (Fig. 46,a). This provided a more satisfactory bottom register than the ancient tenor bores could, and was adopted also in England after French imports had stifled native models built by F. Pace and others with somewhat German features.

Every first and second player of a British orchestra or band played these French-model instruments up to 1930 and brass-bandsmen for much longer, some still, and they should now be preserved along with other outmoded brass instruments against the day when people want to restore authentic nineteenth-century sounds as they have already begun to revive those of the eighteenth century; also for small-combination works composed with the French trombone in mind, like Stravinsky's *Soldier's Tale*, in which the modern trombone, however discreetly handled, lacks the proper transparency and personality; and of course for comedy solos like H. Moss's classic, *The Firefly*, for which the modern instrument is too solemn.

In England the third player, whether in band or orchestra, always played the *G Bass Trombone* which survived the French invasion and was in regular manufacture up to recently (Fig. 46, b). As with all the older bass trombones a wooden handle, attached to the slide stay by universal joint, enables the player to reach the 7th position, with which the downwards compass here irritatingly stops at *C* sharp. Mouthpieces are about 27 mm. wide, 23 mm. deep. Though with wider bore than the tenor, and excellently

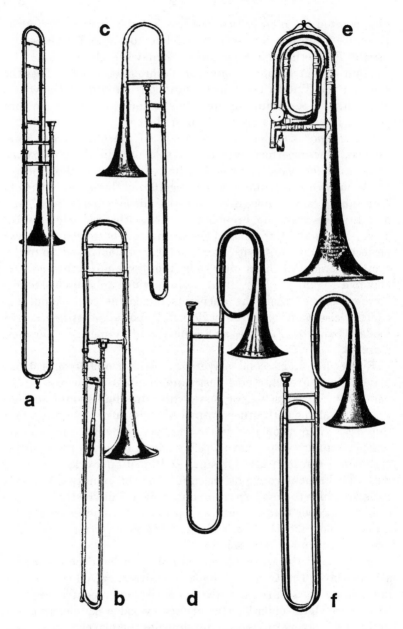

Fig. 46 a. French trombone, 1915; **b.** English G bass trombone, Boosey; **c.** German tenor trombone, 1855 (after Welcker); **d.** F bass trombone, Moritz, *c.* 1900; **e.** bell joint with F attachment, Alexander; **f.** B flat contrabass with double slide, Moritz.

full-sounding at medium dynamics, 'the G' is a difficult instrument on which to produce a blending tone in *forte*. An artist who notably achieved this, William Coleman of the B.B.C. Symphony Orchestra, used Boosey & Hawkes's regular orchestral model in G/D with thumb attachment (below) for D whereby all the lowest notes down to the fundamental can be produced correctly save G' sharp.

The progress of the *German trombone* through the nineteenth century largely followed from the new concept of a bass trombone as a wide-bore B flat instrument. It is likely that mention of *Bassposaune* as the solo instrument of Belcke, and of Queisser in Leipzig (for whom David wrote the Concertino) relate to this instrument; the question is well discussed by Mary Rasmussen in *BQ* V, 1, p. 10. With the invention of the thumb-valve in the bell-joint by Sattler (Leipzig, 1839 and approved by Queisser), which instantly lowers the pitch to F and makes low C possible, this German bass trombone became the B flat/F instrument which it has remained since. The example in Pl. XV has 14·5 mm. slide bore, 22·5 cm. bell; its maker, Joseph Saurle, died in 1863. Dated mid-nineteenth-century tenors (e.g. Fasting, 1847; Barth, 1856) have bores up to 11·5 mm., later reaching 12 mm. or more. The bell already shows the characteristic German wide-radius bow which brings the wide bell-rim clear of the slide without tilting, and the bore expands the whole way through the bell. These examples are still without slide stockings, but they mostly have the full German slide length, 3 cm. longer than elsewhere. Such trombones Wagner, Brahms and Bruckner knew. The 2nd player later came to use a B flat/F of smaller bore than that used by the 3rd player on bass, since to become a common practice in other countries. The sound of the German instrument alone is rather morose, but trombones are usually heard together in harmony or unison, and these massive instruments produce as well as any the inimitable glow of a soft trombone entry in harmony. The chief danger is when Bruckner's unison *ff* is taken too literally and the suave tone overforced to sound brassy, as Berliners have been apt to do, with rough and overbearing effect.

The true F bass trombone, with a coil in the bell (Fig. 46,d) meanwhile continued to be made in Germany well into the present century, mainly for bands though it was used orchestrally for many years in Berlin in the fine model of Moritz.

The true *alto trombone* in E flat (sometimes F) has always been procurable even if seldom listed in the catalogues. Many orchestral first trombonists possess it for occasional use in Alto Trombone parts with very exposed high notes. British players in the narrow-bore days used mainly Courtois altos, but later Alexander, etc.

The *American trombone* was developed first from the French type in a spirit of independence, having already by the 1920s a wide bell, around 18 cm., usually tilted a little by a bend in the opposite branch, to clear the slide. All-purpose trombones have slide bores around 12·4 mm. ('medium') or 13·4 mm. ('medium large'): excellent instruments through which the trombone, at first through jazz (particularly big-band jazz) recovered during this century the proud position among musical instruments which it had so largely lost two centuries before. These models began to be used orchestrally in England during the 1930s and are now familiar over most of the world. A screw collar secures the bell to the slide instead of the old tapered tenon. The left hand can then be safely moved to the bell for operating mutes.[1] American makers have also paid great attention to the B flat/F bass trombone. In magnificent models by Conn (Selmer), Olds, Reynolds, Holton etc., bores reach 14·3 mm. and bells 24 cm. A problem arises with the bigger shifts required when the trombone is switched by the thumb-valve to F. By ratio this brings the 6th position on the F (for the low *C*) nearly 5 cm. beyond the ordinary 7th position and thus virtually off the slide. Also the low *B'*, which would need an extension of some thirty inches, is lacking. The designers therefore added to their later models a second thumb-valve which adds tubing to set the in-strument in a flat E (B flat/F/E trombone). The ordinary F attachment has, of course, the further value of simplifying the execution of passages which otherwise involve big shifts of the slide, and this is the chief reason for the second player using a B flat/F instrument also. Indeed today all three players of the section may use it, and the time has virtually come when, as the works of Mahler to some degree anticipated, composers will be able to regard the compass of all three trombone in the symphony orchestra as descending chromatically to C or below.

---

[1] For practical advice on the trombone generally see especially Denis Wick, 1971. As a slide lubricant there are special preparations, while many use cold cream, pouring on to it the warm water condensed from the breath. Some, however, say that this is acid and bad for the metal.

Contrabass trombone. For *The Ring*, in which Wagner demands of the fourth of the four trombonists a contrabass trombone descending to *E'*, Bayreuth was supplied (by Moritz as far as one can tell) with an instrument in 18-foot B flat provided with a double slide (Fig. 46,f). This has four legs connected by a bow at the top and by two bows crossing each other at the bottom. The shifts become halved and hence the same as those of the ordinary trombone. The device was already well known in Wagner's time, though only with F bass trombones (or in England, G). An early example for a mounted band was mentioned in Chapter 7 (p. 188), while the *double coulisse* appears in the Tuerlinckx and the Schott lists. On the F instruments the double slide is sometimes long enough to provide an 8th position (at 17 inches) for *B'* flat.

A double-slide B flat contrabass contemporary with Wagner's was exhibited by Boosey & Sons in 1862 under the name 'Basso Profondo'. The wide bell contained a large loop through which the left arm passed. It was played at massed brass-band festivals in London and was still in the 1905 catalogue. A version was later made for *The Ring*, in C with nine positions on the slide in order to reach the low *E'*. But in the long run the double slide has yet to prove popular and Wagner's parts are now usually played on some form of bass trombone with plain slide. In London up to the 1950s this was a G/D trombone with a C slide placed in the attachment; the notes from *C* to *A'* flat were then obtained without passing the 5th position and the lower notes followed as pedals. At Bayreuth they now use an F/low C trombone. Elsewhere the parts are often managed effectively on the latest models of B flat/F/E bass trombone mentioned above, the wide bores allowing good use of fundamentals. Meanwhile a fresh design of F contrabass with normal slide was designed by Künitz in 1963 and is made by Alexander. This has two attachments: one (left thumb) lowers by a fourth to C; the other (left middle finger) lowers to D. The tube-length increment given by these two valves together is that which is required to lower by a perfect fifth, putting the instrument in low B flat (just as C and D crooks were coupled on the natural F trumpet to serve for B flat). With these four harmonic series all immediately available, the slide itself has to be moved beyond the 3rd position only for *G'* and *F'* sharp. The design is named *Cimbasso* after the so-named parts in Verdi, which it was brought out in the first place to deal with.

Valve trombones (Fig. 47). Stoelzel does not seem to have made these. The first to do so were in Prague or Vienna in the later 1820s. To Nemetz in Vienna the valved instrument marked the acme of perfection of the trombone, and of course for mounted bands it was particularly suitable. An old Alexander catalogue recommends for these an instrument built with the bell to the

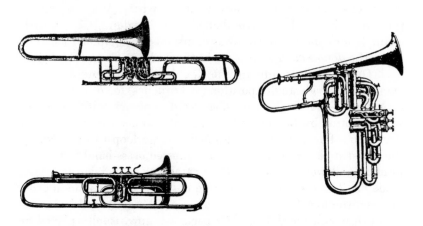

Fig. 47 Valve trombones: German 4-valve tenor; French B flat tenor; on right, with six independent valves, Ad. Sax, Paris.

right of the valves for better balance. Numerous upright (tuba-shaped, Fig. 49) and circular models have also been produced to assist cavalrymen and in Holland also cyclist bandsmen. Apart from this, the valve trombone—though with the constant bore through the valves it cannot compare with the slide instrument in tone, or in intonation and articulation either—has for over a century proved its worth on every continent in cramped theatre pits and also, being virtually indestructable and playable by any-one who knows valve fingering, in local bands which through force of tradition must have a trombone if only in name (in France it is often built in C). It has a certain musical character of its own, par-ticularly well exploited in the rare solos taken by Ellington's Juan Tizol, for instance in 'Twelfth Street Rag'. Moreover, since there is no question of different-sized shifts, valve trombones have been more extensively made in alto and bass sizes, and contrabass too, than slide trombones during this valve era.

A contrabass designed for *The Ring* by Dehmals, Vienna, is in

F with three rotary valves for each hand, all in line. Each set of three has a two-tone 3rd valve, and the second set is tuned to be used in conjunction with the 2nd and 3rd valve combination of the first set—a compromise system also employed on some tubas. Much better are Sax's *Independent pistons* (1852). Three valves for each hand are placed at right angles (Fig. 47); the six correspond individually to positions 1 to 6 on a slide. On lowering the 1st valve the windway passes through its valve loop and so back to the bell. On raising this and lowering the 2nd valve the windway passes through the 1st piston to the 2nd, through the loop attached to this, and back through both pistons to the bell; and so on, so that when the 6th valve is lowered, the rest being 'up', the windway passes through all the previous pistons, through the 6th valve loop, and back through all the pistons to the bell. When no valves are lowered the windway passes through all pistons and a terminal loop and so back again to the bell, and this gives the 7th position. There are no combinations, so that each 'position' is perfectly tuned. The technique is less cumbersome than may at first appear, since any valves *below* that which is giving the note may be held down if convenient. Despite all the tubing the instrument is quite light to hold, and the system was fitted by Sax to most other brass instruments, though it actively reached the present century only on the trombone and apparently only in Belgium where, made by Mahillon and by Lebrun, it was for a long time one of the delights of the Brussels opera, sounding especially good in cheerful passages with grace-notes in *La Bohème*.

TENORS AND TUBAS

Upright valved basses must have appeared just before 1830, though the earliest dated specimen seems to be Uhlmann's 'valved ophicleide', 1839 (Salzburg Collection 152, illustrated in Baines, 1966, No. 799). Made from Austria to Belgium, most are in ophicleide shape with double-piston valves placed vertically on the mouthpipe, though in some cases these valves lie across the instrument (like rotary valves since). This second arrangement was said to suit cavalry bombardons, presumably through being held lower and more slanted. A selection of bombardons in the Brussels Collection is shown in Pl. XVI. A few retain the B flat pitch of the ophicleide, but with three valves the compass then stops at *E*—or at *E* flat with the two-tone 3rd valve which has always been common on the Continent with the large brass instruments. The majority are in tuba-pitch F, up to 145 cm. tall with valve bore reaching 18 mm. The bore profile from bell rim back to the valves is in some cases virtually identical with that of the whole of an ophicleide, being then continued by the narrow tubing required for the valves and thence to a deep, somewhat conical mouthpiece with narrow rim. The sound can be attractive, warm and close-knit, quite lacking the touch of coarseness which earned the ophicleide its solo in *Benvenuto Cellini.*

In Paris, where Guichard had designed valved ophicleides from 1832, Périnet nine years later claimed a superior conversion in a *Piston basse* in which something of the overall conicity of the ophicleide and hence, it was hoped, more of its character, was preserved by using valves of increasing bore: he planned two for each hand, the 4th valve, nearest the bell, having a barely practicable travel of 35 mm. or nearly $1\frac{1}{2}$ inches.

Still early in the period of these bombardons, Moritz and Wieprecht, in or just before 1835, produced their *Bass-tuba* (Pl. XVI 5).[1] This very compact but rather heavy F bass has a valve bore of 15·5 mm. and a wide conical bell section with next to no flare. The five Berlin pistons have their tubing arranged untidily but without sharp bends. Originally the 1st and 2nd valves, for the left hand, lowered by a tone and by a semitone. The three for the right hand provided: a large tone, to make an exact two tones with the 1st valve; large semitone, to make an exact tone-and-a-half with the 1st valve; and a perfect fourth. Thus for *D* flat, 1st and 3rd; *C*, 5th alone; from this down to *A'* flat by adding the 3rd and 4th valves; and adding to these the 1st and 2nd to reach low *F'* sharp above the fundamental as best one could. Moritz's tuba won much admiration and must surely have been envisaged by Wagner in the opening of the *Faust* Overture, which no contemporary bombardon could have managed. In sub-

---

[1] The name 'tuba' had been revived in Gossec's instrumentation of his music for Voltaire's re-interment, 1791: the *tuba curva* (viz. Roman *cornu*) is required in three pitches, each to sound one note; in another piece various *trompes antiques* (viz. *tubae*) add their h3 and h4. Cherubini soon afterwards included the *tuba curva* in a *Hymne à la Victoire,* and then Méhul, in *Joseph.* An example is preserved in the Paris Collection. Halary then coined the name '*clavitube*' for his keyed bugle, and finally, after the Moritz *Bass-tuba,* Sax made a *Sax-tuba,* a kind of valved *cornu,* for Halévy's *Juif Errant*: specimens of this last are in the Berlin and New York Collections. Note also *Tube* in Ex. 35.

sequent models the valve arrangement was usually altered to agree with standard fingering elsewhere: the right hand then has a normal three including the two-tone 3rd valve; the left hand has a large whole-tone valve (which can be held down when playing E flat bass parts), and the perfect fourth—or this last valve only. The two-tone valve, incidentally, alarming though it is for a player unaccustomed to it, can be a great help in march basses, avoiding perpetual cross-fingering in the 'oom-pah' on *F-C-E-C* (or a tone lower in E flat, holding down the extra whole-tone valve).

In Italy, whither the bombardons arrived from Austria, an example dated 1841 by Apparuti of Modena, preserved in the museum at that city, has the tall Uhlmann form, and with it we must return to that singular name '*Cimbasso*' which heads the part below the trombones in Verdi's scores up to *Aïda*. The word dates from before Verdi's works, appearing for instance in the manuscript score (Brit. Mus. Add. 30916) of L. Ricci's *La Chiara di Rosemberg*, first produced in 1831, at the Scala, Milan. The part is here a perfectly ordinary one below trombones as might have been written for any bass horn or other deep instrument of the time. Another spelling is met in a printed catalogue of the Kraus Collection, Florence, compiled in French by the collector's son in 1878 before the instruments were sold (most of them to the Heyer Collection, then in Cologne). This reads after two serpents: '360. *Simbasso* avec 4 clefs' and '361. *Idem* avec tête de serpent, 4 clefs'. These would be *bassons russes*. From the resemblance of some of many dragon bells to a baboon or mandrill, the name may perhaps have had a connection with the word *scimia* (or *simia*), in a nickname 'monkey bass'.[1] Verdi's own parts, however, are clearly for some kind of valved bass in F until his preference apparently changed to a valved bass trombone (in the Milan *Gazetta musicale*, 1871, he demands '4 tromboni' in the strength of an opera orchestra). Even so, some of his later parts are said to

---

[1] *Note to the Dover Edition.* Many of the uncertainties regarding the name 'cimbasso' are dispelled by the expert article by Renato Meucci, 'Il cimbasso e gli strumenti affini nell'ottocento italiano', *Studi Verdiani* V (Parma, 1989). Here again the question of the name's origin has to be left to hypothesis. The most likely seems to be the abbreviation in scores and parts for 'corno basso' ('c. basso' or 'c. in basso')—indicating first the wooden bass horn and subsequently its successors in the role (ophicleide, bombardon etc.)—becoming the spoken, and thence written, 'cimbasso'. Evidence to this is seen in contemporary instrumentation treatises and other sources, of which the article gives a full list.

have 'tuba' pencilled in, while later on, where the score of
Puccini's *Turandot* has *Trombone contrabasso*, at the première at
the Scala in 1926 the player was listed as '*Basso tuba*'. Rampone,
the Milan makers, have long stocked under this last name a thin,
narrow-bore BBb tuba (Fig. 48), reckoned to be the correct instrument for the Cimbasso parts.

Among tenors and altos in addition to the bell-front tenors mentioned earlier in this chapter, Moritz made some very compact

Fig. 48 Left to right Rampone, *Basso-tuba* in BB flat (1948 catalogue);
Moritz, *Kaisertuba*, BB flat or CC, pre-1910; **Below** Boosey, BB flat Bass,
compensating 3rd valve.

upright models with the virtual absence of bell-flare typical of Berlin. Wieprecht, who no doubt had a hand in their design, used an *Althorn* in the Jäger Guards from 1837, no doubt of this type. A specimen in the Munich Städtisches Instrumentensammlung measures only seven inches (12·5 cm.) across the bell and has a two-tone 3rd valve. About the same time in France the doubtful value of the alto ophicleide prompted Guichard to produce the *Clavicor*, patented in 1838. This upright tenor, often with a screw bell, has three Stoelzel valves, two for the right hand and the 3rd valve for the left. This last, placed nearer to the mouth-pipe than the others, has a smaller bore. Some clavicors were built in keys up to F, but most of the many surviving examples are in 8-foot C with a B flat crook. The bell profile, long and rather narrow, was evidently found by scaling up the diameters of a cornet bell by a factor of about two-and-a-half, then continuing it back to the valves in approximately a cone. The conical mouth-piece (cup width 23 mm.) fits into a trombone-sized socket. The tone is not bad though not strong. From 1839 clavicors were also made with the three valves arranged normally, and were so copied in London with various modifications by Pace and Köhler and widely used in British bands through the 1840s and 1850s, usually under the name 'Alt horn' (Fig. 49).

At this point enters Adolphe Sax. Born in the year preceding Waterloo and thirty miles from it, Sax fled from his debts in Brussels to arrive in Paris in 1842 with thirty francs to his name. There he managed to set up a workshop in an old shed, trained a few workmen, and at once set down to his plan of replacing the existing motley of band instruments, valved and otherwise, by an integrated family, namely his Saxhorns. These, first made in the following year and patented in 1845, were principally based—as the name 'sax-*horn*' witnesses—on the German valved bugles, tenors and tubas, but with modifications which brought them into line with his own ideas and with each other. Sax later compared his bass with Moritz's tuba: a narrower starting diameter, but becoming wider in the middle (i.e. getting quickly past the valves); his bell was less wide up to a few inches from the rim, where it flared to a much larger size. At the 9-foot pitch he provided both a wide-bore B flat *basse* and, for lighter tonal weight, a narrow B flat *baryton* with an improved clavicor kind of bore matching the higher members of the series. He also arranged the Berlin pistons more neatly and made them more solidly, guided by lug and groove instead of Wieprecht's fixed pin, which tends to wear out rather quickly.

Sax initially employed a bell-front format for the saxhorns down to baritone (Fig. 49) but he used an upright form throughout his corresponding family of *Saxotrombas* or *saxhorns de cavallerie* (whence 'tromba', with fractionally smaller bores) in order—or so says Forestier's Saxhorn *Méthode*—to forestall dire consequences when a horse threw its head back, though this has normally been prevented from the Middle Ages onwards by the martingale. The saxhorns themselves were also after a year or two made in the same upright model (named 'tuba' in Fig. 49). By 1847 every size could be supplied with a 4th valve, set at right angles to the others for the left hand, in the manner which has remained normal in France and England, where the little finger is rarely used for a valve as it is regularly in Germany and America. In pitch the saxhorns ranged from E flat *soprano* and B flat *contralto* ($4\frac{1}{2}$-foot.) down to the BB flat *contrebasse* which was added by 1851 (Pl. XVI). Also from this year is the piccolo or *petit saxhorn* in B flat *sur-aigu*, which Berlioz scored for twice (also Kastner in a cavalry music in *Les Cris de Paris*, 1857, while Jullien included it in a touring band in England about the same time). Berlioz writes for this only up to sounding *c'''*—he would no doubt have gone higher with today's techniques. At the other extreme, Sax experimentally built a *saxhorn bourdon* in FF with the avowed object of demonstrating that the smallest man could play the biggest instrument; a sub-bass in EE flat by Couesnon, in the Boosey & Hawkes Collection, has valve bore 20 mm., while yet larger was a BBB flat bass used in America in the Gilmore band, 1893, described by Bessaraboff (p. 407) as 208 cm. tall with 80-cm. bell and valve bore 25 mm., almost one inch. Another, by Besson, is now in the possession of the Harvard University Band.

Sax gives in his saxhorn tutor his system for tuning the valve slides (in fact the same system as in Meifred's horn *Méthode*): first fix *g'*, then tune *b'* (2nd valve) by ear, the 1st valve on *d"* and *f"* also by ear, and finally sound *d"* with 1st and 3rd to tune the latter. In practice, of course, everyone has his own method of tuning valves.

The drama of the public contest in the Champ-de-Mars between Sax's hastily organized line-ups, both infantry and cavalry, and those opposed to him on older patterns makes amusing reading in the accounts by Kastner and De Pontécoulant (II, 266).

Sax's large infantry band of saxhorns and clarinets was compared favourably with the older and basically *Harmonie* combinations, which suffered, it was said, from 'the enormous gap in the middle harmonies, the thin cutting tone of the oboes mixing ill with the rest, the swollen-faced bassoonists with no carrying power whatever, and despite some good use of valve horns, the sterile buzzing of hand-horns in the open air, still worse on the march'. In retrospect one might have enjoyed this, but Sax was deemed to have won, and naturally his subsequent contracts for the army infuriated the established Paris makers—an impressive list including Besson, Courtois, Périnet, Raoux, Halary, and Gautrot (the last being successors to Guichard, later to become Couesnon) —who claimed that Sax's instruments so far from being inventions could be seen hanging up in any German maker's front shop. The ensuing litigation finally brought Sax to ruin, though without extinguishing his name: 'Saxhorn' has remained in France the recognized generic for the upright band instruments— though colloquially known simply as *alto* etc.—as made thenceforth by his former opponents. Some began to imitate the saxhorns almost from the moment that Sax first made them. Indeed, from the drawings shown in Lavignac (by Soyer, Part II, vol. 3, 1455–6) as having been produced in an unsuccessful lawsuit of 1856 in the name of Rivet, who apparently acted as cover-up for Gautrot, then the latter was making and selling such instruments, described as *Néo-Altos* and *Bombardons*, which, though with Stoelzel valves, already in 1844–5 had the broader, squatter format which we have all known so well in the models of the Paris and London makers since (Fig. 50). On the other hand one cannot escape the impression that the drawings look more like 1856 than 1844, while the small sizes seem to be the larger size literally scaled down on paper, valve buttons and all, which in practice cannot be.

The upright saxhorns as subsequently built are listed below, the upright B flat *contralto* having been dropped, since at this pitch everyone played the cornet or the flugel-horn. In British brass bands the parts for all five species observe the French notation as used by Sax, being written in transposed treble clef (c′ = h2) so that music-reading tuition is the same throughout; the fifth species below then sounds two octaves plus a tone lower than written.

1. E flat *alto*, at first also called *ténor*, the instrument for which Berlioz so charmingly conceived a solo part in *The Trojans* (in the

Fig. 49 From the advertisement of Henry Distin & Co., Cornet & Sax-horn Manufactory, 31 Cranbourn St., London, *c.* 1849, showing almost entirely French imports, most of them designs by Sax. 'Tuba' denotes the upright saxhorn.

'Royal Hunt' and subsequently transferred to horn). English 'Tenor Horn', used in brass bands only, with three parts, Solo, 1st and 2nd.

2. B flat *baryton*, Engl. 'Baritone' (Fig. 50); two parts in a brass band; formerly also a part in military-band arrangements (the part which was originally termed 'Alt Horn'); one could still occasionally see a baritone in a Guard's band in London as late as 1929.

3. B flat *basse*, with its much wider bore to serve both as a bass and as a full-toned tenor soloist. English 'Euphonium', with one part in each type of band. This name is said to have been invented by a German musician, Sommer, in 1843 for his own species of ophicleide-conversion which, after improvement in Vienna, he exhibited across Europe as far as London. Details of it are vague, even as to the original pitch (B flat, but also low E flat if Distin is correct in Fig. 49, No. 1). In Germany the wide-bore instrument corresponding to the English euphonium is held to have first been the outcome of it.

4. E flat *contrebasse*, Engl. 'E flat Bass'. As built a tone higher in F, with compensating 4th valve, this was the regular orchestral tuba in London until superseded by the newer E flat bass known through its extra-wide bore as 'EE flat' bass.

5. B flat *contrebasse*, Engl. 'BB flat Bass'. On this a compensating 3rd valve is the most useful for bands (Fig. 48). This low BB flat pitch, or a tone above it (16-foot C) has long been the preferred pitch in America for an orchestral tuba, in Holland and now elsewhere too. The tubist then needs a second, smaller instrument, e.g. euphonium, to cope with some very high parts written specifically for the tuba as known in France.

This French orchestral tuba is a wide-bore *basse* in 8-foot C (Fig. 40) developed by Besson, first with five valves. These include a two-tone 3rd valve which also serves for three semitones in conjunction with the 4th valve. The 5th valve is the '*transpositeur*', lowering by a semitone to facilitate fingering in sharp keys. In 1880 Besson added the 6th valve which, lowering by a perfect fifth, makes possible a low D' and offers useful alternative fingerings in the bottom octave generally. The complete fingering is given by Brousse in Lavignac, II p. 1679.

East of the Rhine the corresponding band instruments are termed: 1. *Althorn*; 2. *Tenorhorn*; 3. *Bariton*; 4. *Bass*; 5. *Kontra-*

Fig. 50 Left to right Althorn, bell-front, Moritz; Tenorhorn, oval model, Alexander; B flat baritone, Couesnon.

bass. For the smaller instruments the upright models ('tuba-form') are alternative to bell-front and oval forms (Fig. 50), but how much they owe to Sax and how much to contemporary makers in Germany and Austria is not throughout clear. With the continual international exhibitions ideas were passed round very fast, and looking at the matter from the West one is inclined to overlook the enormous influence of some very inventive and energetic makers who worked within the old Austrian Empire, both in Vienna itself and in that historic focus of brass history, Bohemia. While the permanent influence of Sax extended beyond France in full force only to Belgium and England, to reach Italy and the United States with diminished force, the Austrian sphere of influence spread over Russia, to the Far East as European bands became adopted there, and southward to the Mediterranean countries and Latin America—in fact most areas where the local band will almost certainly include together a bell-front tenor horn, valve trombone, and circular bass. The latter was introduced in Vienna, by Stowasser, 1849 (*Helicon*) first following the pro-portions of the flareless Berlin Bass-tuba (Pl. XVI). Made in F, E flat or BB flat, the helicon is placed over the head to rest upon the left shoulder; in some models a piece of dummy tubing com-pletes the circle. It has since been made in most Western countries (Fig. 51), but without seriously rivalling the upright bass save in the case of the American sousaphone (in E flat or BB flat) which Conn developed from 1898, at first as a helicon with wide bell pointing upwards, then in the now familiar form with detachable bell with a rapid flare up to 66 cm. across pointing forwards, raised above the head, and latterly made in fibreglass. The helicon format has also been applied to all band instruments from E flat alto downwards at one time or another for special types of band.

In Bohemia by far the most influential maker was Sax's Czech contemporary Wenzel Cerveny (in Czech, Červený—the first syllable as in English 'chervil') who set up in Königgratz (today Hradec Králové) sixty miles east of Prague in the same year that Paris opened its gates to the formidable Belgian. Like Sax, Cerveny was perpetually inventing and was equally admired for the workmanlike solidity of his products. The account of the firm's early progress by Schafhäutl (*AMZ*, 1882, pp. 855 ff) names as the first creation a *Cornon*, 1844, the first of the innumerable sub-stitute horns for military bands.[1] It was to be played with a horn

[1] Including: *tenor cor*, Besson (Paris) *c.* 1860, in C (B flat crook), and

mouthpiece and was first made in wide-bore horn format. But to suit mounted bands, in which the valve horn can be awkward to manipulate, Cerveny changed the *Cornon* to upright form, with four valves (with Cerveny always rotary) and a four-position switch valve (*Ton-wechsel*, 1846, Fig. 51) connected to loops having the function of crooks from F to D—not wholly a new idea, something like it having been used in French 'omnitonic' horns earlier in the century (described by Morley-Pegge, Chap. 4), but a straight-forward application which is typically Central-European. The *Ton-wechsel* was also fitted to other instruments, as in Plate XV, here having five positions, for C, B flat, A, A flat and G, the valves of course being tunable to match.

Cerveny's four-valved *Baroxyton*, 1853, was claimed as the first 9-foot B flat instrument to possess a compass down through the contrabass octave to E' flat, having a two-tone third valve and the 4th valve tuned to a perfect fifth—somewhat as in Besson's C tuba later in Paris. It was built in oval form and was possibly one of the first to have this form which is so popular in Germany for altos and tenors, though people often look rather uncomfortable holding it. The maker further claimed that his BB flat *Kontrabass* of c. 1845 was the prototype for everyone else's, including that of Sax.

Most of his inventions were single species, but he produced in the late 1860s a family ('whole *Concert-Register*') of circular wide-bore *Cornetts*, virtually valved Pless horns, which, played together during hunting parties, later won from the Tsar of Russia the title 'Kaiser-Alexander-Quartet' and from the King of Prussia a Ritterkreuz for the inventor. Then in 1882 Cerveny devised a valved bass (*Kaiserbaryton*) with an almost truly conical bore throughout achieved by use of valves of graded bore. The tone-quality was said by Pierre in Paris to be extremely sweet and sympathetic, approaching that of a cello. Here too the idea had been thought of in Paris previously (e.g. Périnet's *piston basse*),

---

developed in London by Distin, by about 1867, made in 6-foot F (E flat crook or slide). This last, made left- or right-handed and played with a conical mouthpiece larger than that of the French horn, was manufactured to the end of the F Horn era and in some countries is still, named in France *cor alto*, in Portugal *clavicorno*, in Italy *genis corno*— i.e. an E flat alto (*genis*) in horn form—and in America *mellophone* (latterly made by Conn with forward-projecting bell for jazz). German equivalents are listed as *Altkorno*, etc.

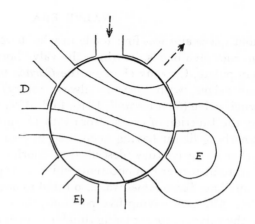

Fig. 51 Plan of Cerveny's *Tonwechsel*, 1846, each clockwise turn of 45° bringing in a larger loop, for E, E flat and D, downwards from F. **Below** E flat helicon, Boosey.

but Cerveny persevered with it in his first model of *Kaiser-tuba* in BB flat, the name honouring the Austrian Emperor and eventually filtering through to England via the trade exhibitions as 'Emperor bass': a bass with maximum dimensions, save (in the original model) for a relatively small bell flare with 36-cm. rim. As since made in Germany with a wider flare and normal valves, the *Kaiser-bass* (Fig. 48) is the largest of the tubas formerly classified as half-size, three-quarter-size, etc; as were those in F or E flat also. To assist the intonation of these one or two valves may be added to the four-valved instruments, though only quite recently, thus: 5th valve (left hand) tuned to approximately a three-quarter tone, to be equivalent to a semitone in combination with the 4th valve (right little finger); and perhaps a 6th valve tuned to a minor third or two tones for *ad hoc* combination with the 4th valve on other low notes.

Cerveny's inventions, some of them trivial, could easily be paralleled by a dozen or more by Sax which have not been mentioned, and yet more by other makers of the period in almost every European country and America: Mahillon in Brussels; Distin in London (e.g. his Ballad horn or Voice horn, 1858, circular with bell facing forwards, in C with B flat crook, intended for playing from song copies with piano accompaniment); Higham in Manchester; Pelitti in Milan, and the extraordinary upright trombone, *bimbonifono*, devised in Florence by G. Bimboni over the years 1849–70, with seven rotary valves in series, actuated by both hands in the woodwind manner (description and diagrams in Gai, 1969, pp. 231–3). All bear witness to a continuingly eager and expansive climate in brass-instrument thinking amidst which it is enormously impressive but not miraculous that Wagner should have sought his new colours for *The Ring*. Each one of these could be matched in one respect or another to types thought of by manufacturers and bandmasters during the period when the operas were composed. Thus particularly the *Wagner tubas* (as they are always professionally described in England even if some purists insist on 'tuben' as in Wagner's scores). These are 9-foot tenors and 12-foot basses in oval form, of medium bore and provided with a mouthpipe which tapers to receive a horn mouthpiece, and with left-handed valves, the instruments being played by the second quartet of hornists with their own mouthpieces.

Wagner had already begun to compose *Rheingold* before he included the tubas. In the first sketch, 1853, the initial appearance of the Valhalla theme in the second scene is marked 'Pos. dolce', i.e. trombones. Nevertheless we learn from the researches of Von Westernhagen that it was in the same year, on a summer evening journey up to St. Moritz, that the idea of an extra brass group first came to him. The tubas appear in the full score of 1854. Eleven years later (September 1865) a letter from the composer to King Ludwig refers to 'the extra instruments' which he had been scoring for in *The Ring* and which he had become acquainted with some time previously in Paris 'at the maker Sax, whose invention they were'. Wagner goes on to tell of his failure to find those '*Sax'schen Instrumente*' or even possible substitutes for them in the military bands in Munich, or in Vienna either, and of the dilemma in which this placed him as he proceeded with the instrumentation.

Von Westernhagen points out that Wagner must have made that visit to Sax during his short stay in Paris in October 1853. The instruments which interested him were presumably the sax-horns (for which the term 'tuba' in Distin's advertisement, Fig. 49, may have been mistakenly picked up at Sax's factory). Evidently by the time of this letter of 1865 Wagner had not yet envisaged tubas which horn-players would play with their own mouthpieces. This was possibly a suggestion of Richter, horn-player himself, who joined the composer's staff a year or two later. What instruments were used in the 1869 performance at Munich seems to be unknown; but Richter was later sent round Germany to order what was needed for the Bayreuth première of *The Ring* in its entirety, and the new tubas were delivered by 1875. The tradition, and the likelihood, is that Moritz supplied them (Fig. 52).

They were then made also by other makers, Kruspe, Uhlmann, and particularly Alexander, whose models (with four valves) are the best-known today (Pl. XV). In all the parts, also in the score of *Rheingold*, they sound, whether in treble or bass clef, respectively a tone and a fifth lower than written ($c' =$ h4). In the other scores they appear in E flat and B flat, sounding a sixth and a ninth lower (but in bass clef, a third higher and a tone lower) which the composer thought would be easier for the conductor; an exception is in the Prelude to *Götterdämmerung*, where they are written in B flat and F in brass-band style ($c' =$ h2) and sound a ninth and a twelfth lower. Other countries attempted to find substitutes for Wagner's amazingly successful innovation, in

such as saxhorns, and special *cornophones* by Besson. This came to an end around 1930, in which year Sir Thomas Beecham obtained for the London Philharmonic a proper set from Alexander.

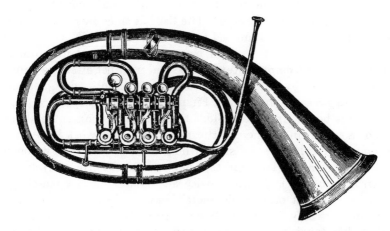

Fig. 52 Tenor Wagner tuba in B flat, Moritz, pre-1910 from catalogue.

Bruckner and Strauss were both slightly tempted by Wagner's tubas. The Tenor Tuba in *Don Quixote* was evidently first to have been a Wagner tuba: Strauss tells in *Instrumentationslehre* how several times he had written for a B flat Tenorhorn, and had found that as a melody instrument the ordinary military *Bariton* (euphonium) was preferable to the 'harsh, awkward Wagner-tubas with their demoniac sound'. This is not in the least how we hear these instruments nowadays: arresting indeed, but not wild. Perhaps the players which Strauss used to hear had been forcing the tone; or perhaps he anyhow preferred the rotund sound of the euphonium, which is the usual instrument for his and other non-Wagnerian parts marked Tenor Tuba, as in *The Planets* by Holst.

Quite differently from this, the Wagner tubas are now said to have become popular among younger players in America, for example in Hollywood, as bell-up horns for film and television music. Which shows how brass history never stands still. A visitor to, say, Bill Lewington's shop in London is greeted by the rich sight of over two score different species or sub-species of brass instrument, each invented originally for some particular purpose and now probably also used experimentally or regularly by symphony musicians or jazz musicians for something else.

And now too the historical revival. After harpsichords and viols had been made for many years, Finke started in Germany in the 1950s to build baroque trombones (e.g. with slide bore 9·9 mm. and 9·5 cm. bell in the tenor). The list has since increased as the demand has grown. Meinl & Lauber of Geretsried (W. Germany) offer replicas of most types of baroque and classical instrument including *Zug-trompete* after Veit; keyed trumpet after the handsome original by Doke; hand-horn with crooks, designed on Viennese precepts by Horace Fitzpatrick; and many more. Nor need this be all. In other fields of historical instrument-making such as woodwind, much of the most successful work today has been accomplished by craftsmen who started on their own without previous training. To begin to make a natural horn or trumpet, even a 'buisine', is for the novice an exhausting and scorching prospect: correct or suitable metals have to be found, and the instruments may first come all out of tune. But wood-turners and others have their problems too, and at the time of writing, Philip Bate in London is constructing a 'minstrel's trumpet' for a well-known professional trombonist who also plays ophicleide. So, with a last figure (from Viollet-le-duc's *Dictionnaire raisonné du mobilier*) and in complete deference to the professional makers upon whom brass playing must always depend, we may perhaps be allowed to wish the amateur horn- and trumpet-smith of the future the best of fortune.

Bibliography

═══

BIBLIOGRAPHY of works cited in the text and some works for further reference, up to 1974. The imprint of books where not stated is London.

Acta Mus.: *Acta Musicologica*, International Musicological Society, Basel, etc. 1928–.

AfMF: *Archiv für Musikforschung*, Leipzig, 1936–. (Continuation of *Zeitschrift für Musikwissenschaft*.)

AfMW: *Archiv für Musikwissenschaft*, Bückeburg, 1918–27; 1952–.

Allen, Derek, 'Belgic coins from Southern Gaul', *Journ. Prehistoric Soc.*, 1958.

Allen, J. Romilly, *The Early Christian Monuments of Scotland*, Part III, Edinburgh, 1893.

Altenburg, J. E., *Versuch einer Anleitung zur heroisch-musikalischen Trompeter- und Pauker-Kunst*, Halle, 1795. Facs. reprint, Dresden, 1911. (Engl. translation by E. Tarr, 1974.)

AMZ: *Allgemeine musikalische Zeitung*, Leipzig, 1798–.

An. Mus.: *Anuario Musical*, Barcelona, 1946–.

Arban, *Grande méthode complète de Cornet à pistons et de Saxhorn*, Paris (1864).

Atlas: Vertkov, K., et al., *Atlas muzykalnykh instrumentov narodov SSSR*, (Atlas of popular musical instruments of the USSR), Moscow, 1963.

Bach, Vincent, *Embouchure and Mouthpiece Manual*, Mount Vernon, N.Y., 1954.

Bahnert, H., Herzberg, T., & Schramm, H., *Metallblasinstrumente*, Leipzig, 1958.

Baines, A., *European & American Musical Instruments*, 1966.

—, (ed.), *Musical Instruments through the Ages*, 1961 etc.: 'The Older Brass Instruments', by C. W. Monk; 'The Horn and the Later Brass', by R. Morley-Pegge.

—, 'Two Cassel Inventories', *GSJ* IV.

Barbour, J. Murray, *Trumpets, Horns and Music*, Michigan, 1964.

—, 'Franz Krommer and his Writing for Brass', *BQ* I, 1.

Basedow, H., *The Australian Aboriginal*, Adelaide, 1925. (Chap. XXX.)

Bate, P., *The Trumpet and Trombone*, 1966.

—, 'Saxhorn', *Grove* (5th edn.).

Beaver, W. N., 'A further Note on the Use of the Wooden Trumpet in Papua', *Man*, 1916, p. 24.

Behn, F., *Musikleben im Altertum und frühen Mittelalter*, Stuttgart, 1954.

Berger, J., 'Notes on some 17th-century compositions for Trumpets and Strings in Bologna', *MQ*, 1951.

Berger, K., *The March King and his Band*, New York, 1957. (On Sousa.)

Berlioz, H., *Voyage Musical en Allemagne et en Italie*, Paris, 1844. Reprint, Farnborough, 1970.

— *Modern Instrumentation and Orchestration*, 1858. (Translation of *Traité de l'Instrumentation*, Paris, 1844.)

Berr, F., & Caussinus, *Méthode complète d'Ophicléide*, Paris (*c.* 1837).

Bessaraboff, N., *Ancient European Musical Instruments*, Boston, 1941.

Besseler, H., *Die Musik des Mittelalters und der Renaissance*, Potsdam, 1931.

— 'Die Entstehung der Posaune', *Acta Mus.*, 1950.

Blackwood, B., *Both Sides of the Buka Passage*, 1935.

Blandford, W. F. H. Articles include: in *Musical Times* on the horn, 1922, 1925, 1926, 1936 (listed Morley-Pegge, 189); on other brass, 1939, 1940; and *Monthly Mus. Record*, 1931, 1935.

Blochet, E., *Les peintures des Mss. orientaux de la Bibliothèque national*, Paris, 1914–.

Blome, R., *The Gentleman's Recreation*, 1686. (Hunting.)

Bonanni, F., *Gabinetto armonico*, Rome, 1722.

Borren, C. van den, 'La musique pittoresque dans le ms. 222 C 22 de la Bibliothèque de Strasbourg', *Bericht über den musikwissenschaftlichen Kongress in Basel (1924)*, Leipzig, 1925.

Bossert, G. (Stuttgart Hofkapelle inventory of 1589), *Württembergische Vierteljahrhefte für Landesgeschichte*, 1912.

Bouquet, M.-Th., 'La Cappella musicale dei Duchi di Savoia, 1450–1500', *Rivista Italiana di Musicologia*, III, Florence, 1968.

Bowles, E. A.: Various articles on medieval horns, trumpets and tower musicians in *BQ* V, 3; *AfMW* 1963; *Acta Mus.* 1966.

BQ: *Brass Quarterly*, ed. Mary Rasmussen, Durham, New Hampshire, 1957–64.

Bragard, R., & de Hen, F. J., *Les instruments de musique dans l'art et l'histoire*, Rhode-St-Genèse, 1967.

Brand, E. D., *Band Instrument Repairing Manual*, Elkhart, Indiana, 1939.

Bridge, J. C., 'Horns', *Journ. Architectural, Archaeol. and Hist. Soc. for . . . Chester*, 1905.

Brøgger, A. W., et al., *Osebergfundet*, Oslo, 1917–28.

Broholm, H. C., et al., *The Lures of the Bronze Age*, Copenhagen, 1949.

Bruce, J., of Kinnaird, *A narrative of the travels . . . into Abyssinia*, 1790. The passage quoted is taken from J. W. Moore's *Complete Encyclopaedia of Music*, Boston, 1854, p. 935.

Buhle, E., *Die musikalischen Instrumente in den Miniaturen des frühen Mittelalters*, I, Die Blasinstrumente, Leipzig, 1903.

Bukofzer, M. L., *Studies in Medieval and Renaissance Music*, 1951.
Byrne, M., 'Instruments for the Goldsmiths Company', *GSJ* XXIV.
— 'The Goldsmith-Trumpet-makers of the British Isles', *GSJ* XIX.

Caecilia, Mainz, 1822–.
Cameron, L. C. R., *The Hunting Horn: What to blow and How to blow it.*
Swaine, Adeney, Brigg, c. 1905, reprint 1950. (With facsimile of the
'Ancient Hunting Notes' from *The Sportsman's Dictionary*, 1744.)
Carse, A., *Musical Wind Instruments*, 1939.
— *The Orchestra from Beethoven to Berlioz*, 1948.
— 'The Prince Regent's Band', *Music & Letters*, July 1946.
Cherry, N., 'A Corelli Sonata for Trumpet...', *BQ* IV 3, 4.
Chinnery, E. W. P., 'Further Notes on the Wooden Kipi Trumpet and
Conch Shell by the Natives of Papua', *Man*, 1917.
Closson, E., *Le MS dit des Basses Danses de la Bibl. de Bourgogne*,
Brussels, 1912.
Coles, J. M., 'Irish Bronze Age Horns and their relations with North
Europe', *Proc. Prehist. Soc.*, New Series XXIX, Cambridge, 1963.
Collection de 116 Airs et Fanfares, Paris (c. 1825; trompes de chasse).
Comettant, J. P. O., *Histoire d'un inventeur au XIXe siècle*, Paris, 1860.
(Life of Adolphe Sax.)
Crane, F., 'The Derivation of some 15th-century Basse-Danse Tunes',
Acta Mus. 1965.
—, *Extant Medieval Musical Instruments*, Iowa, 1972.
Cucuel, G., *La Pouplinière...*, Paris, 1913.

Daremberg & Saglio, *Dictionnaire des antiquités grecques et romaines*,
Paris, 1877–1919. (Articles 'Cornu', 'Funus', 'Gladiator', 'Lituus',
'Tuba', etc.)
Dart, T., 'The Repertory of the Royal Wind Band', *GSJ* XI.
Dauprat, L. F., *Méthode de Cor-alto et Cor-basse*, Paris, 1824.
Dauverne, ainé, *Méthode de Trompette*, Paris (pre-1848).
Davison & Apel, *Historical Anthology of Music: Oriental, Medieval
and Renaissance Music*, Harvard, 1947.
Day, C. R., *Descriptive Catalogue of Musical Instruments ... at the
Royal Military Exhibition, London, 1890*, 1891.
DDT: *Denkmäler deutscher Tonkunst*, 1892–.
D'Harcourt: see Harcourt.
Dieppo, A. G., *Méthode de trombone*, Paris, c. 1840.
Domnich, H., *Méthode de Premier Cor et de Second Cor*, Paris, 1808.
Downs, A., 'The Tower Music of a 17th-Century Stadtpfeifer', *BQ*
VII 1. (On Johann Pezel.)
DTB: *Denkmäler der Tonkunst in Bayern*, 1900–.
DTÖ: *Denkmäler der Tonkunst in Österreich*, 1893–.
Duvernoy, F., *Méthode pour le Cor*, Paris, 1803.

Ehmann, W., 'New Brass Instruments based on old models', *BQ* I 4.
Eichborn, H. L., *Die Trompete in alter und neuer Zeit*, Leipzig, 1881.
Reprint, Wiesbaden, 1968.

— 'Ein neues Waldhorn', *ZfI* Apr. 1883.
— *Das alte Clarinblasen auf Trompeten*, Leipzig, 1894.
Eisel, J. P., *Musikus autodidaktos*, Erfurt, 1738.
Eitner, R., 'Briefe von Jorg Neuschel in Nürnberg . . .', *Monatshefte für Musikgeschichte*, 1877.
Eliason, R. E., 'Early American Valves for Brass Instruments', *GSJ* XXIII.
— *Keyed Bugles in the United States* (Smithsonian Studies in History and Technology: No. 19), Washington, 1972.
Ellis, A. J., 'On the History of Musical Pitch', *Journ. of the Society of Arts*, March 1880.
Emsheimer, E., 'Zur Typologie der schwedischen Holztrompeten', *Studia instrumentorum musicae popularis*, I, Stockholm, 1969.
Eppelsheim, J., *Das Orchester des Lully*, Tutzing, 1961.
Eustathius: *Commentarii ad Homeri Iliadem*, III. Leipzig, 1829.

Fantini, G., *Modo per imparare a sonare di Tromba*, Frankfurt, 1638. Facs. reprint, Milan, 1934.
Farkas, P., *The Art of Brass playing*, Brass Publications, Bloomington, Indiàna, 1962.
Farmer, H. G., *Memoirs of the Royal Artillery Band*, 1904.
— *Military Music*, 1950.
Ferrières, Henri de, *Le Livre du Roy Modus et de la Royne Ratio*, ed. A. Pauphilet, *Jeux et sapience du Moyen Age*, Paris, 1940.
Fétis, F. J., *Biographie universelle des musiciens*, Paris, 2nd edn., 1860–65. (Esp. on French musicians.)
— 'Cors à pistons', *Revue Musicale de Fétis*, 1828.
— *Rapport*, Exposition universelle, Paris, 1867.
Fink, G. W., 'Wichtige Verbesserung der Posaune', *AMZ* 1839. (On Sattler's thumb valve.)
Fitzpatrick, H., 'Notes on the Vienna Horn', *GSJ* XIV.
— 'An 18th-Century School of Horn-makers in Bohemia', *GSJ* XVII.
— *The Horn and Horn-playing*, 1970.
Fleischhauer, G., *Etrurien und Rom*. Musikgeschichte in Bildern, II 5, Leipzig, 1964.
Fleming, H. F. von, *Der Vollkommene Teutsche Jäger*, Leipzig, 1719, 1724.
—, *Der Vollkommene Teutsche Soldat*, Leipzig, 1726.
Forestier, J., *Méthode pour le Cornet à pistons*, Paris, c. 1835.
Francoeur, L. J., *Traité générale . . . des instruments d'orchestre*, 1812. (Choron's edition of Francoeur's *Diapason général* . . ., 1772).
Frevert, W., *Die deutschen Jagdsignale*, Berlin, 4th edn. 1960.
Freyhan, R., *Die Illustrationen zum Casseler Willehalm-Codex*, Frankfurt, 1927.
Fröhlich, F. J., *Vollständige theoretisch-pracktische Musikschule*, Bonn, 1811.

Gai, V., *Gli strumenti musicali della corte medicea e il museo . . .'Luigi Cherubini' di Firenze*, Florence, 1969.
Galpin, F. W., *Old English Instruments of Music*, 1910.

Gerber, E. L., *Historisch-biographisches Lexikon der Tonkünstler*, Leipzig, 1790–92; *Neues Historisch-biographisches Lexikon*, 1812–14.

Gessner, C., *Descriptio Montis Fracti*, Zurich, 1555.

Gleich, F., *Handbuch der modernen Instrumentirung für Orchester und Militairmusikcorps*, Leipzig, 1853.

Goldschmidt, H., 'Das Orchester der italienischen Oper im 17. Jahrhundert', *SIMG* II, 1900.

Gombosi, O., 'Zur Vorgeschichte der Tokkate', *Acta Mus.* 1934.

Gontershausen, Welcker von: see Welcker.

Gregory, R., *The Horn*, 1961.

— *The Trombone*, 1973.

Grove's Dictionary of Music & Musicians, 5th edn., 1954.

GSJ: Galpin Society Journal. 1948–.

Halfpenny, E. Articles in *GSJ*: 'William Shaw's "Harmonic Trumpet"' (XIII); 'William Bull and the English Baroque Trumpet' (XV); 'Two Oxford Trumpets' (XVI); 'Early British Trumpet Mouthpieces' (XX); 'Smith, London' (XXI); 'Four 17th-century British Trumpets' (XXII); 'Notes on Two Later British Trumpets' (XXIV).

— 'Musicians at James II's Coronation', *Music & Letters*, 1951.

— 'Tantivy . . .', *Proc. Royal Musical Assoc.*, 1954.

Halle, J. S., *Werkstäte der heutigen Künste*, III, Leipzig, 1764.

Haller, K., *Partituranordnung und musikalischer Satz*, Tutzing, 1970.

Hammerstein, R., *Die Musik der Engel*, Munich, 1962.

Hampson, J. N., *Besses-o' th-Barn Band*, Northampton, *c.* 1893.

Harcourt, R. & M. d', *La Musique des Incas et ses survivances*, Paris, 1925. (Plates in separate volume.)

Hardouin, *Trésor de Vénerie* (1394), ed. Michelant, Metz, 1856.

Harrison, F. & Rimmer, J., *European Musical Instruments*, 1964.

Heartz, D., 'A 15th-century Ballo . . .', *Aspects of Medieval and Renaissance Music: a Birthday Offering to Gustave Reese*, 1967.

Heinitz, W., *Instrumentenkunde*, Potsdam, 1929.

Hen, F. J. de, *Beitrag zur Kenntnis der Musikinstrumente aus Belgisch Kongo*, Tervuren, 1960.

Hickmann, H., *La Trompette dans l'Egypte Ancienne*, (Supplement to: *Annales du service des antiquités de l'Egypte*, Cahier 1), Cairo, 1946.

—, *Aegypten*. Musikgeschichte in Bildern, II 1, Leipzig, 1961.

Hind, H., *The Brass Band*, 1934.

Hinde, R., *Discipline of the Light Horse*, 1778.

Höfer, F., *Instrumentationslehre mit besonderer Berücksichtigung der Kirchenmusik*, Regensburg, 1913. (Posaunenchor.)

Hoover, C. A., 'The Slide Trumpet of the 19th Century', *BQ* VI 4.

—, 'A Trumpet Battle at Niblo's Pleasure Garden', *MQ* 1969.

Horsley, I., 'Wind Techniques in the Sixteenth and Early Seventeenth Centuries', *BQ* IV 2.

Hyatt-King, A., 'Mountains, Music, and Musicians', *MQ* 1945. (Alphorn music and composers.)

Hyde, J., *A New and Complete Preceptor for the Trumpet and Bugle Horn*, *c.* 1798.

Instrumentenbau Zeitschrift, Sieburg, 1946–.
Izikowitz, K. G., *Musical and other Sound Instruments of the South American Indians*, Göteborg, 1935. Reprint, East Ardley, Yorks., 1970.

Jan, K. von, on instruments of Antiquity in: Baumeister, A., *Denkmäler des klassischen Altertums*, III, Munich, 1884–88.
Jones, T., 'The Didjeridu', *Studies in Music*, University of Western Australia, I, 1967.
Julyan, Lt. Col. W. L., 'History of the Hunting Horn', *The Field*, Oct. 1947.

Kalbrenner, A., *Wilhelm Wieprecht, sein Leber und Wirken*, Berlin, 1882.
Kappey, J. A., *Brass Band Tutor*, c. 1871.
—, *Military Music*, (1894).
Karomatov, F., *Uzbekskaya Instrumentalnaya Musyka*, (Uzbek instrumental music), Tashkent, 1972.
Karstädt, G., *Lasst lustig die Hörner erschallen!*, Hamburg, 1964.
Kastner, J. G., *Cours d'instrumentation*, Paris, 1839, 1844.
—, *Traité générale d'instrumentation*, Paris, 1837, supplement 1844.
— *Manuel général de musique militaire*, Paris, 1848.
— *Les Danses des morts*, Paris, 1852.
Keepnews, O., & Grauer, B., *A Pictorial History of Jazz*, n.d.
Kirby, P. R., 'The Trumpets of Tut-ankh-amen and their successors', *Journ. R. Anthropol. Instit.*, 1947.
—*The Musical Instruments of the Native Races of South Africa*, Johannesburg, 1953.
Kirchmeyer, H., 'Die Rekonstruktion der "Bachtrompete"', *Neue Zeitschrift für Musik*, 1967. (The Steinkopf-Finke Clarino.)
Kleefeld, W., 'Das Orchester der Hamburger Oper, 1678–1738', *SIMG* I, 1889.
Klier, K. M., *Volkstümliche Musikinstrumente in den Alpen*, Kassel, 1956.
Kling, H., *Modern Orchestration and Instrumentation*, Engl. transl. New York, 1902 etc.
Kuhlo, E. & J., *Posaunenbuch*, Anstalt Bethel, 1910.
Kunst, J., *Music in New Guinea, Three Studies*, The Hague, 1967.

La Borde, J. B. de, *Essai sur la Musique ancienne et moderne*, 1780.
Lafontaine, H. C. de, *The King's Musick*, 1909. (Court records up to William and Mary.)
Lamaña, J. M., 'Los instrumentos musicales, en los ultimos tiempos . . . de la Casa de Barcelona', *An. Mus.* XXIV, 1969.
Langwill, L. G., *Index of Musical Wind-Instrument Makers*, 3rd edition, Edinburgh, 1972. (Indispensable. Catalogues of Collections in Bibliography.)
Larrea, A. de, 'La Saeta', *An. Mus.* IV, 1949.

LaRue, J., & Brofsky, H., 'Parisian Brass Players, 1751–93', *BQ* III 4.
—, & Wolf, G., 'Finding Unusual Brass Music', *BQ* VI 3.
Lavignac & de la Laurencie, *Encyclopédie de la Musique* . . ., Paris, 1913–. Part I (Antiquity, Asia etc.); Part II, Vol. 3, Soyer, A. M., 'Des instruments à vent', 1927.
Lennep, H. van, 'De Midwinterhoorn: Een oud Nederlands instrument', *Honderd Eeuwen Nederland*, II 5–6, The Hague, 1959.
Leo, emperor, *Tactica*, ed. Checo, Basel, 1554. (Chap. IX.)
Lesure, F., *Music and Art in Society*, Pennsylvania, 1967.

Madurell, J., 'Documentos para la historia de los maestros de capilla . . . y menestriles en Barcelona', *An. Mus.* III, 1948.
Mahillon, V.-C., *Catalogue descriptif & analytique du Musée Instrumental du Conservatoire royal de Bruxelles*, 5 vols., Ghent, 1893–1922.
Majer, J. F. B. C., *Museum Musicum*, 1732. Facs. reprint, Kassel, 1954.
Mandel, C., *Treatise on the Instrumentation of Military Bands*, 1859.
Marche, Olivier de la, *Les Mémoires*, Lyon, 1562.
Marcuse, S., *Musical Instruments: a Comprehensive Dictionary*, New York, 1964. (Includes most of the instruments which there is not space to describe here.)
Marix, J., *Histoire de la Musique et des Musiciens de la Cour de Bourgogne sous le règne de Philippe le Bon*, Strasbourg, 1939.
Marolles, G. de, *Monographie abrégée de la trompe de chasse*, Paris, n.d.
Mauricius, emperor, *Arte militara*, ed. H. Mihaescu, Bucharest, 1970.
Meadows Taylor, Capt., 'Catalogue of Indian Musical Instruments . . .', *Proc. Royal Irish Academy*, 1864.
Meifred, P. J., *Méthode pour le Cor chromatique ou à Piston*, Paris, 1840.
Menke, W., *History of the Trumpet of Bach and Handel*, transl. from the German by G. Abraham, 1934.
Mersenne, M., *Harmonie universelle*, Paris, 1636. Facs. reprint, Paris, 1965 (Vol. III on instruments).
Meyer, E. H., 'Die Bedeutung der Instrumentalmusik am Fürstbischöflichen Hofe zu Olomouc . . .', *Die Musikforschung*, 1956.
MGG: Musik in Geschichte und Gegenwart, Kassel, 1949–.
Military Band Journals published in London from *c.* 1845 include those of Boosé, Gratton Cooke, Jullien, Koenig, and Wessel. (Some in British Museum.)
Miller, G., *The Military Band*, 1912. (Arranges the 'Unfinished' Symphony, 1st movement, bar by bar.)
Morley-Pegge, R., *The French Horn*, 1960.
—, Important articles in *Grove* (5th edn.) include 'Bass-Horn', 'Bassetrompette', 'Horn', 'Key Bugle', 'Ophicleide', 'Serpent', 'Valve'.
Morrow, W., 'The Trumpet as an Orchestral Instrument', *Proc. Musical Association*, 1895.
MQ: Musical Quarterly, New York, 1915–.
Musica Antiqua Bohemica, Prague . . .
Musical Directory, Register & Almanach, Rudall Rose & Carte, 1853–69; continued as *Musical Directory, Annual & Almanach*.

Neefe, K., 'Die historische Entwicklung der Kgl. Sächsischen Infanterie- und Jägermusik in 19. Jahrhundert', *Neue Zeitschrift für Musik*, Leipzig, 1896.

Nemetz, *Neueste Posaun-Schule*, Vienna, c. 1830.

Nickel, E., *Der Holzblasinstrumentenbau in der freien Reichsstadt Nürnberg*, Munich, 1971.

Nicot, J., *Thresor de la Langue Françoyse*, Paris, 1606.

Nikiforov, P. I., *Mariiskie narodnye muzykalnye instrumenty*, (Popular instruments of the Mari), Ioshkar-Ola, 1959.

'Old Guard, An', *The Coach Horn*, Köhler, 1888.

Oman, C. W. C., *The Art of War in the Middle Ages*, 1885 etc.

Panoff, P., *Militär Musik*, Berlin, 1938.

Payne, I. W., 'Observations on the stopped notes of the French Horn', *Music & Letters*, 1968.

Pierre, C., *La Facture Instrumentale à l'exposition universelle de 1889*, Paris, 1890.

Pietzsch, G., 'Die Beschreibungen deutscher Fürstenhochzeiten . . . als Musikgeschichtliche Quellen', *An. Mus.* XV, 1960.

Piggott, Stuart, 'The Carnyx in Early Iron Age Britain', *The Antiquaries' Journal*, 1959.

Pirro, A., 'Remarques sur l'execution musicale de la fin du 14e au milieu du 15e siècle', *Report of International Society for Musical Research, 1st Congress, Liège, 1930*.

—, *Histoire de la musique de la fin du XIVe siècle*, Paris, 1940.

Polyphonia Sacra, Plainsong & Medieval Music Society, 1932.

Pompecki, B., *Jagd- und Waldhornschule*, Neudamm, 2nd edn. 1926.

Pontécoulant, A. de, *Organographie: Essai sur la Facture Instrumentale*, Paris, 1861.

Praetorius, M., *Syntagma Musicum*, Wolfenbüttel, 1619. Reprint, Kassel, 1929 (Vol. II, 'De Organographia'). Facs. reprint (Vols. I–III), Kassel, 1958.

Purday, Z. T. (publisher), *Tutor for the Royal Keyed Bugle* . . . 'by a Professor of Eminence', c. 1835.

Ramalingan, V. S., *Trumpet music and Trumpet style in the Early Renaissance*, Dissertation, University of Illinois, 1965.

Rasmussen, M., among articles in *BQ* especially: 'Gottfried Reiche and his 24 Neue Quatricinia' (IV 1); 'Two Early 19th-century Trombone Virtuosi: Queisser and Belcke' (V 1); 'English Trumpet Concertos in some 18th-century printed collections' (V 2); 'A Concertino for Chromatic Trumpet by J. G. Albrechtsberger' (V 3); 'MS Wenster Litt.I 1–17b (Universitetsbibl., Lund) . . .' (V 4); 'A Bibliography of 19th- and 20th-century Music for Mixed Voices with Wind- or Brass-ensemble Accompaniment' (VI 3–VII 3).

— *A Teacher's Guide to the Literature of Brass Instruments*. Brass Quarterly, Durham, New Hampshire, 1964.

Reiss, J., 'Pauli Paulirinus de Praga, Tractatus de musica', *ZfMW* 1925.

Ricks, R., 'Russian Horn Bands', *MQ* 1969.

Rimmer, J., *Ancient Musical Instruments of Western Asia*, British Museum, 1969.

Ringer, A. L., *The Chasse; historical & analytical bibliography of a musical genre*, Dissertation, Colombia University, 1955.

Rode, T., 'Zur Geschichte des Horns oder Waldhorns', *Neue Berliner Musikzeitung*, 1860.

Roeser, V., *Essai d'instruction à l'usage de ceux qui composent pour la clarinette et le cor*, n.d. (1764?). (Unique copy in Library of Brussels Conservatoire. A modern edition has been announced.)

Rognone, F., *Selva di varii passaggi*, 1620. Reprint, Biblioteca musice Bononiensis, section II no. 153, Bologna, 1970.

Rose, A., *Talks with Bandsmen*, 1895?.

Roy and Miller, *Tutor for the Keyed and Valve Trumpet*, c. 1835. (Evidently an adaptation of Roy's Method published by Schott, Mainz, ten years earlier.)

Sachs, C., *Geist und Werden der Musikinstrumente*, Berlin, 1928. Reprint, Hilversum, 1965. (Ethnology of musical instruments.)

—, *The History of Musical Instruments*, New York, 1940.

—, 'Chromatic Trumpets in the Renaissance', *MQ* 1950.

Sadokov, R. L., *Tysyacha oskolkov zolotovo Saza* ('The golden Saz') Moscow, 1971.

Sárosi, B., *Die Volksmusikinstrumente Ungarns*, Leipzig, 1967.

Sauerlandt, M., *Die Musik in fünf Jahrhunderten der Europäischen Malerei*, Leipzig, 1922.

Sax, A., *Méthode complète pour saxhorn et saxotromba*, Paris, 1851.

(Sax, A.), *Musée Ad, Sax*, (catalogue of sale), Paris, 1877.

Schaeffner, A., *Les Kissi: une société noire et ses instruments de musique*, Paris, 1951.

Schlesinger, K., 'Horn', *Encyclopaedia Britannica*, 11th edn., 1910. Also other instrument articles in the same.

Schlosser, J., *Die Sammlung alter Musikinstrumente*, Vienna, 1920. (The Collection of the Kunsthistorisches Museum, Vienna.) Reprint 1973.

Schneider, W., *Historisch-technische Berschreibung der Musikalischen Instrumente*, Merseburg, 1834.

Schubart, C. F. D., *Ideen zu einer Aesthetik der Tonkunst*, Vienna, 1806. Reprint, Leipzig, 1924.

Schubert, F. L., *Alle gebrauchlich Musikinstrumente*, Leipzig, 1866.

Schuler, M., 'Die Musik in Konstanz während des Konzils 1414–1418', *Acta Mus.* 1966.

Schünemann, G., 'Sonaten und Feldstücke der Hoftrompeter', *ZfMW* 1935.

—, *Trompeterfanfaren, Sonaten* . . . (*Erbe deutscher Musik*, I, 7), Kassel, 1936.

Schwab, H. W., *Konzert*. Musikgeschichte in Bildern, IV 2, Leipzig, 1971.

Seaman, G., 'The Russian Horn Band', *Monthly Musical Record*, 1959.

Sendry, A., *Music in Ancient Israel*, 1969.

Shaw, G. B., *Music in London*, 1890–94.

Shone, A. B., 'Coaching Calls', *Musical Times*, 1951.

Sichart, L. H. von, *Geschichte der Königlich-Hannoverschen Armee*, Hannover, 1866–98.

SIMG: Sammelbände der Internationalen Musikgesellschaft, Leipzig, 1899–.

Singer, C., et al., *History of Technology*, Oxford, 1956. (Esp. Vol. II.)

Smirnov, B., *Iskusstvo Vladimirskikh Rozhechnikov*, (The art of the Vladimir rozhoks), Moscow, 1959.

Smithers, D. L., 'The Trumpets of J. W. Haas', *GSJ* XVIII.

—, 'The Hapsburg Imperial *Trompeter* and *Heerpaucker* Privileges of 1653', *GSJ* XXIV.

—, *The Music & History of the Baroque Trumpet before 1721*, 1973.

Söderberg, B., *Instruments de musique au Bas-Congo*, Stockholm, 1956.

Southern, E., 'Some Keyboard Basse Dances of the 15th Century', *Acta Mus.*, 1963.

Speer, D., *Grund-richtiger Unterricht der Musikalischen Kunst*, Ulm, 1687, 1697.

Spenser, Baldwin, *Native Tribes of the Northern Territory of Australia*, 1914.

Squire, W. Barclay, 'Purcell's Music for the Funeral of Mary II', *SIMG* IV 2, 1903.

Straeten, E. van der, *Musique aux Pays-Bas*, Brussels, 1867–. (Vol. IV for Flemish town bands in the Renaissance.)

—, *Les Ménestrels aux Pays-Bas du XIIIe au XVIIIe siècle*, Brussels, 1878.

Sundelin, A., *Die Instrumentierung für sämmtliche Militär-Musik-Chöre*, Berlin, 1828.

Sykes, M., 'Notes on Musical Instruments in Khorasan', *Man*, 1909.

Szadrowsky, H., 'Die Musik . . . der Alpenwohner', *Jahrbuch des Schweitzer Alpenclub*, 1867–8.

Talbot, J., see Baines, A., 'James Talbot's Manuscript (Christ Church Library Music MS 1187), I. Wind Instruments', *GSJ* I.

Tayler, D., 'Music of some Indian tribes of Colombia', *Recorded Sound* (British Institute of Recorded Sound), 1968.

Terry, C. S., *Bach's Orchestra*, 1932.

Teuchert, E., & Haupt, E. W., *Musik-instrumentenkunde in Wort und Bild*, Leipzig, 1911, 1928. (Vol. III.)

Tinctoris: see Baines, A., 'Fifteenth-century Instruments in Tinctoris's *De Inventione et Usu Musicae*, *GSJ* III.

Titcomb, C., 'Baroque Court & Military Trumpets and Kettledrums', *GSJ* IX.

Trichet, P., *Traité des instruments de musique*, ed. Lesure, F., Paris, 1957.

Tucker, A. N., *Tribal Music and Dancing in the Southern Sudan*, n.d.

Tully, *Tutor for the French horn*, c. 1840.

Turberville, G., *The Noble Arte of Venerie*, 1575. Facs. reprint, Oxford, 1908.

Turner (publisher), *Complete Tutor for the Coach Horn, Post or Tandem Horn, Bugle and Cavalry Trumpet*, (1898).

Turrini, G., 'L'Accademia filarmonica di Verona dalla Fondazione (Maggio 1543) al 1600 e il suo Patrimonio musicale antico', *Atti e memorie della Accademia di Agricoltura, Scienze e Lettere di Verona*, Verona, 1941.

Valdrighi, L. F., *Cappelle, concerti e musiche di Casa d'Este dal secolo XV al XVIII*, Modena, 1884.

Valentin, C., *Geschichte der Musik in Frankfurt-am-Main*, Frankfurt, 1906.

Vandor, I., 'LaNotazione musicale strumentale del Buddismo tibetano', *Nuova Rivista musicale Italiana*, Rome, 1973.

Vertkov: see *Atlas*.

Vessella, A., *La Banda*, Milan, 1935.

Viney, V., *Receuil de musique à l'usage des groupes & sociétés de Trompes de Chasse*, Paris, 1929.

Virdung, S., *Musica getutscht*, Basel, 1511. Facs. reprint, Kassel, 1931.

Vobaron, *Méthode de trombone*, Paris, c. 1833.

Vogel, M., *Die Intonation der Blechbläser*, Düsseldorf, 1961.

Wachsmann, K. P.: Trowell, M., & Wachsmann, K. P., *Tribal Crafts of Uganda*, 1953. Part II, 'The Sound Instruments'.

Weber, G., 'Ueber Ventilhorn und Ventiltrompete mit drei Ventilen', *Caecilia*, 1835.

Weigel, C., *Abbildung der Gemein-nützlichen Haupt-stände*, Regensburg, 1698.

Welcker, H., von Gontershausen, *Neu-eröffnetes Magazin musikalischer Tonwerkzeuge*, Frankfurt, 1855.

Werner, A., 'Die alte Musikbibliothek . . . an St. Wenzel in Naumburg', *AfMW* 1927.

Werner, E., 'Musical Aspects of the Dead Sea Scrolls', *MQ* 1957.

Westernhagen, C. von, *Die Entstehung des 'Ring'*, Zurich, 1973.

Wheeler, J., 'New Light on the Regent's Bugle', *GSJ* XIX.

—, 'Further Notes on the Classic Trumpet', *GSJ* XVIII.

Wick, D., *Trombone Technique*, 1971.

Wille, G., *Musica Romana*, Amsterdam, 1967.

Wolf, J., 'Ein Breslauer Mensuraltraktat', *AfMW* 1918.

Wolff, H. C., *Oper*, Musikgeschichte in Bilder, IV 1, Leipzig, 1970.

Wörthmüller, W., 'Die Nürnberger Trompeten- und Posaunenmacher des 17. und 18. Jahrhunderts', *Mitteilungen des Vereins für Geschichte der Stadt Nürnberg*, Nürnberg, 1954–5.

Wright, F. (ed.), *Brass Today* (Besson), 1957.

Wright, R., *Dictionnaire des instruments de musique*, 1941.

Wulstan, D., 'The Sounding of the Shofar', *GSJ* XXVI.

Zedler, J. H., *Universal-Lexicon*, Leipzig, 1732–.

ZfI: *Zeitschrift für Instrumentenbau*, Leipzig, 1880–.

ZfMW: *Zeitschrift für Musikwissenschaft*, Leipzig, 1918–.

Ziskal, J., 'Eine Wettertrompete in Böhmen', *Zeitschrift für Oesterreichische Volkskunde*, 1896, p. 191.

Supplement to the Bibliography

Barclay, Robert, 'Preliminary Studies on Trumpet Making Techniques in 17th and 18th Century Nürnberg,' *Studia Organologica, Festschrift für J. H. van der Meer*, Tutzing, 1987.

Benade, Arthur H., *Fundamentals of Musical Acoustics*, New York, 1976 (Dover reprint, 1990).

Bendinelli, Cesare, *Tutta l'arte della Tromba* (1614), ed. Edward H. Tarr, Kassel, 1973. (See also Tarr, Edward H.)

Bevan, Clifford, *The Tuba Family*, 1978.

Brüchle, B., and Janetzky, K., *A Pictorial History of the Horn*, Tutzing, 1978.

Campbell, Murray, and Greated, Clive, *The Musician's Guide to Acoustics*, 1987.

Coover, James, *Musical Instrument Collections, Catalogues and Cognate Literature*, Detroit, 1981.

Dahlqvist, Reine, *The Keyed Trumpet and its Greatest Virtuoso, Anton Weidinger*, Nashville, 1975.

—, 'Some Notes on the Early Valve,' *GSJ* XXXII, 1980.

Dudgeon, Ralph T., 'Joseph Haliday, Inventor of the Keyed Bugle', *Journal of the American Musical Instrument Society*, IX, 1983.

Eliason, Robert E., *Early American Brass Makers*, Nashville, 1981.

Fischer, Henry G. (in *Historic Brass Society Journal*, I, 1989).

Haine, Malou, *Adolphe Sax*, Brussels, 1980.

Heyde, Herbert, *Musikinstrumenten-Museum der Karl-Marx-Universität Leipzig, Katalog, Band 3, Trompeten, Posaunen, Tuben*, Leipzig, 1980; do. *Band 5, Hörner und Zinken*, Leipzig, 1982.

—, *Das Ventilblasinstrument, seine Entwicklung im deutschsprachigen Raum*, Wiesbaden, 1987.

Historic Brass Society Journal, New York, 1989–.

Horwood, Wally, *Adolphe Sax*, Bramley, Hants, 1980.

Lawson, Graeme, & Egan, Geoff, 'Medieval Trumpet from the City of London,' *GSJ* XII, 1988.

MacCracken, Thomas J., 'Die Verwendung der Blechbläsinstrumente bei J. S. Bach unter besonderer Berücksichtigung der Tromba da tirarsi,' *Bach-Jahrbuch*, 1984.

Meucci, Renato, 'Roman Military Instruments and the *Lituus*', *GSJ* XLII, 1989.

—, 'Il Cimbasso e gli strumenti affini,' *Studi Verdiani*, V, Parma, 1989.

Myers, Arnold, 'Fingering Charts for the Cimbasso and other Instruments,' *GSJ* XXXIX, 1986, p. 134.

Springer, G. H., *Maintenance and Repair of Wind and Percussion Instruments*, Boston, 1976.

Tarr, Edward H., *Cesare Bendinelli, The Entire Art of Trumpet Playing* (1614), *Complete English Translation and Commentary*, Nashville, 1975.

—, *The Trumpet*, 1988.

Van der Meer, John H., *Verzeichnis der Europäischen Musikinstrumente im Germanischen Nationalmuseum, Nürnberg*, I, *Hörner und Trompeten . . . Idiophone*, Wilhelmshaven, 1979.

Virgiliano, Aurelio, *Il Dolcemilo* (MS *c*. 1600), ed. M. Castellani, Florence, 1979.

Webb, John, 'Notes on the Ballad Horn,' *GSJ* XXXVII, 1984.

—, 'Designs for Brass in the Public Record Office', *GSJ* XXXVIII, 1985.

Index

===

Page numbers in *italic* refer to music examples

A CATALOG OF SELECTED
DOVER BOOKS
IN ALL FIELDS OF INTEREST

A CATALOG OF SELECTED
DOVER BOOKS
IN ALL FIELDS OF INTEREST

DRAWINGS OF REMBRANDT, edited by Seymour Slive. Updated Lippmann, Hofstede de Groot edition, with definitive scholarly apparatus. All portraits, biblical sketches, landscapes, nudes. Oriental figures, classical studies, together with selection of work by followers. 550 illustrations. Total of 630pp. 9⅛ × 12¼.
21485-0, 21486-9 Pa., Two-vol. set $29.90

GHOST AND HORROR STORIES OF AMBROSE BIERCE, Ambrose Bierce. 24 tales vividly imagined, strangely prophetic, and decades ahead of their time in technical skill: "The Damned Thing," "An Inhabitant of Carcosa," "The Eyes of the Panther," "Moxon's Master," and 20 more. 199pp. 5⅜ × 8½. 20767-6 Pa. $4.95

ETHICAL WRITINGS OF MAIMONIDES, Maimonides. Most significant ethical works of great medieval sage, newly translated for utmost precision, readability. Laws Concerning Character Traits, Eight Chapters, more. 192pp. 5⅜ × 8½.
24522-5 Pa. $4.50

THE EXPLORATION OF THE COLORADO RIVER AND ITS CANYONS, J. W. Powell. Full text of Powell's 1,000-mile expedition down the fabled Colorado in 1869. Superb account of terrain, geology, vegetation, Indians, famine, mutiny, treacherous rapids, mighty canyons, during exploration of last unknown part of continental U.S. 400pp. 5⅜ × 8½. 20094-9 Pa. $7.95

HISTORY OF PHILOSOPHY, Julián Marías. Clearest one-volume history on the market. Every major philosopher and dozens of others, to Existentialism and later. 505pp. 5⅜ × 8½. 21739-6 Pa. $9.95

ALL ABOUT LIGHTNING, Martin A. Uman. Highly readable nontechnical survey of nature and causes of lightning, thunderstorms, ball lightning, St. Elmo's Fire, much more. Illustrated. 192pp. 5⅜ × 8½. 25237-X Pa. $5.95

SAILING ALONE AROUND THE WORLD, Captain Joshua Slocum. First man to sail around the world, alone, in small boat. One of great feats of seamanship told in delightful manner. 67 illustrations. 294pp. 5⅜ × 8½. 20326-3 Pa. $4.95

LETTERS AND NOTES ON THE MANNERS, CUSTOMS AND CONDITIONS OF THE NORTH AMERICAN INDIANS, George Catlin. Classic account of life among Plains Indians: ceremonies, hunt, warfare, etc. 312 plates. 572pp. of text. 6⅛ × 9¼. 22118-0, 22119-9, Pa., Two-vol. set $17.90

ALASKA: The Harriman Expedition, 1899, John Burroughs, John Muir, et al. Informative, engrossing accounts of two-month, 9,000-mile expedition. Native peoples, wildlife, forests, geography, salmon industry, glaciers, more. Profusely illustrated. 240 black-and-white line drawings. 124 black-and-white photographs. 3 maps. Index. 576pp. 5⅜ × 8½. 25109-8 Pa. $11.95

AMERICAN CLIPPER SHIPS: 1833–1858, Octavius T. Howe & Frederick C. Matthews. Fully-illustrated, encyclopedic review of 352 clipper ships from the period of America's greatest maritime supremacy. Introduction. 109 halftones. 5 black-and-white line illustrations. Index. Total of 928pp. 5⅜ × 8½.
25115-2, 25116-0 Pa., Two-vol. set $17.90

TOWARDS A NEW ARCHITECTURE, Le Corbusier. Pioneering manifesto by great architect, near legendary founder of "International School." Technical and aesthetic theories, views on industry, economics, relation of form to function, "mass-production spirit," much more. Profusely illustrated. Unabridged translation of 13th French edition. Introduction by Frederick Etchells. 320pp. 6⅛ × 9¼. (Available in U.S. only)
25023-7 Pa. $8.95

THE BOOK OF KELLS, edited by Blanche Cirker. Inexpensive collection of 32 full-color, full-page plates from the greatest illuminated manuscript of the Middle Ages, painstakingly reproduced from rare facsimile edition. Publisher's Note. Captions. 32pp. 9⅜ × 12¼.
24345-1 Pa. $5.95

BEST SCIENCE FICTION STORIES OF H. G. WELLS, H. G. Wells. Full novel *The Invisible Man*, plus 17 short stories: "The Crystal Egg," "Aepyornis Island," "The Strange Orchid," etc. 303pp. 5⅜ × 8½. (Available in U.S. only)
21531-8 Pa. $6.95

AMERICAN SAILING SHIPS: Their Plans and History, Charles G. Davis. Photos, construction details of schooners, frigates, clippers, other sailcraft of 18th to early 20th centuries—plus entertaining discourse on design, rigging, nautical lore, much more. 137 black-and-white illustrations. 240pp. 6⅛ × 9¼.
24658-2 Pa. $6.95

ENTERTAINING MATHEMATICAL PUZZLES, Martin Gardner. Selection of author's favorite conundrums involving arithmetic, money, speed, etc., with lively commentary. Complete solutions. 112pp. 5⅜ × 8½.
25211-6 Pa. $3.50

THE WILL TO BELIEVE, HUMAN IMMORTALITY, William James. Two books bound together. Effect of irrational on logical, and arguments for human immortality. 402pp. 5⅜ × 8½.
20291-7 Pa. $8.95

THE HAUNTED MONASTERY and THE CHINESE MAZE MURDERS, Robert Van Gulik. 2 full novels by Van Gulik continue adventures of Judge Dee and his companions. An evil Taoist monastery, seemingly supernatural events; overgrown topiary maze that hides strange crimes. Set in 7th-century China. 27 illustrations. 328pp. 5⅜ × 8½.
23502-5 Pa. $6.95

CELEBRATED CASES OF JUDGE DEE (DEE GOONG AN), translated by Robert Van Gulik. Authentic 18th-century Chinese detective novel; Dee and associates solve three interlocked cases. Led to Van Gulik's own stories with same characters. Extensive introduction. 9 illustrations. 237pp. 5⅜ × 8½.
23337-5 Pa. $5.95

Prices subject to change without notice.

Available at your book dealer or write for free catalog to Dept. GI, Dover Publications, Inc., 31 East 2nd St., Mineola, N.Y. 11501. Dover publishes more than 175 books each year on science, elementary and advanced mathematics, biology, music, art, literary history, social sciences and other areas.